S0-CVC-946

SAHAGÚN
TRANSITION

OKLAH
DISCO

SERIE

Robert Co
Ronald Sc

ADVIS

Maya Ang
Jonathan (
Jacques De
Nurrudin
Shoshana
Henry Lo
Sandra M
Dominick
Vincent B
Richard M
J. Hillis M
Marjorie
Edward W
Thomas
Gayatri C
Cornel W

Oklahoma Project for D

SAHAGÚN AND THE TRANSITION TO MODERNITY

Walden Browne

University of Oklahoma Press : Norman

Library of Congress Cataloging-in-Publication Data

Browne, Walden, 1964–
    Sahagún and the transition to modernity / Walden Browne.
        p. cm. — (Oklahoma project for discourse and theory ; v. 20)
    Includes bibliographical references and index.
    ISBN 0-8061-3233-7 (alk. paper)
    1. Sahagún, Bernardino de, d. 1590—Philosophy.   2. Nahuas—Missions.
3. Aztecs—Historiography.   4. Franciscans—Missions—Mexico.   5. Franciscans—
Theology.   6. Philosophy, Modern.   I. Title.   II. Series.

F1219.S13917 B76 2000
972'.018'092—dc21

99-047301

Sahagún and the Transition to Modernity is Volume 20 of the Oklahoma Project for Discourse and Theory.

1 2 3 4 5 6 7 8 9 10

To Sally, Nicholas, and Alexander

CONTENTS

SERIES EDITORS' FOREWORD

The Oklahoma Project for Discourse & Theory is a series of interdisciplinary texts whose purpose is to explore the cultural institutions that
constitute the human sciences, to see them in relation to one another, and
perhaps above all, to see them as products of particular discursive practices. To this end, we hope that the Oklahoma Project will promote dialogue within and across traditional disciplines—psychology, philology,
linguistics, history, art history, aesthetics, logic, political economy, religion, philosophy, anthropology, communications, and the like—in texts
that theoretically are located across disciplines. In recent years, in a host of
new and traditional areas, there has been great interest in such discursive
and theoretical frameworks. Yet we conceive of the Oklahoma Project as
going beyond local inquiries, providing a larger forum for interdiscursive
theoretical discussions and dialogue.

Our agenda in previous books and certainly in this one has been to
present through the University of Oklahoma Press a series of critical volumes that set up a theoretical encounter among disciplines, an interchange
not limited to literature but covering virtually the whole range of the
human sciences. It is a critical series with an important reference in literary
studies—thus mirroring the modern development of discourse theory—
but including all approaches, other than quantitative studies, open to
semiotic and post-semiotic analysis and to the wider concerns of cultural
studies. Regardless of its particular domain, each book in the series will
investigate characteristically post-Freudian, post-Saussurean, and post-
Marxist questions about culture and the discourses that constitute different cultural phenomena. The Oklahoma Project is a sustained dialogue
intended to make a significant contribution to the contemporary understanding of the human sciences in the contexts of cultural theory and
cultural studies.

The title of the series reflects, of course, its home base, the University of Oklahoma. But it also signals in a significant way the particularity of the *local* functions within historical and conceptual frameworks for understanding culture. *Oklahoma* is a haunting place-name in American culture. A Choctaw phrase meaning "red people," it goes back to the Treaty of Dancing Rabbit Creek in Mississippi in 1830. For Franz Kafka, it conjured up the idea of America itself, both the indigenous Indian peoples of North America and the vertiginous space of the vast plains. It is also the place-name, the "American" starting point, with which Wallace Stevens begins his *Collected Poems*. Historically, too, it is a place in which American territorial and political expansion was reenacted in a single day in a retracing called the Oklahoma land run. Geographically, it is the heartland of the continent.

As such—in the interdisciplinary Oklahoma Project for Discourse & Theory—we are hoping to describe, above all, multifaceted *interest* within and across various studies of discourse and culture. Such interests are akin to what Kierkegaard calls the "in-between" aspect of experience, the "inter esse," and, perhaps more pertinently, what Nietzsche describes as the always *political* functioning of concepts, art works, and language—the functioning of power as well as knowledge in discourse and theory. Such politics, occasioning dialogue and bringing together powerfully struggling and often unarticulated positions, disciplines, and assumptions, is always local, always particular. In some ways, such interests function in broad feminist critiques of language, theory, and culture as well as microphilosophical and microhistorical critiques of the definitions of truth and art existing within ideologies of "disinterested" meaning. They function in the interested examination of particular disciplines and general disciplinary histories. They function (to allude to two of our early titles) in the very interests of theory and the particularity of the postmodern age in which many of us find ourselves. In such interested particulars, we believe, the human sciences are articulated. We hope that the books of the Oklahoma Project will provide sites of such interest and that in them, individually and collectively, the monologues of traditional scholarly discourse will become heteroglosses, just as such place-names as *Oklahoma* and such commonplace words and concepts as *discourse* and *theory* can become sites for the dialogue and play of culture.

ROBERT CON DAVIS
RONALD SCHLEIFER

Norman, Oklahoma

ACKNOWLEDGMENTS

I would like to thank Professors Hans Ulrich Gumbrecht, Mary Louise Pratt, James A. Fox, and Yvonne Yarbro-Bejarano at Stanford University for their extremely generous guidance and support during the writing of this book. Sally Elizabeth Pontius edited much of the original text; her insights were invaluable. Jesús Bustamante García, Mónica Quijada, José Luis de Rojas, and Fermín del Pino made my Fulbright year in Spain especially productive and humane. Yasushi Ishii, Sachiko Takita, Luis Millones, and Julie Evans offered intellectual and moral support at several crucial junctures. John Chance, Emily Umberger, Michael Schreffler, Ian Robertson, Doug Smith, and the rest of the Nahuatl study group gave me a home away from home at Arizona State University during my stay in Phoenix. I am grateful to the editors of the University of Oklahoma Press for their hard work and dedication to the project. My copy editor for the Press, Barbara Siegemund-Broka, is responsible for much of the clarity of the text as it now stands.

A few portions of the book were previously published as short articles. An early version of the section of chapter 4 on the "crisis of exemplarity" in Sahagún's work was published as "The Crisis of Exemplarity in Sahagún's *Historia universal de las cosas de la Nueva España* and *Psalmodia christiana*," in Mary H. Preuss, ed., *Beyond Indigenous Voices* (Lancaster, Calif.: Labyrinthos, 1996). A very embryonic version of the section in chapter 4 on mimesis was published in German translation as "Die Organisation von (Mensch und) Dingen Zum historischen Ort der Modernität in Fray Toribio de Motolinía, Fray Bernardino de Sahagún und Fray Augustín de Vetancurt," in Horst

Wenzel, ed., *Gutenberg und die Neue Welt* (Munich: Wilhelm Fink Verlag, 1994), 251–62. An earlier version of much of chapter 3 was published as "When Worlds Collide: Crisis in Sahagún's *Historia universal de las cosas de la Nueva España*," *CLAHR* 5:2 (1996): 101–49.

All translations are my own, unless otherwise noted.

SAHAGÚN AND THE TRANSITION TO MODERNITY

INTRODUCTION

The Franciscan friar Bernardino de Sahagún was born in 1499 or 1500 in the province of León, Spain. He studied at the University of Salamanca, in Salamanca, Spain. In 1529, five years after the first group of Franciscan friars made their way across the ocean to the recently conquered New Spain (Mexico), Sahagún left Spain for good with a group of missionaries led by Fray Antonio de Ciudad Rodrigo. From 1536 to 1539 Sahagún taught Latin at the Colegio de Santa Cruz de Tlaltelolco[1]—a school established to educate (originally for the priesthood) young boys from noble Nahua families. Some of these boys would later assist Sahagún in the compilation of his most famous work: *Historia universal de las cosas de la Nueva España*. From 1545 to 1556, Sahagún was back in Tlaltelolco to help with the reorganization of the foundering colegio. Sahagún passed most of the second half of his life away from "official" positions in his order. Much of this time was spent working on what would become his enormous written legacy. In fact, most of his surviving writings date from the second half of his ninety-year life span.

Sahagún is mostly remembered today as the author of the *Historia universal*—an extremely large collection of texts in Nahuatl with loose Spanish translations that cover a wide gamut of precolonial and colonial Nahua culture. The most polished—but still incomplete—version of this history is commonly referred to as the *Códice florentino* (*Florentine Codex*) because of its present location in Florence, Italy. Sahagún's history is the single most important source for what is known—or what is assumed to be known—about the precolonial

3

and colonial Nahuas. Some of Sahagún's other extant work consists of notes or *"memoriales"*—now in Spain—that represent various stages of the composition of the *Historia universal.* He also composed a work entitled *Coloquios y doctrina christiana*—a reconstruction of a dialogue between Nahua elders and the first twelve Franciscans in New Spain that has survived only in fragmentary form. Of all Sahagún's works, only the *Psalmodia christiana* (1583) was printed during his lifetime. The Psalmodia is a collection of canticles or sermons written in Nahuatl as a substitute for the "idolatrous" songs of the Nahuas. Several sermons written in Nahuatl, a spiritual exercise, a denouncement of an indigenous soothsaying calendar (the *Arte adivinatoria*), and other works have survived and are scattered across the world in various collections.[2]

In general, scholars do not know as much as they would like about the life and character of Sahagún. Most of what they do know comes from Sahagún's interspersed autobiographical comments in the numerous prologues he wrote for his history. The rest of the picture must be deduced or filled in from the nature of his vast written output. With the exception of Fray Gerónimo de Mendieta's portrayal of Sahagún in his *Historia eclesiástica indiana,* there are few vivid descriptions of Sahagún from people who actually knew him. And, as I shall show, even Mendieta's description needs some qualification.

In the year 1590, at the age of ninety, Sahagún died in Mexico City after catching a cold. According to Gerónimo de Mendieta, when Sahagún first fell ill his companions insisted he be taken to an infirmary in Mexico City in order to be treated, or at least, if he did not want to be cured, so he could be buried with "his old saintly companions" (Mendieta, 664). In Mendieta's account, Sahagún responded to his companions with these words: "Quiet, you silly fools, leave me alone. My hour has not yet arrived." And to the nurse, "These silly fools my brothers have made me come here without necessity" (664). Sahagún was right. He did not die then but a few days later. Back in Tlaltelolco, Sahagún announced, "Now, yes, the hour has arrived." He ordered that all the Nahuas he had educated at the Colegio de Santa Cruz be summoned, and he bid them a final farewell. He was then taken back to Mexico City where he died "blessed in the Lord" (665).

There is no reason to question the accuracy of Mendieta's account of Sahagún's death since he knew him personally and was in a good position to hear accurate reports about the manner in which he died. Nevertheless, the story highlights one of the most important and self-consciously posited obstacles to present-day historiography—a field charged with the responsibility of summoning ghosts back from the dead. The so-called facts of Sahagún's death are inseparable from a highly charged, socially constructed web of meanings and implications that has not remained consistent over time.

The account of Sahagún's death is part of a Franciscan necro-logical tradition in which, as might be expected, negative attributes of the deceased are passed over in silence, but positive attributes are highlighted to demonstrate how the friar's life was a faithful imita-tion of Christ's and Saint Francis's.[3] The Franciscan order stood out for the amount of emphasis it placed on following Christ and Saint Francis as models and in the way that it used this mimetically acquired exemplarity silently to change the world at large (Daniel). Franciscans believed that Saint Francis's life was a reenactment of Christ's on many levels and that, according to Thomas of Celano, at the hour of his death "all the mysteries of Christ" were "*fulfilled* in him" (Habig, 536, my emphasis). Another of Saint Francis's biogra-phers—Saint Bonaventure—provides the following words after describing how he died:

Surely he was the most Christ-like of men! His only desire was to be like Christ and imitate him perfectly, and he was found worthy to be adorned with the marks of his likeness; in his life he imitated the life of Christ and in his death he imitated his death, and he wished to be like him still when he was dead. (Habig, 739–40)

According to Bonaventure, Saint Francis "hung, body and soul, upon the Cross with Christ" (737).

Saint Francis's biographers go to great lengths to establish parallels—or something more than a parallel—between his last days and those of Christ. At least two of these parallels resurface in Mendieta's account of Sahagún's death. First, Sahagún knows the hour of his death. Holy people are often credited with foreknowledge of the hour of their death because it represents both a prophetic gift and the culmination of a kind of spiritual perfection. This is true of Christ's life, and it is true of Saint Francis's—and of Mendieta's description of Sahagún's. Moreover, even though both Sahagún and Saint Francis are said to have known when they were going to die, their companions did not. Sahagún's brethren miscalculated the moment of death just as Saint Francis's did (e.g., Habig, 1040). Both men were spirited back and forth between towns so that they would die in the proper place. Second, Mendieta points out that Sahagún summoned his former students to his side shortly before his death. Similarly, both Christ and Saint Francis are described as summoning their disciples to their sides shortly before their deaths at just the right time. In addition, Mendieta ties Sahagún's longevity to the fact that he was "full of good works" (664)—implying indirectly that it is sin that causes death.

These descriptions of Sahagún's death gain import when considered in light of the system of cultural values that operated at the time. Death—the most universal and undeniably real of nature's truths—is as culturally encoded as anything else. I have used this anecdote about Sahagún's death to dramatize the concept of (historical) reality that underlies my entire work.[4] This is a book on Sahagún, but, just as important, it is also a book on how Sahagún is perceived. It starts with the premise that people cannot simply lift themselves out of their historically malleable cognitive limitations into an omniscient or transhistorical view of things, but that these limitations can be identified and explored to a certain extent. Stated another way, the central premise of this book is that Sahagún is *not* like modern-day individuals because his (socially constructed) knowledge of the reality belonged to a different time and place.

Although this premise should be obvious, it runs completely counter to much—if not most—Sahagún criticism.

My goal is to estrange the reader from Sahagún—or at least the Sahagún who looks a lot like a modern-day scholar. In the first part of the book I show how the present shapes the contemporary academic understanding of Sahagún. I attempt, in the second part, to relocate Sahagún in interpretive contexts that are perhaps alien to the modern world but that would have been extant during his own time. I acknowledge an element of impossibility in my endeavor, as I do not believe scholars will ever be able entirely to divorce their interpretation of Sahagún from the here and now in which they operate. Nevertheless, the premise that Sahagún was not like the modern individual adds a level of complexity to Sahagún studies that I feel has been sorely lacking. I hope that by self-consciously interpreting Sahagún in terms of several discursive contexts, I can go beyond some of the simplistic labels that surround him—labels that create interpretive blind spots and close off discussion before it even gets started.

My views will not be popular with some Sahagún scholars because they challenge some deeply entrenched and ethically charged conclusions of an enormous (and repetitive) body of criticism. Sahagún is credited with suffering a Christlike intellectual martyrdom because of a nefarious conspiracy that reached as high up as the royal chambers of Philip II; with being the "father of modern anthropology"; with epitomizing everything good about Renaissance humanism; and with truly seeking to relate to the Nahuas on their own terms. I challenge all of these views, mostly in the first part of the book. My arguments question whether or not today's political, ethical, and aesthetic sympathies are really the same as Sahagún's. Some "Sahagunistas" will perceive this as an act of heresy, but I believe it is not.

I do not dispute the importance and interest of Sahagún's work— quite the contrary. My major bone of contention with many previous Sahagún studies is that they sum up an understanding of Sahagún too rapidly and in too narrow a fashion. These interpretations may seem useful at first, but they preclude nuance. For instance, the stubborn idea that Sahagún was an anthropologist obstructs an understanding of the ways in which he was a man of his own time and could not have been the inventor of an academic discipline that emerged in the nineteenth century in a context quite alien from his world.

In the first part of the book I play the unsavory role of devil's advocate vis-à-vis a set of firmly entrenched—almost canonical—conceptualizations of Sahagún. Contrary to popular belief, however, the role of devil's advocate in the Catholic church's canonization of saints is never allocated to heretics. It is a position of great responsibility and is taken very seriously. It is bestowed on high-ranking, qualified, ethical persons who are clearly in the fold of the church. Partly due to the role of the devil's advocate, not every candidate for sainthood is canonized. Nevertheless, this rejection rarely means that the candidate is stigmatized or posthumously excommunicated; and the process produces a richer historical picture of the candidate and his or her time than would otherwise have been available.[5] If this part of the book does nothing more than force critics to reconsider their views on Sahagún, it will have served its function.

In the second part of the book I leave behind the head-on engagement with Sahagún scholarship and attempt to approach his work in ways that go beyond pat interpretive labels. My central thesis in this part is that the majority of Sahagún's work must be interpreted as a symptom (or as symptoms) of the disintegration of the medieval worldview. Sahagún was caught in an epistemological tug-of-war between medieval and early-modern modes of thought and structures of knowledge that was galvanized into existence and shaped by the particular circumstances of his encounter with the Nahuas of New Spain.

I believe that Sahagún presents an interesting test case of how medieval ways of knowing in general gave way to the modes of thought associated with modernity. In Europe, the advent of modernity was a slow and drawn-out process—so drawn out that it is possible to see fundamental structures of the Middle Ages as far forward in time as the eve of the French Revolution.[6] Because of the sudden and dramatic way in which Sahagún was forced to reexamine the universality of his worldview in light of an entirely alien one (that of the Nahuas), modern scholars have a unique opportunity to observe an accelerated test case of the breakdown of medieval hermeneutics.

In many respects, Sahagún's response to the breakdown of medieval ways of knowing was unique. Modern Europe developed intricate responses to the sinking ship of medieval hermeneutics over a very long period of time. Sahagún did not have this luxury, so his remedies often prove to be original. In a sense, Sahagún was forced to produce his own "modernity"—a modern view of the world that is unique to his situation in the Americas. This notion runs counter to the commonly held belief that Europe invented modernity and then—and only then—exported it to the New World.[7]

My definitions of the medieval and modern periods—of medievalism and modernity—are not strictly chronological. As I already stated, the transition from the Middle Ages to modernity was neither simple nor immediate. Also, I am working with definitions of medieval and modern that are primarily tied to the evolution of conceptualizations of linguistic signs—evolving notions about the true location of meaning and the making of meaning in either the world, the mind, or God's eye. I define "medieval" as the belief that knowledge is a preexisting, divinely ordained, unified corpus that medieval interpreters elucidate and protect against the eroding forces of time through the use of memory—but rarely produce themselves. Medieval people believed that all knowledge of the cosmos was ultimately *revealed* only through the grace of God. I define "modern" as the opinion that the human mind, or "subjectivity," is the place where knowledge is produced. In short, knowledge in early modernity was thought of as "perspectival": the early modern individual saw himself or herself as an observer who was *eccentric* to, or at a distance from, the world.[8]

These definitions obviously do not coincide with all the definitions of medieval and modern that are currently in circulation. They especially do not coincide with definitions that assign specific dates along a single timeline of a world history or equate "modern" with "better." I do not subscribe to the notion that the modern period is superior to the medieval period or vice versa. Each age answers its own fundamental questions in its own way, and it can be said that an age comes to an end when these questions can no longer be answered adequately in the same fashion. The adequacy of these answers is contextually determined. Different ages should be approached the same way anthropologists ideally approach other cultures: with a strong sense of relativism and—as Clifford Geertz argues in "Anti Anti-Relativism"—the belief that relativism does not mean nihilism or the abandonment of one's own system of values.[9]

My thesis that Sahagún is caught in a tug-of-war between medieval and modern ways of knowing is the unifying thread throughout my arguments in the second part of the book. But rather than imposing a limited, monocular interpretation of Sahagún, this thread allows me to approach Sahagún from several different interpretive frameworks without condemning the book to being a random collection of essays. Each chapter in the second part analyzes Sahagún's work in terms of two or more themes that seem important to an understanding of how Sahagún dealt with the disintegration of medieval hermeneutics in the specific context of New Spain. These themes are not necessarily subsumable to each other, nor do they contradict each other. In a sense, I go over the same ground several times, but each time with a different set of interpretive tools. This approach suggests, I hope, that it is possible to sustain an extremely complex interpretation of Sahagún without losing the forest for the trees. It is in this sense that my medieval/modern paradigm does not operate as a label but as a catalyst for interpretive complexity.

In recent years it has become fashionable for European and Euro-American scholars to attempt to explain the precolonial and colonial mind. I admittedly indulge in some of this in the book, but in general I am suspicious of the practice. For reasons I will go into later, I believe scholars have often mistaken good intentions for the ability to plumb the depths of "alterity."[10] Much of this scholarship comes off like the donning of cowboy boots by city dwellers: it is supposed to bring the city dweller closer to the world and the mystique of cattle herding but, in the end, only accentuates the differences between the two social groups.¹¹ For many, this is an unpleasant topic, but I believe it is crucial to press hard on this issue and keep it in the forefront of discussion if discourse on Sahagún and the Nahuas is to go anywhere new. In general, understanding will only emerge if scholars are willing to recognize their historical, cultural, and cognitive limitations and keep the recognition of these limitations in play throughout their work.

My preoccupation with alterity explains why I take the singular step of concentrating on Sahagún and treating him as an "Other." Sahagún's most important work—the *Historia universal*—is about the Nahuas. The most common misconception about this work is that the precolonial and colonial world of the Nahuas is easily accessible to present-day scholars because the extraordinary efforts of Sahagún render it transparent. Sahagún has served as the vehicle through which scholars have approached much of the colonial Nahua world because they have unconsciously assumed that his point of view—his methodology—coincides with their own purportedly objective one. I do not believe this is the case. Only by understanding the ways in which Sahagún was different from the modern individual can scholars begin to reconstruct the social contexts that gave his world meaning. Only by reinstating some of this context (if only artificially, through historical memory) can there ever by any hope of understanding how Sahagún's cognitive filters—or "sieves," as he called them—influenced his depictions of the Nahuas.

Throughout this book I treat Sahagún, the Nahuas, and myself as three interfaces that brush up against each other but never really coalesce. This is not a book about recuperating lost authenticities because, in this historical moment, I question whether there are any lost authenticities available for recuperation. Building on a poem by William Carlos Williams, James Clifford calls this phenomenon "the pure products go crazy." In *The Predicament of Culture,* Clifford

argues that in the twentieth century there has been an unprecedented overlay of traditions that has produced a "pervasive condition of off-centeredness in a world of distinct meaning systems, a
state of being in culture while looking at culture, a form of personal and collective self-fashioning" (9). Clifford rejects the view
that history is entropically losing both its unity and authentic identities. He argues, rather, that personal and cultural identity must be
understood as a tension between nostalgia for a supposedly authentic
past and the modern need continuously to reinvent oneself in a
world where the status of given, pure, authentic pasts is increasingly
problematic or suspicious:

> Modern ethnographic[12] histories are perhaps condemned to oscillate
> between two meta-narratives: one of homogenization, the other of emer-
> gence; one of loss, the other of invention. In most specific conjunctures
> both narratives are relevant, each undermining the other's claim to tell "the
> whole story," each denying to the other a privileged, Hegelian vision. (17)

For Clifford, personal and cultural identity must be understood
more as emergence or invention than as decay. Moreover, since "one
is always, to varying degrees, 'inauthentic': caught between cultures,
implicated in others" (11), one's scholarly work should be deeply
suspicious of "any transcendent regime of authenticity" (10)—any
cultural or critical apparatus that attempts to deny the profound
historical contingency of any interpretation of the world.

The interpretive complexity for which I argue is one response to
the historical contingency Clifford describes of any view that
attempts to explain (away) Sahagún or the Nahuas, but in the end
it, too, proves inadequate. Interpretive complexity dilutes so-called
certainties about Sahagún and the Nahuas. With the accumulation
of details, it may seem like more is being understood about
Sahagún and the Nahuas, but ultimately their "true" identities will
remain opaque. For some, this sense of interpretive inadequacy
would seem to undermine the legitimacy of the role that historians,
literary critics, and other scholars are supposed to play in society.

This view, however, is mistaken. It is the role of scholarship systematically to question ideas accepted as certainties and provide the space for other hermeneutic possibilities. Inadequacy is a paradigm, not a stigma.

PART 1

THE CRITICAL, SYMBOLIC, AND HISTORICAL CONSTRUCTION OF FRAY BERNARDINO DE SAHAGÚN

1

SAHAGÚN'S ENTRANCES INTO HISTORY

An Episodic Examination of How Sahagún Became an Object of Scholarly Desire

Who was Fray Bernardino de Sahagún? Although a considerable part of his work has resurfaced over time, very little is known about Sahagún, the man. Nevertheless, over time Sahagún has come to occupy an important symbolic role for intellectuals and historians of colonial Mexico and precolonial Mesoamerica. In the first section of this chapter, I do not answer the question of who Sahagún was. Rather, I examine how it is possible that, in what I refer to as the "historical reception" of Sahagún, historians have come to identify with him. I am less interested in the obvious fact that the past is always interpreted or reappropriated from the standpoint of the present than in *how* this process occurs on a cognitive level and how the peculiar case of Sahagún lends itself to an exaggerated evolution of historical anachronisms. In the second section, I examine the reception/confiscation of Sahagún's main work by the bureaucratic government of Philip II and the problems this confiscation presupposes for understanding Sahagún's plight. The confiscation of Sahagún's principle work is often dramatically alluded to as a case in point of *vertu persecutée*—proof of a government conspiracy designed to eradicate the work of those who look beyond the more temporal concerns of colonial politics. The confiscation of Sahagún's manuscript without a doubt constitutes one of the more unfortunate colonial political decisions of the time, but it would be wrong to assume that Philip II had a personal ax to grind with Sahagún and his fellow missionaries.

The third section of this chapter is primarily concerned with the work of an obscure Italian travel-writer who wrote in French: Jules-Césaire (Giacomo Costantino) Beltrami. It is not my intent to vindicate the work of Beltrami, for I believe, by modern standards, his work is devoid of any scholarly merit. Nevertheless, during the first half of the nineteenth century Beltrami was a well-known and admired writer whose ideas were taken quite seriously. The pivotal symbolic role Sahagún holds in his *Le Mexique* offers a unique occasion to observe not only how Sahagún has undergone a symbolic transformation according to the precepts of each time period, but also how the nineteenth-century rehabilitation of Sahagún's work coincides with the epistemological tensions that hovered on the horizon in the early stages of the consolidation of contemporary scientific and humanistic disciplines. The numerous colonial and precolonial manuscripts including Sahagún's that were rediscovered throughout the nineteenth century were found less by chance than because, from the early nineteenth century on, travelers and scholars such as Beltrami sought them out in an unprecedented fashion. Something had changed in the mind-set of Europeans of the early nineteenth century that explains why figures such as Sahagún came to have so much importance in some contemporary disciplines. What appears now as the intellectual "messiness" of Beltrami's thoughts stems from the fact that Beltrami stood on the threshold of a centrifugal dispersion or splintering of knowledge into what would later be seen as a natural disciplinary division between the various sciences and humanities. A close examination of the apparent messiness of Beltrami's thinking reveals the historical contingency involved in the deceptively transparent notion that Sahagún held the same intellectual and ethical concerns as today's scholars.

On an overarching level, it can be said that all three sections of the chapter focus on the problems inherent in any attempt to "re-anthropomorphize" a Sahagún who has been reified through the distance in time that separates the modern individual from him and through the dehumanizing structures inherent in political bureaucracies. I have chosen to avoid creating an exhaustive inventory of

Sahagún's symbolic trajectory from the sixteenth century to today in order to concentrate on three problems that I think will prove more useful in the long run in the task of reorienting the contemporary understanding of Sahagún's work. The problem of how Sahagún lends himself so easily to symbolic manipulation, the problem of what really motivated the government of Philip II to confiscate Sahagún's magnum opus, the *Historia universal*, and the problem of how Sahagún has been taken up with such vigor since the beginning of the nineteenth century as a standard-bearer for modern scholarly ethics and methods must be examined before contemporary trends in Sahagún criticism can be placed in proper perspective.

1. Sahagún's Corporeal and Historical Presence

Through the denial of the "flesh"—as Saint Francis understood the word[1]—Franciscans turned away from the worldly and toward the heavenly. The very denial of the flesh, however, converted the body into a vehicle for devotion and conversion through example.[2] Hence, the ideal Franciscan's body was not his own; it was modeled on Christ's body and on that of Saint Francis. Much, if not most, of the saint's *Rule of 1221*—simple clothing, fasting, work, begging, and so forth—was intended to create an exemplary body at the expense of the flesh (Habig, 31–53). In chapter 10 of the *Rule of 1221*, Saint Francis begs "the friar who is sick to thank God for everything," for otherwise, "he does not *seem* to be a real friar because he cares more for his body than for his soul" (Habig, 40–41, my emphasis). Given Saint Francis's urgent requests to his brethren, it is not surprising that Franciscans tended to downplay the display or description of the body when it ran counter to the saint's ideals.

For the most part, portrayals of Fray Bernardino de Sahagún reflect this Franciscan tendency, but there are a exceptions. Briefly, here are three of the few descriptions of Sahagún's corporeal presence that run counter to the tendency and seem to offer a glimpse of a flesh-and-blood Sahagún. In his *Monarquía indiana* (1615), Fray Juan de Torquemada says that Fray Bernardino de Sahagún was so handsome as a youth that his religious superiors hid him away from the eyes of women (3:486). In what would otherwise be a nondescript mention of New Spain's geography, Sahagún himself recounts how he climbed the impressive heights of the mountain range Iztactépetl in search of idols (*Códice florentino*, hereafter abbreviated *CF* XI:232v). On another occasion, while in Xochimilco, Sahagún dove underwater in order to remove an idol and replace it with a stone cross (*CF* XI:233v).

Sahagún's numerous biographers delight in repeating these anecdotes because there is so little else that—even indirectly—refers to Sahagún's physiognomy or demeanor. Moreover, none of the commonly reproduced pictorial depictions of Sahagún is contemporary to his life. Despite the regularity with which certain of his physical attributes are depicted, no one knows what Sahagún looked like.[3]

More often than not, Sahagún's biographers begin with a lament over how little is known about his life.[4] Not only are pages filled with what scholars would like to know about Sahagún but do not, time and time again Sahagún's biographers emphasize the dubious veracity of their information. For example, each new biographer is wont to note that there is absolutely nothing that either confirms or denies the possibility that Sahagún was from a *converso*[5] family. To cite another example, there is no apparent source for the idea, which first surfaced in Jules-Césaire Beltrami's *Le Mexique*, that Sahagún's family name was Ribeira (2:168). Yet, despite its highly doubtful veracity and even more doubtful relevance, discussion of the name is used to fill up pages. The articulation of the erroneous nature of information on Sahagún paradoxically creates an illusion of biographical presence. It is as if whittling away at all the foundationless nontruths could someday lead to a hidden kernel of truth.

There are both simple and complex reasons why a reconstruction of Sahagún's life, a resuscitation of his bodily presence, seems to be of paramount importance. The most obvious reason is the nature of his written legacy. Sahagún left a fragmented corpus whose imposing size is in inverse proportion to explicit biographical information on its author. Moreover, the very same feature that is used to explain the importance of the ethnographic descriptions in the *Florentine Codex*—Sahagún's apparent lack of an authorial voice coupled with his supposed deferral to named, but nevertheless homogenized, indigenous informants—runs counter to modern sensibilities of authorship. Sahagún's apparent self-effacement creates the illusion that there is an objective, empirical text that is of primary importance to ethnohistorians. Sahagún is frequently lauded for being among the first ethnographers to separate his voice from the voice of his informants.[6] The apparent lack of precedents for this achievement has, in turn, made historians want to know better the man who accomplished it. Sahagún's self-effacement and the elusiveness of his authorial voice serve, therefore, both as the cause of his fame and as the obstacle that seems to impede understanding of him.

Added to the search for Sahagún's elusive authorial voice is the desire to vindicate his work against what appears to be its original unfavorable reception. With modern-day sensibilities, it seems incomprehensible that Sahagún's work was not valued more in his day. Sahagún struggled against indifference and factions that were both internal and external to the Franciscan order to continue his work, only to have it confiscated in the end by the government of Philip II. That Sahagún suffered from these trials there is little doubt. Fray Gerónimo de Mendieta, a contemporary of Sahagún, notes with irony in his *Historia eclesiástica indiana* that Sahagún's work was ostensibly confiscated for use by an official chronicler in Spain, but that his manuscript would probably be used in Spain to wrap up spices (663). It seems natural to empathize with Sahagún despite the distance across time of his predicament.

It is not my intent to disparage the quixotic attempt to resuscitate through historiography the life of Sahagún, but to understand it. The present-day reader is continuously propelled farther and farther away from Sahagún's lifetime and context, but few are surprised by Alfredo Chavero's suggested inscription on a proposed monument to Sahagún in Mexico: "To / fray Bernardino de Sahagún / protector of the vanquished / teacher of the Indians / and / preserver of our history / homage / of admiration and gratitude" (Chavero,

Sahagún, 5). The fact that Sahagún has preserved "our history"—the history of the Mexican people—by mediating the distance that separates his time from the present seems straightforward enough. Yet, if it is in fact "our" (Mexico's present) history, why is it not already a self-evident part of every Mexican citizen's consciousness? Why is a mediation needed to restore it? It is more logical to say that, through the use of an emblematic Sahagún, Mexicans incorporate into their lives a past that was previously foreign to them—not their own. Moreover, it is telling that the dedication on this memorial is addressed directly to Sahagún and not to his memory. By addressing the memorial—the homage—directly to Sahagún as if two-way communication were still possible, Sahagún is seemingly converted into an active, living participant in the process of establishing the historical past.

Today in León, Spain, a statue of Sahagún, bearing the following inscription, looms over viewers: "FRAY BERNARDINO DE SAHAGUN / SAHAGUN 1499–MEXICO 1590 / MISSIONARY AND EDUCATOR OF THE PEOPLE / THE FATHER OF ANTHROPOLOGY IN THE NEW WORLD / DAY OF THE REGION OF LEON / 2 JUNE 1966 / THE PROVINCE OF LEON / TO FRAY BERNARDINO DE SAHAGUN SAHAGUN XI–VI MCMLXVI." This statue was erected a few short months after one in Salamanca that bears a similar inscription (Ballesteros Gaibrois, 151–52). With its somewhat tardy commemoration, the province of León (re)claimed Sahagún as part of its own history. The scramble in 1966 to stake claim to Sahagún's memory was not without a muted polemical side. At the end of his *Vida y obra de fray Bernardino de Sahagún*, in a kind of playful one-upmanship of Mexico, Manuel Ballesteros Gaibrois rubs in his claim that Spain took first place in the race to erect a monument to Sahagún (152). Only in Spain, it seems, could Mexico's own history be truly appreciated.

The competitive nature of these monuments in Spain was a response to the growing number of Mexican intellectuals in the 1960s who argued that Sahagún was the "father of anthropology in the New World."[7] The emphasis placed on the University of Salamanca as Sahagún's alma mater, and on León as his birthplace, allowed

Spanish intellectuals to take some of the credit for his achievement. The aura of permanence that now surrounds these monuments obscures the ideological, colonial tug-of-war in which they were first conceived. Moreover, the sculpted and engraved stone used for the monuments lends an air of concreteness to a figure who is, in reality, much more difficult to understand than is often openly admitted. It is obvious that the past is always perceived from the vantage point of the present, but how the case of Sahagún lends itself so easily to this process despite what ordinarily might be regarded as insurmountable obstacles is worth examining with greater care.

In "'Narrating the Past Just as if It Were Your Own Time': An Essay on the Anthropology of Historiography," Hans Ulrich Gumbrecht argues that the only metahistorical and intercultural constant in historiography is a "prereflexive anthropological need to transcend the limits of our lifetime"—a human need to thematize (but not necessarily to narrate) the past as if it were a part of, or a precursor to, the present (71).[8] Gumbrecht argues that it "is precisely because the structures of the life world and everyday worlds are behavioral orientations mediated by socialization and are not innate that we are able to count on a—particularly human—need to transgress them" (74). This transgression occurs through a peculiar use of memory, for, as Jacques Le Goff points out in *History and Memory*, "memory is the *raw* material of history" (xi, my emphasis).

Neither the content nor the structure of memory, however, is ever a constant. For example, in "Sahagún and Hermeneutics: A Christian Ethnographer's Understanding of Aztec Culture," John Keber has pointed out that, due to modern sensibilities, Sahagún is less well remembered now as a zealous missionary who was willing to use coercion (63). If it is true that memory always implies a separation of the past out from the present, it is also true that there is a great deal of variation in how this separation takes place (Le Goff, History, 1–20). For example, in primarily oral cultures, the distinction between past and present seems blurry from the perspective of literate cultures (Ong, 42–43). Memory, when it occurs, seems primarily personal, but as Gumbrecht's observations suggest, memory is inextricably caught up in the mediated nature of the structures of the "life-world."[9]

Peter L. Berger and Thomas Luckmann argue in *The Social Construction of Reality* that the social reality of everyday life is "apprehended in a continuum of typifications, which are progressively *anonymous* as they are removed from the 'here and now' of the face-to-face situation" (33, my emphasis).[10] In *The Structures of the Life-World*, Alfred Schütz and Thomas Luckmann offer an important distinction between how one experiences the past and how one experiences the present through typifications. Schütz and Luckmann argue that personal memories of one's own experiences of others will be perceived as experience of past social reality, and since these others were present in simultaneity with one's life (because one interacted with them), one can in hindsight "follow along in its inner duration the step-by-step construction of meaning contexts under [one's] attention" (1:88). That is, the typifications that constituted the structure of the life-world that oriented the relationship an individual had with others (i.e., contemporaries) are still available to that individual through memory. For example, I am mentally able to reconstruct a conversation I had with a friend as well as the elements that gave the conversation its contextual meaning. This is not so with the world of my predecessors: not only is this world definitively concluded—as Schütz and Luckmann go on to say—the "biographical articulation in which the individual experiences were joined together is definitely completed" (1:88). Whereas both the worlds of contemporaries and predecessors are approached through typifications, I can expect to act in relation to my contemporaries but not in relation to my predecessors or ancestors: "My behavior can be oriented to the behavior of my ancestors only insofar as their acts can become because-motives for my actions, but with regard to my ancestors I cannot effect anything more. Social relations that are essentially reciprocal cannot exist with ancestors" (1:88–89).

Schütz and Luckmann's point has at least two important consequences. First, in the case of a predecessor, not only is it impossible to reconstruct an intersubjective relationship with the predecessor through memory, but the farther away the predecessor is both spatially and temporally, the more difficult it becomes to reconstruct even indirectly the meaning contexts in which the predecessor lived. Since there is always a biographical element interacting with the structures of the life-world, over time the structures of the life-world as mediated through society inevitably shift: Sahagún's life-world is quite removed from the modern world. Second, since the predecessor is experienced through an individual's typifications as invariable due to his or her inability to enter into an intersubjective relationship with that individual, predecessors are inevitably alien or anonymous to a certain degree from the perspective of an individual's own actualized life-world: no one today can check his or her image of Sahagún against a living, flesh-and-blood Sahagún. If, as Gumbrecht suggests, history results from the need to transgress the boundaries separating current, actualized life-worlds from those of a previous time, and since, in making history, this transgression must be realized through the use of modern typifications, it is to be expected that predecessors will seem to present themselves as accessible in varying degrees. This is because aspects of these predecessors will vary a good deal in the degree and in the manner in which they resonate in modern typifications—if they resonate at all.

Since the past offers so little about Sahagún's life, modern-day typifications are forced to carry almost the entire burden of reconstructing his life. To put it more precisely, the absence of information on Sahagún's life means that there is little or nothing that contradicts the preordained typifications now applied to Sahagún— nothing or little that forces an adjustment of them. Moreover, since these typifications are the same ones that a modern-day person would use to reconstruct through memory his or her relation with a contemporary, it is not surprising that Sahagún would seem to appear to share that person's sensibilities—to feel close to his or her life-world. Regarding Sahagún, personal memory and historical memory are conflated, and across the centuries historians such as Joaquín García Icazbalceta have remembered Sahagún the way one remembers an old friend: "His memory should be eternal, and, for us, always pleasing" (García Icazbalceta, 376).

The absence of information on Sahagún's life forces modern readers to fill in the gaps, and as a result, he always feels strangely familiar to those readers. This same absence of information, however, continuously indicates that Sahagún is far away in both a spatial and temporal sense. The emphasis Sahagún's biographers place on a few statements that allude to his bodily presence constitutes an attempt to conjure up a dialogue—or a virtual dialogue—with a living Sahagún. The fact that there are so many biographies about someone of whom very little is known should raise the question of whether or not the conversation is truly a monologue, in which Sahagún serves as a vehicle for modern readers to talk to themselves about themselves. Rather than arguing that the absence of information on Sahagún's life impedes the writing of his biography, I would like to examine why this absence seems to have facilitated the writing of so many biographies rather than mere critical interpretations of his surviving work.

2. Interpreting the Confiscation of the *Florentine Codex*

Virtually every biographical statement written on Sahagún takes up the problem of why the government of Philip II confiscated Sahagún's major work. The tendency of Sahagún's biographers to identify with his plight, however, has produced a series of contradictions that are straightened out when Sahagún's victimization is not interpreted as a form of vertu persecutée or as a personal vendetta directed by Philip II against Sahagún.[11]

On 22 April 1577, Philip II ordered Martín Enríquez, the viceroy of New Spain, to confiscate Sahagún's magnum opus, the *Florentine Codex*.[12] In the same royal warrant, Philip II went on to order that no further ethnographic work similar to Sahagún's be written down: "and be informed *not to consent in anyway that anyone write things concerning superstitions and the way in which the Indians lived, in any language,* because this is what suits the service of God and ours" (Fernández del Castillo, 513, his emphasis). It is probable that Sahagún was not the only victim of the king's warrant. Although it was carried out for missionary purposes, non-government-sponsored ethnographic work on pre-Hispanic customs in general was suddenly considered dangerous. For example, the *Historia de las Indias de Nueva España e Islas de la Tierra Firme* (1581) by Fray Diego Durán, a Dominican—a text that is similar in many respects to Sahagún's work—was lost until the second half of the nineteenth century, when it was subsequently published for the first time in Mexico by José Fernández Ramírez (Esteve Barba, 226–28). This sense of danger also surrounded most of the other histories of the New World from the latter half of the sixteenth century that were not directly sponsored by the government.

Superficially, then, it would seem that Sahagún's work in particular provoked the ire of Philip II's government and led to the suppression of other similar projects. On closer examination, however, this does not turn out to be the case. In the same warrant for the confiscation of the *Florentine Codex*, Sahagún is personally exonerated: "and even though it is understood that the zeal of said Fray Bernardino had been good, and with the desire that his work bear fruit, it has become apparent that it is not suitable that this book be printed nor move around in those parts, because of some causes for concern" (Fernández del Castillo, 513). Sahagún's exoneration implies that the government of Philip II was making a conscious change in policy. As I shall show , Philip II's government previously not only tolerated work similar to Sahagún's, in some cases it encouraged it. Moreover, historians are faced with the fact that, although there was a growing intolerance of writing projects not initiated by the government, the government did not desist in sponsoring its own projects. The fact that government projects such as the *Relaciones geográficas* sometimes contained indigenous customs while nongovernment writing projects languished also indicates a conscious shift in government policy.

In *Utopía e historia en México*, Georges Baudot first analyzed the political situation in Spain and its dominions that led to the confiscation of Sahagún's work (471–504). Baudot points out several trends in political thinking that converged in the final prohibition against ethnographic work in the New World, but it seems that two events in particular occasioned the quick and definitive response of Philip II's government. Philip II's response, as Baudot describes it, was in part prompted by a grandson of Motecuhzoma Xocoyotzin, Diego Luis de Motecuhzoma, who in 1576 petitioned the Council of Indies to recognize him as the sole heir of his grandfather. Diego Luis de Motecuhzoma's petition was symptomatic of the growing number of both Spaniards and Nahuas seeking to contest and legitimate various aspects of the distribution of power in Mexico. Ironically, the Council of Indies dealt with Motecuhzoma's petition by sending him back to Mexico so that his voice would be drowned out by the numerous other indigenous *tlahtoque* (royalty) with similar claims (499).[13]

The second event Baudot cites is even further removed from Sahagún's immediate circumstances. After 1569, the viceroy of Peru, Francisco de Toledo, sought to terminate any lingering Inca resistance to Spanish rule (499–500). Toledo's administrative innovation was to comb indigenous history for examples of tyranny in order to legitimate his measures. As D. A. Brading describes in *The First America*, Toledo's plan culminated in a farcical ceremony in which Inca nobles were forced to listen to a public reading of Pedro Sarmiento de Gamboa's *Historia indica* and sign documents assenting to its accuracy (138–46). What both Baudot's and Brading's analyses illuminate is the Spanish government's sudden realization that the history of America, like any other history, was subject to manipulation and that its manipulation could have immediate and far-reaching political consequences that needed to be controlled by the state in order to secure political stability.

Sahagún was in the wrong place at the wrong time. The confusing nature of the confiscation of the *Florentine Codex* stems from the fact that it coincided with a conscious change in governmental policy. Sahagún willingly—even happily—polished up and handed over the *Florentine Codex* to Fray Rodrigo de Sequera, to whom he dedicated the work, confident in the knowledge that it was requested

by Juan de Ovando, president of the Council of Indies (*CF* II:2r).
Sahagún was apparently unaware of the intent behind the royal
warrant to confiscate his work, and he did not perceive the confiscation as a penalty; but there is no reason to think Sahagún was a
naive dreamer who should have known better than to entrust his
life's work to the mechanisms of Philip II's bureaucratic government. In order to understand the context in which Sahagún's
manuscript was confiscated, it is necessary to digress a little and say
something more about the nature of bureaucracy and the nature of
Philip II's government.

Before 1577, Philip II's government was already highly bureaucratic. With regard to the New World, however, it was only halfway
down the road to bureaucracy, in the modern sense of the word.
Modern bureaucracy is characterized by the *institutionalization* of the
very structures that assure its continuation. Niklas Luhmann has
shown in *A Sociological Theory of Law* that modern positive law is not
legitimated from above (by God or a king, for example) but rather
through the mechanisms that assure its evolution and continuation:
namely, the institutionalization of the decision-making process of
legislation. Modern law, therefore, distinguishes itself in that its
potential for change and modification is one of its constituent elements. As Luhmann argues, one of the major consequences of the
positivization of modern law is an increase in indifference toward
the individual (163–64).[14]

The same holds true for political bureaucracy. In *Teoría política en
el Estado de Bienestar*, Luhmann argues that modern society is characterized by an increase in overall complexity that is related to the
increase in the "functional differentiation" of social systems such as
law, economics, and politics. The functional differentiation Luhmann
refers to entails the increasing inability for any one social system to
represent or to cope with the problems of society on an overarching
level.[15] Luhmann argues that the transition in Europe to a modern
society is characterized by a movement away from a stratified society
(in which the nobility occupied a privileged position that permitted

them to represent society as a whole—a *pars pro toto* relation) to a functionally differentiated society (in which no social system is hierarchically superior to another; Luhmann, *Teoría*, 44).

Political bureaucracy is more than just an undesirable residue of modern politics. Political bureaucracy is a *constitutive* element of the modern political state. What is subsequently perceived as political bureaucracy was initially a response to the increasing complexity of demands placed on decision-makers. Bureaucracies begin as organizational systems designed to *facilitate* decision-making by reducing complexity to a narrow field of options. Nevertheless, the more an organizational system is fine-tuned in order to cope with specific questions, the more "indifferent" it will be to everything else (*Teoría*, 43). Attempts to correct this indifference result in the creation of yet more bureaucracy. The systemic segmentation implicit in bureaucracies leads to the erosion of society as a centralized whole. Rather than deferring to the authority of a king, for example, modern bureaucracies are positivized systems whose authority is self-reflexively produced (*Teoría*, 111–17).

Precisely at the moment that Sahagún's work was confiscated, the Council of Indies was instigating important bureaucratic reforms that took the Spanish government one step closer to its positivization. The import of these reforms is most transparent in the questionnaires the Spanish government sent to the New World in order to improve its decision-making process. The questionnaire of 1573, by far the longest and most detailed, consisted of a hundred and thirty-five different instructions. Writing from El Escorial outside Madrid, Philip II ordered "the verifications, descriptions, and accounts of *the complete state* of the Indies and of *each thing and its parts*, in order that those who govern in both the spiritual and the temporal understand better and determine how to govern" (Solano and Ponce, 16–17, my emphasis). The questionnaire goes on to reiterate several times that "a complete account" must be given in response to the questions. Philip II wished to possess all the necessary information in order to guide his subjects in the spiritual as well as the temporal aspects of the world. More than once, the questionnaire

specifically asks for information on pre-Hispanic indigenous customs: "in sum, everything they might have had in their infidelity
and of that, that which should be taken away from them and that
which should be preserved" (23, 28). The questionnaire also specifically asks that members of the religious orders assist in the gathering
of information (19).

The questionnaire of 1573 was requesting exactly the kind of
information Sahagún was already collecting. Moreover, Sahagún's
goals do not seem to have been at variance with the goals of the
questionnaire. For example, Sahagún says that "in order to preach
against these things, it is necessary to know how they used them in
the time of their idolatry" (CF I:1r). In describing the good as well
as the bad, Sahagún's wish to show that the Nahuas were not "less
apt for our Christianity if they were to be duly cultivated in it" was
in perfect concert with the goals of the questionnaire (CF I:3r).

The questionnaire of 1573 demonstrates that, just a few years
before Philip II's famous warrant of 1577, Sahagún's work could
have received a positive reception at the Council of Indies. The
questionnaire of 1577, however, shows how quickly and how radically the government's goals had changed. The questionnaire of
1577, ordered by Philip II and composed by Juan López de Velasco,
no longer sought "entera noticia" (complete information). The questionnaire of 1577, consisting of just fifty succinct requests, asked for
"brief" and "clear" responses. Compared to the questionnaire of
1573, the requests are pared down and more specific. Moreover, the
questionnaire of 1577 goes further in dictating the structure the
responses should—and often would—take (Solano and Ponce,
79–87).

The switch from the request for a complete report to the request
for a brief and clear report implies a profound shift in the philosophy of government. A complete report implies a style of government in which the king or his representatives expected to make
decisions only after examining the complete panorama of facts. A
brief and clear report implies a style of government in which the
king or his representatives no longer felt that the virtual omniscience

implicit in a complete report was possible. Rather, decisions were to be made after examining a limited group of facts generated *by* the government. The functional differentiation of government exposed by this change of policy signals an undermining of the absolute sovereignty of the king. In this switch of policy, the control over the wheels of government passed from the hands of a centrally located, quasi-omniscient king to the governmental system itself. The switch is symptomatic of the split in modern European societies between the king and the state. In modern European societies, the centrality of the sovereign is in varying degrees replaced by the self-perpetuating mechanisms of a centralized state. From the end of the reign of Philip II on, the thirteenth-century definition of a king set forth by Alfonso X in *Las siete partidas* would be increasingly eroded:

And the saints said that the king is put on Earth in God's stead, in order to perform justice, and give each one his right. And for that reason they called him the heart and the soul of the people. . . . And just as the heart is one, and through it all the parts of the body receive their unity in order to be a body, so are all those of the kingdom, even if they be many (because the king is and should be the only one), and for this reason they should all be with him, in order to serve him and help him in the things he must do. ("Segunda partida, Título I, Ley V. Que cosa es el Rey")

In *Felipe II*, Geoffrey Parker has shown how Philip II's style of government grew out of his uphill struggle to maintain control over the increasingly complex political world of his dominions. Known as the "king of papers," Philip II attempted to do without a "cabinet" government and insisted on personally signing each and every one of his dispatches (48). Philip II, a great collector of things, sought to maintain the unity of his kingdom by situating himself in the geographical center of Spain and surrounding himself with reports rather than people in order to make his decisions. By 1560, the number of papers crossing the king's desk was mind-boggling, and by 1571 the king was required to make an average of forty decisions a day (51).[16]

Philip II's insistence on maintaining the unity of his kingdom through the personal surveillance of rapidly accumulating reports meant that many contradictory decisions were made (49). The difficulty any single person would have in handling all the decisions that needed to be made also meant that important decisions were made using criteria from another area. To a large extent, for example, the problems of the Low Countries were handled as if they were problems originating in the Americas and vice versa.

The appointment in 1566 of Juan de Ovando to investigate the Council of Indies grew out of two basic problems that Philip II could no longer neglect. First, no one in the Council of Indies was up to date on which laws were in effect. Second, very few members of the Council of Indies actually knew anything about the Americas (Parker, 143). The questionnaires of 1573 and 1577 were intended to compensate for this lack of knowledge. The questionnaire of 1577 produced a very large corpus of information on the New World known now as the *Relaciones geográficas* (see Solano and Ponce, *Cuestionarios*). The idea that the *Relaciones* were produced by the government and for the government in an attempt to centralize the decision-making process is supported by the fact that very little use was made of the knowledge stored in these documents by nongovernment personnel until modern historians rediscovered them. The government of Philip II operated on the assumption that, if it acquired enough information, it could make the right decisions from afar; but the growing complexity of the dominions overwhelmed these efforts. Even the attempt in the questionnaire of 1577 to coordinate how and what knowledge would be generated was thwarted by the complexity of a government that still tried to make centralized decisions through the king.

When Sahagún's work was confiscated, the Spanish government was being pulled in too many different directions by the demands of its faraway dominions. Ironically, the bureaucratic structures that Philip II put in motion in order to fight the decentralization of his reign—bureaucratic structures like the one implicit in the questionnaire of 1577—turned out to be the very same forces that in the end would undermine the actual authority of the king.

Sahagún's magnum opus was not confiscated by the bureaucratic government of Philip II so that it could be destroyed. It was confiscated because, having received notice of its existence, the government of Philip II wished to incorporate it into its new project of centralizing the production and processing of information on the New World. Not only was the *Florentine Codex* not destroyed, a laborious copy of its contents (the Tolosa manuscript) was made in Spain in an attempt to preserve the nonpictorial information it contained (Bustamante García, *Fray Bernardino,* 328–46). The sheer amount of work this copy implies belies the notion that Philip II's government was against preserving information on the indigenous world. What the government of Philip II *was* against was non-government-sponsored historical or ethnographic projects in the New World.

Although Sahagún certainly had his share of difficulties with his companions in New Spain,[17] he was not the victim of a personal vendetta. Sahagún was the victim of the indifference of an increasingly bureaucratic government that was relying more and more on categorical decision-making schemas rather than on the circumstances of any individual situation. The recent transition to this style of government explains why Sahagún was content to turn over his work to the government. Sahagún was oblivious to the potential consequences; the entirely inhuman indifference of far-reaching bureaucracies (with which modern individuals are now familiar) was unforeseen in his time.[18]

The modern individual is familiar with the feeling that someone should be held accountable in a bureaucratic structure—yet, as an afterthought, it is also accepted that often this person simply does not and cannot exist. Bureaucratic structures are social systems that have gone a long way toward existing over and beyond the individuals who rely on them. In the everyday life-world, human beings act on others on the assumption that they, too, can be acted on. Schütz and Luckmann point out, however, that the growth of the state along with the development of mass media "have promoted a far-reaching anonymization of some (important) social relations"

(2:96).[19] In modern times, the immediacy of human acts—the foundation stone of the human life-world—is increasingly confronted with the "mediacy" of *unilateral* acts. Increasingly, in modern times, something can happen to a person without there being any way to reciprocate the act—partly because the act was unilateral, partly because it was not an act originating in the immediacy of a face-to-face situation.

The temptation to view Sahagún as the victim of a personal vendetta or of a conspiracy directed primarily at him is similar in at least one regard to the temptation to assume, as his biographers tend to do, that he is just like the modern individual. Both temptations share the (natural) tendency to apply the structures of the immediate life-world to structures that are cut off from the presence and immediacy that constitute the cornerstone of human understanding.[20]

Perhaps Fray Gerónimo de Mendieta was not too far off when he assumed that the *Florentine Codex* was being used to wrap up spices in Spain. Jesús Bustamante García has convincingly argued that the *Florentine Codex* was given by Philip II as a wedding gift to Francis I and Bianca Capello, who married in Italy in 1579 (*Fray Bernardino*, 342). Bustamante's hypothesis implies that Philip II valued the *Florentine Codex* partly as an objet d'art, and the Tolosa manuscript is the copy he ordered to be made of the material in Spanish translation that Sahagún had so painstakingly gathered. This, surely, was not what Sahagún had in mind when he sent his manuscript to Spain; if he had expected this, he never would have gone to the trouble to commission illustrations and copy down the original Nahuatl. Whether it was used to wrap up spices, or was seen as a quaint picture book most suitable to be given away as a wedding present, or was perceived as yet more information to be sorted and analyzed at some later date, the uses to which the *Florentine Codex* was put were far-removed from the more immediate concerns of Sahagún and his fellow missionaries in New Spain. Given the fact that Sahagún poured so much of his life into the writing of the *Florentine Codex*, its confiscation does constitute a kind of victimization; but despite what many critics and historians may have hoped, it was not the kind of victimization that makes saints into martyrs.

3. A Nineteenth-Century Rediscovery of Sahagún

The monumental status of Fray Bernardino de Sahagún's corpus is in marked contradistinction to the paucity of concrete information about his personal life. Sahagún's tendency to downplay—but not soften—his moral views sets him apart from the legions of writers of the time who clamored to have their views on the Spanish conquest of Mexico heard and heard again. As I argued earlier, the dearth of information on Sahagún's life coupled with his tendency to express his views sotto voce have permitted an extremely malleable historical memory of him.

As each succeeding generation has looked back on Sahagún, he has undergone a subtle—but nonetheless profound—series of symbolic transformations. In seventeenth-century Mexico, for example, a highly flattering description of Sahagún was included in Fray Agustín de Vetancurt's *Teatro mexicano* (113), a work Benjamin Keen has characterized in *The Aztec Image in Western Thought* as primarily concerned with providing the incipient *criollismo*[21] of late seventeenth-century Mexico with a suitably dignified past (187–89). This inclusion of Sahagún in an ideological project designed to construct the foundations of a Creole hegemony can be contrasted with that of Sahagún's contemporary, Fray Gerónimo de Mendieta, in his *Historia eclesiástica indiana*. Begun in 1573, Mendieta's work must be read in light of the growing tensions that were developing between the Mendicant orders in New Spain and the government of Philip II. Like Vetancurt, Mendieta was interested in chronicling the achievements of the Franciscan missionaries in New Spain; but far from being incipient criollismo, Mendieta's main concern was with vindicating an order that was increasingly coming under fire from secular authorities. Mendieta's ironic passage concerning the fate of Sahagún's life's work at the hands of secular authorities—a passage to which I alluded earlier—is symptomatic of Mendieta's overall purpose of justifying the Franciscan position in the political struggle over who would control the indigenous population's bodies and souls: "He had such little luck, this blessed father, in the work of his writings, that these eleven books that I speak of were cautiously removed by a governor of this land and sent to Spain to a chronicler who requested papers on the Indies, but which will be used there to wrap up spices" (Mendieta, 663). Mendieta's veiled barb at the unnamed governor is one case in a long line of examples that support Mendieta's view that Spanish officials were scoundrels who should not have access to his projected Franciscan and indigenous utopia.[22]

The memory of Sahagún was well tended by Mendieta and Vetancurt, and each one saw Sahagún as an important part of their respective visions. Other succinct and relatively isolated references to the life or work of Sahagún during the seventeenth and eighteenth centuries by writers and historians including Antonio de León Pinelo, Luke Wadding, Nicolás Antonio, Fray Juan de San Antonio, Juan José de Eguiara y Eguren, Francisco Xavier Clavijero, Juan Bautista Muñoz, and Angelo María Bandini helped keep the trail fresh for those who would later look back in time for clues about Sahagún.[23] Nevertheless, it was the nineteenth century that saw the memory of Sahagún grow in stature at an exponential rate. In his survey of nineteenth-century Mexican writers of ethnohistory, Howard F. Cline notes that during the post-1821 period Mexican historians were primarily concerned with providing their new nation with a shared historical legacy that could set it off from other nations.[24] Cline goes on to say that the post-1821 writers were different from colonial writers in that colonial writers did not share any *single* patriotic goal. After 1821, historical interpretations of the indigenous and colonial Spanish past were channeled into efforts at establishing a Mexican national identity, and as Cline points out, much of current Mexican historiography is still governed by these concerns (370–71).[25]

It is not too surprising that many of the major figures in nineteenth-century Mexican historiography such as José Fernández

Ramírez, Manuel Orozco y Berra, Joaquín García Icazbalceta, Francisco del Paso y Troncoso, and Alfredo Chavero are also the historians with the keenest interest in Sahagún. The nineteenth-century resurgence of interest in Sahagún is mainly attributable to the editorial zeal with which these historians sought to piece together the Sahagún corpus as part of a greater program to establish foundational texts for the new nation. For Mexican historians who were grappling with how to reconcile the indigenous past with the Spanish colonial past, Sahagún seemed to offer an irresistible example. Here was a devout man who dedicated his life to recording the indigenous past in a seemingly scientific way and who seemed to rise above the political intrigues and shenanigans of his Spanish contemporaries—even if he was frequently affected by them. Sahagún seemed—and still seems to many—the perfect reconciliation between what Cline denotes as the two predominant historiographical schools in nineteenth-century Mexico: the "indigenistas" and the "hispanistas" (371).

The conversion of Sahagún into a symbol of Mexican nationalism is not difficult to understand—even if on closer examination, like all nationalistic thematizations of the past, it lacks a certain coherence. What *is* less apparent, however, is why a large number of European writers came to identify with this cause and sought—implicitly or explicitly—to make substantial contributions to the construction of a Mexican national identity, often through their contributions to criticism on the Sahagún corpus. An examination of the work of the nineteenth-century travel writer Jules-Césaire (Giacomo Costantino) Beltrami will help answer this question.

The major nineteenth-century European contribution to Sahagún studies was made, of course, by Eduard Georg Seler (1849–1922),[26] but it is my contention that much insight into the expectations of the spurt of newly arrived nineteenth-century European writers on Mesoamerica can be garnered by examining the work of Beltrami, an earlier and much lesser known—and in that sense, less successful—author. Longstanding acceptance of the value of Seler's work has "naturalized" it; this is not the case with Beltrami's.[27] Seler's rigorous and painstaking scholarship was developed in the second half of the nineteenth century in the context of fully established academic disciplines that are now taken for granted but that in no way can be considered to predate the period of nascent European nationalisms. The same can be said for the scholarship of European figures who concerned themselves with Sahagún such as Rémi Siméon (author of *Dictionnaire de la langue nahuatl ou mexicaine*, 1885), Eugène Boban, and Cayetano Rosell.[28] Beltrami's writings, however, predate the time—still current—when unstudied amateurs would be ridiculed if they really thought they could make serious contributions to the various arcane fields of science. At the end of the eighteenth century and the beginning of the nineteenth the situation was the opposite. As Mary Louise Pratt points out in *Imperial Eyes: Travel Writing and Transculturation*, the arrival of the "Linnaean systematizing project had a markedly democratic dimension, popularizing scientific inquiry as it had never been popularized before" (27). By merely cataloguing what they saw, whether plants or customs, travel writers such as Beltrami felt they were making a significant contribution to the progress of science. The fact that Beltrami has dated himself so much in this sense allows for substantial insight into what was at stake for many of these nineteenth-century European writers.

Jules-Césaire Beltrami is primarily—if not exclusively—remembered today for the pages he dedicated in his *Le Mexique* (1830) to the life and work of Sahagún. Beltrami's section on Sahagún was reprinted by Bernardino Biondelli in 1858 as a preface to his publication of Sahagún's *Evangelio* as *Evangeliarium Epistolarium et Lecionarium Aztecum sive Mexicanum ex Antiquo Codice Mexicano nuper reperto depromptum* (Bustamante García, *Fray Bernardino*, 91–96). It is mostly this version that is known today, and Beltrami's larger work, *Le Mexique*, is now almost never—if ever—read in its entirety. Nevertheless, in his day Beltrami was a well-known figure who was famous for having discovered the source of the Mississippi River—a feat considered quite noteworthy at the time.[29] Antonello Gerbi notes in *The Dispute of the New World* that François Auguste-René de Chateaubriand, for example, based his descriptions of a Mississippi he had never seen on Beltrami's *Notizie e lettere* (358n).[30]

Although *Le Mexique* was composed in an epistolary form directed to an unnamed countess, Beltrami wrote with the confidence that the observations he made during his travels through Mexico, like those he had made in North America, would be of interest to a larger audience: "Perhaps my letters will fall some day into the hands of the public; they will be read by reasonable men, by good Christians, when Jesuitism will have finally ceased to profane Heaven and to corrupt the Earth" (2:315).

Beltrami referred to his journey as a "pilgrimage"; but unlike traditional pilgrimages, which are defined and given their meaning by the journey to and from a particular place of worship, Beltrami was headed nowhere in particular. It was Beltrami himself—a man with, in his own opinion, particular observational skills—who provided the added symbolic sense and narrative thread of a pilgrimage to his haphazard journey through Mexico. I will argue that Beltrami's exaggerated sense of himself as a traveler endowed with special observational skills is neither an anomaly nor a secondary aspect of Beltrami's narrative. Rather, it is the symptom of a profound epistemological shift that was occurring in European thought at the end of the eighteenth and the beginning of the nineteenth century in which the subject, rather than a given natural order, was increasingly being relied on to determine what constituted knowledge.[31] By studying this shift through the work of Beltrami, I hope to explain why European thinkers became more and more obsessed with creating an archival and archeological past for Mesoamerica and its inhabitants. I propose to do this by placing Beltrami's comments on Sahagún in the larger context of *Le Mexique* and then by examining his work as a symptom of the epistemological tensions of his times as evidenced in the work of Immanuel Kant. This critical approach may seem peculiar, since Kant is so far removed from the world of Sahagún. Beltrami's depiction of Sahagún, however, was not. In his earlier *Pilgrimage in America*, Beltrami explicitly places himself under the aegis of Kant's philosophical system

(98–99). It is through a Kantian perspective that Beltrami viewed and portrayed Sahagún.

Part way through his narrative, Beltrami describes the tenth letter of his *Le Mexique* as "eternal," for he felt that he had shed significant light on the "chaos of absurdities, fables, and impostures" that surrounded the history of ancient Mexico (2:167). Beltrami's achievements had not come to an end, however, because he had an even greater find to report: the rediscovery of an unpublished Sahagún manuscript (the *Evangelio* in Nahuatl).

Beltrami felt his rediscovery of the manuscript was important because of its potential usefulness to science and to Mexican nationalism and because of what he felt Sahagún represented:

Generous souls, always sensitive to that which, in some way, relates to the regeneration of peoples, moreover will be interested in this monument because of the memory of one of these men whom, like those of Las Casas, true Christian sentiments have distinguished from a turpitude on this side of the Atlantic that came to desolate these unhappy lands: one sees there the fine remnant of the illustrious philanthropist and monk, Bernardino de Sahagún. His precious works, so worthy of the most beautiful fame, were destroyed or hidden because his sentiments had better served the Evangelist and Humanity than the politics and greed of the Spaniards. This find will crown my small Mexican toils. (2:168)

For Beltrami, Sahagún was a solace amid the memories of European horrors (2:168), a man who should have been canonized, and would have been, if he had chosen to serve monarchs instead of humanity (2:168, 171). According to Beltrami, humanity was the hero of Sahagún's heart and pen, but politics and greed (embodied in the Spaniards) conspired against him (2:170) even after he was forced to leave Spain, where "the frock is nothing more than a cloak for vice and passions" (2:169). Beltrami considered Sahagún the most important man of letters in colonial New Spain. He describes him as "the Dante, the Pascal, the Gessner, the Johnson, the classical model, in short, for the language of the country [Nahuatl]" (2:169). Amid the "savage conspiracy" (2:172) against Sahagún and his work, only the indigenous population was capable of appreciating his pure religiosity. The emotional import Beltrami attached to the memory of Sahagún is made even more explicit in the exaggerated devotion of his supposed visits to his tomb: "His remains are the most precious relic of this convent of Saint Francis; they are the sublunary object most worthy of veneration that I have encountered during my Mexican pilgrimage. I believe that I must have been taken for an Indian, for I was often seen full of devotion before his tomb" (2:171).[32]

Beltrami finishes his letter with an explanation of what he feels is the scientific importance of his discovery.[33] In accordance with the precepts of Gottfried Wilhelm Leibnitz, Giambattista Vico, and an incipient European philology (which grew out of the search for the origins of peoples and nations through the comparison of languages) Beltrami believed Sahagún's manuscript offered the key to unraveling the history of the Mexicans (2:176–78). Beltrami's final words reveal the confidence he had in the importance of his find: "I will be happy to have opened up, in this manner, a new field of science and literature to you, Countess, to our friends, and to society. I send you my greetings" (2:179). By recuperating the manuscript of an appropriately politicized Sahagún, Beltrami credits himself, no less, with having founded a new field of disciplinary study.

From Beltrami's pages on Sahagún I would like to highlight two important aspects. First, Sahagún represented for Beltrami a beacon in the darkness of the Spanish colonial period. Sahagún was symbolically important to Beltrami for scientific, nationalistic (political), and moral reasons. Second, it is important to note that Beltrami wants to take credit solely for these important discoveries. Beltrami's guides and archival assistants are faceless, nameless beings who seem all but irrelevant to the light Beltrami sheds on Mexico. It is fair to wonder whether Beltrami really discovered the Sahagún manuscript amid the reams of colonial documents in Mexico, or whether some librarian showed it to him.[34] These two aspects of Beltrami's pages on Sahagún must be examined in light of what precedes and follows them in the text of *Le Mexique*.

In *Imperial Eyes*, Pratt has laid out the critical foundation for understanding travel narratives such as Beltrami's. Pratt's work on Alexander von Humboldt, for example, is especially relevant for the case of Beltrami since Beltrami repeatedly compares his journey through Mexico to Humboldt's. She argues that the "conventions of travel and exploration writing (production and reception) constitute the European subject as a self-sufficient, monadic source of knowledge" (136). Pratt points out that Humboldt constitutes himself in this way through a curious fusion of the specificity of science and an esthetics of the sublime (121). Pratt goes on to show that, in a "mirror dance of colonial meaning-making," European travel and exploration writers such as Humboldt often appropriated preexisting Creole knowledge and glorifications of American nature and antiquity in order to have the privilege of being the ones to bestow (reimport) these gifts on Creoles (136–37). In a context in which Creole nationalists sought to separate themselves culturally from Europe, the European reimportation of rehashed knowledge constituted an attempt to keep the dominance of European knowledge in the picture when it was no longer welcome. To a large extent, this political and intellectual ruse was quite successful, since Humboldt's books became foundational texts in the forging of Creole national identities in the 1820s, 1830s, and 1840s, although maybe not in the way Europeans had anticipated (175, 187).

My use of the word "ruse" might seem exaggerated at first, but travel writers such as Beltrami were often quite explicit in their high estimation of themselves as bestowers of knowledge. Beltrami wrote two lengthy dedications for *Le Mexique*. The first one is dedicated to European sovereigns, but the second one is dedicated to the Mexicans themselves. In "Aux Mexicains" Beltrami states that "the force of your character, your wisely combined institutions, your fine arts [are] almost entirely hidden to the stranger and to yourselves" (1:ix). Beltrami goes on to say that, even if the Mexicans earned their own independence, it is he who has tried to restore their achievements to them: "Unknown peoples, and dignified to be! I have tried, and I had to do it even for the honor of the Human Species, to restore to you your titles of illustriousness, so audaciously concealed or usurped by the deception of jealous conquerors and timid oppressors" (1:x). Beltrami's claim to rediscovering the Sahagún manuscript is what he considers to be the finest example of how he has restored to the Mexican people their past achievements. Ironically, the manuscript Beltrami carried off to Europe is almost certainly not by Sahagún. Moreover, it is hard to argue that Beltrami made it available to a large public since it was only published in a limited edition which is only extant in the special collections sections of a few libraries. The original—whatever it is—is now housed in Italy.[35]

The "jealous conquerors" and "timid oppressors" to whom Beltrami refers are, of course, the Spaniards. Sahagún and Sahagún's manuscripts take on special political and moral significance if they are contrasted with Beltrami's general opinion of Spaniards and Spanish priests. Sahagún, a true Christian in Beltrami's eyes, is the complete opposite of all the other composite peninsular-born Spaniards and Spanish priests he describes in *Le Mexique*.[36] Beltrami never tires of enumerating and repeating the vices of both the peninsular-born Spaniards he encountered during his journey and the most infamous of the Spanish colonial oppressors of the past. Beltrami creates a running joke about the Spanish priests' *"sobrinas"* (nieces)—the word he claims they used to describe their mistresses. At one point, Beltrami even reproduces in lengthy dialogue form an absurd argument he claimed he had with a priest who defended his right to have a mistress. I quote here only a small part:

PRIEST: Nothing in the Sacred Scriptures prohibits marriage to whomever they may be; on the contrary, everything recommends it, and principally the *crescite* and *multiplicamini*; a great publicist from your country has said that the best institution the Jews had was the abhorrence of virginity, and that it is because of their devotion to marriage that they still dominate, in a sense, the world.

BELTRAMI: But you know that the Apostles abandoned their wives as soon as they received the Holy Spirit: and that is what the consecration of priests is assimilated to when they receive their orders.

PRIEST: So it is said; but it is not Jesus Christ who speaks of it. That inhuman, antisocial, barbarian action could never have come from either him or his Apostles. (2:325–26)

Beltrami sums up his views on Spaniards in general at the end of the first volume of his work when he claims that the perverse Spaniards have always been the same as they are blinded by their misguided national pride (1:397–98). Later on, Beltrami makes even clearer what the problem with the Spanish nation is: it is no nation at all. Beltrami explains that Spain is a "gothic edifice constructed out of fragments," with no public spirit or commonly held interests (2:365). Beltrami lends objective authority to his prejudiced statements by crediting them to a dissenting—hence honest—advisor to the Spanish king Ferdinand.

Beltrami's Mexican Creoles offer the other extreme in his moral narrative. If he happens to meet a good priest, he is always quick to point out he is a Creole (1:216). He considers the Creoles in general to be the best Catholics (2:230), and he even finds Mexican women enchanting when they smoke their "*cigaritos*" (sic), even though he himself only will smoke while playing court to "savages" in Mississippi (2:268). Nevertheless, the general high esteem in which Beltrami holds all Mexican Creoles is most apparent when he credits himself with having acquired during his journey "Creole thoughts" (1:240).

If Beltrami's image of Sahagún seems two-dimensional, it is because the images of all the people Beltrami meets in Mexico are two-dimensional. Beltrami populates Mexico with cardboard caricatures of evil Spaniards and good Creoles—using his exaggerated amazement in the face of exceptions to prove the objectivity of his general rule.[37] Sahagún is swept up in Beltrami's greater purpose of demonstrating how worthy the Creoles are of their new-found independence and how deserving the Spaniards are of any ill that might befall them. For Beltrami, Sahagún is the historic figure who best unifies his threefold purpose of supporting Mexican nationalism, identifying true Christianity (as opposed to Spanish religious hypocrisy), and contributing to science.

Unlike Humboldt's works, Beltrami's *Le Mexique* did not go on to become a foundational text in the formation of a Mexican Creole identity. The poverty of Beltrami's text compared to the work of Humboldt is one reason, but another reason is equally, if not more, important. Beltrami's conviction that he was helping to forge the Mexican identity was expressed so openly, it must surely have been somewhat offensive to Creole intellectuals, who prided themselves on being independent intellectually as well as politically. Benedict Anderson points out in *Imagined Communities* that, despite European intellectuals' convictions to the contrary, the rise of independent nation-states in the New World was due more to Creole functionaries (*letrados*) hoping to break out of their imposed economic barriers than to the noble ideals of liberalism and of the Enlightenment (Anderson, 65). Although the early stages of the struggle for independence in Mexico are more ambiguous in that lower classes were involved, it is generally recognized that, early on, the struggle for Mexican independence fell into the same pattern of a triumphing politico-economic elite that is recognizable in other Latin American independence movements. Monarchical—and even supposedly liberal—Spain had become a millstone around the necks of *criollos* (Creoles), who realized during the turn-of-the-century European wars that they did not need Spain as an intermediary. As Ramón Eduardo Ruiz notes in *Triumphs and Tragedy*, "the criollos wanted a government for themselves but no structural changes" (147).

The attempt to explain nationalism in the New World as a direct result of the influence of European liberalism and the Enlightenment can be read as a symptom of an epistemological crisis as well as a political crisis in Europe. In retrospect, there is something desperate about Beltrami's heartfelt need to convince Mexicans that it was he, and not they, who was providing them with the knowledge they needed in order to forge their new identities. The fact that Beltrami goes to such great pains to convince the readers of his credentials as an objective observer indicates just how problematic those credentials were. In what follows, I would like to examine Beltrami's self-authorization as a purveyor of knowledge in light of the epistemological shift that Michel Foucault identified as occurring at the end of the eighteenth century. For Foucault, Kant's *Critiques* mark one of the signposts of this turning point between the eighteenth and nineteenth centuries. The way in which Beltrami establishes his observational credentials parallels a philosophical position inherited from Kant's *Critique of Judgement*. Beltrami, who was a reader of Kant and situated in time at the end of the "Kantian moment," shares with him the European epistemological angst of a knowing subject who no longer holds a discernible ontological link to the object of knowledge. My explanation of the role of Sahagún in Beltrami's work will begin to resemble Russian nesting dolls: the specificity of Sahagún in Beltrami's work is determined by the larger epistemological currents of Beltrami and his time, so it now becomes necessary to examine what Kant signifies in the history of mentalities.

In *Les mots et les choses*, Foucault argues that "that which had changed at the turn of the century, and provoked an irreparable alteration, was knowledge itself as a preliminary and undivided mode of being between the subject that knows and the object of knowledge" (264). Kant's highly systematic attempt to determine the a priori status of the human faculty to reason is symptomatic of a growing late-eighteenth-century preoccupation with bridging the newly opened chasm separating the object of knowledge from the knower. Previous to this epistemological crisis, European thinkers had not felt that the very foundations of human understanding were perilously unstable. Many factors converged to provoke this crisis—not least of which was the growing discrepancy between the biblical account of creation and the growing mass of archaeological evidence of an evolving geological history. Travelers and explorers to the New World unknowingly contributed to the crisis by providing a more and more complex picture of nature and the world that was increasingly difficult to reconcile with a literal reading of the Bible. In *La física sagrada*, to cite one example, Horacio Capel studies the Spanish contribution to the seventeenth- and eighteenth-century scientific debates on the world's geological origins. Capel's study is especially revealing because Spain, as the self-pronounced defender of Catholic orthodoxy, was even more determined to bridge the increasingly large gap separating scientific findings and the biblical account of creation. All the authors Capel examines reveal that the more the incommensurability of the two world-views was glimpsed, the more thinkers came to rely on the power of the observing individual to reconcile them. Moreover, the more problematic the authoritative position of the observing individual became, the more scholars attempted to recur to sharp, unknowable—but nonetheless real—divisions between natural explanations and supernatural explanations—between empiricism and transcendentalism.

Kant's *Critiques* must be understood in light of these tensions, and particularly, the growing tensions between empirical and transcendental explanations of the world. From the nineteenth century on, knowledge was believed to be produced only through the subject. Kant's *Critiques* represent one of the last major European philosophical projects concerned with reconciling a previous notion that knowledge is produced by God and the world with the nineteenth-century notion that knowledge is produced by the subject (a source of knowledge that is not a priori).

Kant's *Critique of Judgement* grew out of his need to unify his conceptions of practical and theoretical reason through the a priori human faculty of judgement. Kant's impasse resided in the fact that, playing by the rules of his own philosophical system, the existence of the faculty of judgement could not be arrived at without first passing through practical or theoretical reason—hence rendering its a priori status questionable. In more general parlance, this philosophical dilemma can be described as the problem of determining the relationship between the organization of human understanding and the organization humans perceive in nature. Kant wanted to show that human understanding brought a teleologically organized knowledge to nature and that nature itself coalesced with this finality, *even though it could not be shown a priori*. Beltrami, as I shall show, shares this predicament, and his Sahagún gets caught up in the wake.

As is well known in literary studies, Kant's concepts of taste, beauty, and the sublime became central elements in his quest to vindicate and reconcile the human subject vis-à-vis an increasingly opaque nature—a nature so rich in complexity that its organizational laws could never be discerned through sheer empiricism. Kant uses his arguments on taste, beauty, and the sublime to arrive at the a priori status of the finality of nature, and in section 66 Kant explicitly brings the a priori principle of the finality of nature together with the need for empirical observation (223).[38]

Beltrami shares with Kant a newly found—if only illusory—confidence in the power and importance of the observer. For Beltrami, the kind of moral relativism implicit in the quotation that follows did not constitute a problem, for following what he refers to repeatedly as his "system," Beltrami acted with the utmost confidence that all his observations were objective, even if they passed first through the channels of his own mind: "It is said that, whatever he does, man only acts relative to himself, and that, even in the most sublime acts of virtue, even in the most pure works of charity, everything is in reference to oneself" (1:295).

Beltrami's defense of his scientific pursuits is expressed even more concretely in Kantian terms. Throughout his journey, Beltrami gathered plants and artifacts, which he stored in large chests (often assumed by thieves and greedy customs officials to contain more expensive items). Beltrami's primary interest was botany, for he felt that of all the sciences, it was the most accessible to all reasoning individuals regardless of their scientific background. Beltrami argues that botany is superior to all the other sciences, with the exception of theology, because it is the most positivistic in enabling one to determine the divine finality behind nature (1:321). As is the case for Kant, nature no longer offers Beltrami self-evident proof of the existence of a divine plan. Nevertheless, Beltrami believes that this divine plan can be perceived through the "solitary" observation of the realm of nature that most freely reveals its hidden organization: the world of plants. Plants are superior to minerals in Beltrami's eyes because the mineral world is too hidden from the average person's eyes to facilitate the natural coalescence between the observer's understanding and the natural order of things (1:317). The same holds true for astronomy, for even though the beauty of the heavens is a fine tribute to God's creative powers, humans can only employ their observational skills with the help of apparatuses such as telescopes (1:322).

Beltrami's arguments could be perceived as a layperson's paraphrasing of Kant, for Kant makes these kinds of arguments in support of his ideas concerning the relationship between the faculty of judgement and the organization of Nature. In fact, in what might be identified as a kind of circularity of influences, Kant was particularly interested in how European explorers to the New World observed nature when they came face-to-face with its wonders. In accordance with Kant's privileging of a direct experience of nature as a way of understanding better the divide that distances human beings from it, Beltrami argues that his form of botany is superior to all others because he eschews the unnecessary distraction of scientific terminology (1:323). In short, his form of botany is superior because it is the most sublime, the most mentally purifying (1:320), the most directly in contact with Nature:

Fleeing from men, searching for solitude, no longer using one's imagination, thinking even less, and nevertheless gifted with a lively temperament that distances us from languishing apathy, one begins to notice everything that surrounds us; and through a very natural instinct, one gives preference to those objects that present themselves as most agreeable. (1:316–17)

The turn of the century epistemological crisis apparent in European thinkers such as Kant had a direct effect on travelers and explorers such as Beltrami and vice versa. Beltrami's exaggerated need to impose his observing self on the New World must be read as a symptom of a European form of knowledge that was no longer stable and needed to convince itself of its well-being by convincing everyone else in the process. Beltrami repeatedly states that he does what he does in the interests of the Mexican Creole population, but all his numerous chests filled with plant specimens and finds such as the Sahagún manuscript are sent to Europe. What can now be perceived as Beltrami's exaggerated faith in the observing subject's power to coincide with a divine finality in Nature not only lies at the root of his scientific pursuits, it lies at the root of his political convictions. It is this same exaggerated faith in the powers of the observing subject that enables Beltrami to, he believed, shed divinely inspired light on Mexican politics despite the darkness that has engulfed the country. The power of knowledge that allows Beltrami to perceive God's plan in plants despite an acknowledged rift between the knower and the object of knowledge serves, too, as the precondition for a politics in which Mexican Creoles, like nature, contain God's plan but require a knowing subject like Beltrami to reveal it. Beltrami's faith in his scientific credentials as an objective observer serve as the cornerstone for all other aspects of his travel narrative. His supposed scientific objectivity is perversely charged with a priori ethical—even divine—content. For Beltrami, science is closely correlated with Christian ethics. Sahagún, a man who lived hundreds of years before, is so symbolically important to Beltrami because he supposedly shared in the same philanthropic quest—or pilgrimage—to shed divine light and knowledge on a country kept in darkness through the moral chicanery of the Spaniards. Beltrami bears testimony to the notion that nineteenth-century European politics and the nineteenth-century European epistemological crisis exist in a symbiotic relationship with each other.

Foucault argues that the nineteenth-century European destabilization of faith in ontological arguments coincides with a growing tendency in Europe to look outside its borders for its own identity and a growing preoccupation with the concept of the "Other" (*Les mots*, 339). Kant marks the final stage of the Enlightenment, when this ontological instability first began to loom large and menacingly on the horizon. Beltrami gains his confidence in the restorative powers of the solitary individual observer through an elaborate Kantian scaffolding that holds it aloft. Throughout the nineteenth century, as the grounds for European knowledge became more and more problematic, the interest in the Other increased to almost obsessive proportions. The less the European subject could rely on the coalescence of the self and the world as a source of knowledge, the more it tried to rely on the construction of knowledge through the construction of the Other. It is for this reason that, for nineteenth-century European thinkers, the appealing perception that Sahagún had successfully bridged the gap between Europeans and the Other gained in resonance and symbolic importance. The allure of this perception of Sahagún is attested to by the number of anonymous colonial texts that have been attributed to him with little or no foundation.[39]

In recent years the image of Sahagún has been "regenerated"— to use one of Beltrami's favorite verbs—in the self-consciously construed crisis of modern anthropology. Whereas nineteenth-century thinkers such as Beltrami believed Sahagún had successfully bridged the culture gap, contemporary critics perceive a Sahagún who struggled with his cognitive and ethical limits the way modern anthropologists self-consciously do now. For many contemporary critics Sahagún represents a man—paralleling their own moral dilemmas—who heroically sought to resolve the incommensurability of European and indigenous cultures as he respectfully recognized the futility of his task. This phenomenon is one of the topics of the next chapter.

2

PATERNITY SUITS AND CASES
OF MISTAKEN IDENTITY

*Current Interpretations of Sahagún's Mind-Set
and Symbolic Importance*

The five-hundred-year anniversary celebration in 1992 of the discovery of America by Christopher Columbus was meant to focus attention on the importance of the event, but the more the event was examined, the less appealing it became. For example, the word "discovery" was replaced at an early stage of the preparations with the theme of an encounter between two worlds in an attempt to mollify the growing number of protesters who found little to celebrate in the arrival of Europeans on the American continent. In contrast to previous centennial celebrations of the event—which included an attempt in the nineteenth century to canonize Columbus—schoolchildren in 1992 were taught to question Columbus's status as a hero and sometimes even to see him as an outright villain.[1] The enormous quantity of biographies, histories, film adaptations, and documentaries prepared in anticipation of the event—sometimes with little more than profit in mind—was met by an increasingly suspicious public. The combination of muted hostility, indifference, and embarrassment surrounding the celebration is typified by the plight of the sailors of the replicas of the Santa María, Pinta, and Niña, who were left stranded in New York with no funds either to make further scheduled stops or to return to their home port in Spain—or even to find temporary lodgings in New York.[2]

The decline of Columbus's popularity as a symbol of the European discovery of the Americas left the public at large without any simple way to comprehend the enormity of what happened when Europeans began to colonize the Americas. It is in this context, and with the social tensions that led up to it in mind, that specialized scholars—if not yet the general public—have become increasingly interested in figures who are perceived to have blurred the boundaries between exploiter and exploited in the American colonies. In recent years, critics have increasingly focused their attention on sixteenth-century Europeans, indigenes, or mestizos—such as Fray Bartolomé de Las Casas, Álvar Núñez Cabeza de Vaca, Felipe Guamán Poma de Ayala, or Diego Múñoz Camargo—who might have been uniquely positioned to grapple with issues of mutual respect and cultural relativity and incommensurability. The recent surge in publications on Sahagún—including editions and translations of his works—is indicative of this same trend, for Sahagún clearly was a gifted polyglot who sought to come to terms, in a *partially* sympathetic manner, with the customs of his parishioners—the Nahuas.[3]

Nevertheless, much recent criticism has jumped to the hasty conclusion that Sahagún saw or dealt with problems of cultural relativity as people today might see or deal with them. Hence, Sahagún has been labeled the father of the culturally sensitized modern discipline of anthropology, and Sahagún's heightened sensitivity has partially been explained as a result of his "humanistic" education—an explanation that rests on the problematic assumption that Renaissance humanism is a clearly definable philanthropic movement that is inherently the moral superior of its medieval predecessor, scholasticism.[4]

Whereas the label "father of modern anthropology" has mostly proven useful in the past as an ideological construct that legitimated nationalistic claims of the Latin American invention of a scientific discipline, the label "Renaissance humanist" has served to confound progress in knowledge with progress in morality. When this misidentification is applied to Sahagún, he is considered morally superior to his medieval-minded colonial predecessors because, it is argued, he was graced with a humanistic education at the University of Salamanca. I believe that the more these labels are employed, the more they lose any explanatory power they initially might have had. I believe that it is certainly imperative that the fruits of modern anthropology be used to enhance understanding of Sahagún and his work. Nevertheless, crediting Sahagún with founding modern anthropology diverts attention away from the fact that Sahagún did what he did in a context that was alien to the nineteenth-century disciplinary organization of knowledge in which anthropology introduced itself into a university setting. In short, anthropology has something to teach modern scholars about Sahagún, but Sahagún has nothing, or very little, to teach today's practicing anthropologists about their own disciplinary problems. Moreover, placing Sahagún clearly on the side of Renaissance humanism in an appeal to his humanity obfuscates the particularity and import of his New World context as well as the curious role his medieval heritage played in his work.

Many scholars' interest in Sahagún's work (i.e., the *Florentine Codex*) stems from their impression that it represents a relatively transparent description of indigenous culture, since Sahagún took care to separate the reports he garnered in Nahuatl from his translations and commentaries. Sahagún used indigenous informants and took care to retain a version in Nahuatl of the information he gathered. On a very superficial level, it is easy to mistake this version in Nahuatl for raw data. Since Sahagún's methodology paralleled an ideal of the feasibility of scientific empiricism that enjoyed popularity before Thomas Kuhn challenged it, Sahagún not only has been heralded as a precursor to the modern scientific methods used in the discipline of anthropology but was cited extensively as the objective last word on authentic Nahua culture.[5] Since over the past few decades both the physical and social sciences have come to question claims of interpretive transparency—in essence, to reexamine the role of the observer in producing knowledge—the valorization of Sahagún's seemingly empirical methodology was bound to be scrutinized anew by critics in an attempt to determine what paradigms or belief systems lay at its base.

John Keber, in an enlightening essay, has approached this problem by sidestepping the issue of Sahagún's stature as the father of modern anthropology and treating him as a figure who inevitably operated within the confines of his Christian belief system.[6] J. Jorge Klor de Alva has taken this approach a step further by attempting to bridge the gap between the limits of Sahagún's Christian parameters and the claim that Sahagún's distinctive methodology still entitles him to be considered the first modern anthropologist or the father of modern anthropology (Klor de Alva, "Sahagún," 35, 52). In a similar vein, Jesús Bustamante, in a work commissioned to address Sahagún's humanism as part of a larger editorial project, adroitly introduced the problematic nature of the concept of humanism in order to add a level of complexity to his argument and avoid the pitfalls of the traditional, limited, moralistic identification of Sahagún as a Renaissance humanist (Bustamante García, "Retórica"). These three essays are diverse examples of Sahagún criticism that either implicitly or explicitly tests the applicability of the two-dimensional labels that have been applied to Sahagún in an attempt to translate his scholarly contributions into terms readily accessible to all.

The first section of this chapter is concerned with the subject of Sahagún's status as the father of modern anthropology[7] in the wake of the recent reassessment of what might constitute a scientific methodology in anthropology. In the second section of the chapter, I analyze the epistemological assumptions that lie beneath the claim that Sahagún is a humanist. A short, third section deals with the equally problematic notion that Sahagún's use of his medieval heritage in his work represents a *smooth* continuation of medieval traditions of scholarship.

1. Anthropologists

In 1928 Alfonso Toro argued that Sahagún's work was more ethnographic and linguistic in content than historical. In 1938, Wigberto Jiménez Moreno elaborated on this statement, arguing that Sahagún's work was truly exceptional because it employed a "scientific method." By scientific method, Jiménez was referring primarily to Sahagún's use of indigenous informants to gather the information that went into the *Florentine Codex*. According to Jiménez, "Sahagún was following, without knowing it, the most rigorous and exacting method of the anthropological sciences" (Jiménez Moreno, xv–xvi). In 1962, while attending a conference in Austria entitled "The Determination of the Philosophy of a Culture," Miguel León-Portilla followed Jiménez's lead and proposed that the proceedings be dedicated to Sahagún in the following manner:

Dedicated to FRAY BERNARDINO DE SAHAGÚN (1500–1590), Franciscan Missionary, Father of Anthropology in the New World. He devoted sixty years of his life to understanding from the inside, in the light of their philosophy, the culture of the ancient Mexicans. He collected hundreds of pre-Colombian texts in the Náhuatl language; he examined them with a critical eye and, finally, offered to his contemporaries a living image of the life and thought of the pre-Hispanic Mexicans in his *General History of the Things of New Spain*, a masterpiece and example of anthropological research for generations to come. (Northrop and Livingston, v)

From this point on, and with some further encouragement from León-Portilla, the idea that Sahagún was the father of anthropology in the New World transformed itself into a commonplace in colonial studies. At some point in time, this relatively innocuous claim gave way to the more general and more controversial notion that Sahagún is the father of modern anthropology, period.[8]

In recent years, this polemical claim has run up against a more deep-seated question or problem. Many contemporary anthropologists are self-consciously grappling with the problems of what constitutes a scientific method in anthropology and whether or not they want to glorify the origins of the discipline at all. Rightly or wrongly, this topic has been perceived by scholars both inside and outside the field as a kind of disciplinary vulnerability that facilitates, and even legitimates, a blurring of academic territories. One result of this phenomenon is the identification some scholars have made between anthropologists and individuals from the past who, at first glance, would seem to have nothing at all in common with the discipline. Carlo Ginzburg, for example, places anthropologists and inquisitors of the Holy Office on the same plane in "The Inquisitor as Anthropologist."[9]

To cite another example, in "Dialogue as Conquest: Mapping Spaces for Counter-Discourse," José Rabasa attempts to establish an epistemological link between the enterprise of conquistadores such as Hernán Cortés and the work of modern anthropologists. He states, "This paper will show how dialogue was an invention of the conquistadores. It aims to elaborate an experimental, perhaps perverse, genealogy of the conventional anthropological enterprise and of recent dialogical experiments as well" (134). In his "perverse genealogy," Rabasa detects in anthropology a nefarious link to discourses of conquest. Rabasa traces this link to Cortés's use of dialogue to gain the upper hand in the conquest of Mexico. In fact, Rabasa refers to Cortés as a "proto-anthropologist," tying this statement to the following, more general claim: "One readily grasps the image of the anthropologist as conqueror in the equation *knowledge is power*" (134, his emphasis).[10]

Like Rabasa, J. Jorge Klor de Alva responds to anthropology's recent methodological self-consciousness with a more ethically ambiguous or complex founding-father figure, although his tone certainly is not quite as inflammatory as Rabasa's. Klor de Alva's work is worth examining in greater detail, partly because he displays what I believe is an ongoing problem in the field of colonial studies—the obsession with founding fathers whose natures metamorphose as fast as definitions of the discipline of anthropology evolve. Nevertheless, I examine his work mostly because the intricacy of his arguments lends itself more easily to a sustained examination of Sahagún's symbolic status as the father of modern anthropology and what is lost when this perspective dominates the discussion. Like Miguel de León-Portilla, Klor de Alva is a staunch proponent of the idea that Sahagún is the father of modern anthropology.[11] In the essays I will discuss, however, he inserts this idea into the context of the heated debate about the origins and methods of today's discipline.

In "Sahagún and the Birth of Modern Ethnography," Klor de Alva's brilliant insight that Sahagún's ethnographic methodology is influenced by practices of the Catholic confessional is embedded in the curious, further-reaching claim that Sahagún "genuinely" is "the first modern anthropologist" (35). In the essay, Klor de Alva juxtaposes two mutually incompatible theoretical perspectives in a self-conscious attempt to reaffirm the redemptive or exemplary status of Sahagún's work in the aftermath of a post-1968 trend in scholarship that has led critics to reexamine and redefine notions of intellectual foundations and disciplinary patrimony. Klor de Alva describes the essay as an outline for a book-length study of Sahagún's role in the "colonization of the intimate life of the natives of New Spain," "the deployment of confessional practices as part of a disciplinary regime," and "the birth of modern anthropology as a mechanism for the extraction of (practical) local knowledge" (31). Klor de Alva's boldest claim is that the contemporary "crisis of representation" in the human sciences—as signaled by Foucault, Jean-François Lyotard, Hayden White, and others—is to a large extent the "same crisis of representation" experienced by Sahagún in sixteenth-century New Spain. Klor de Alva believes that only the prejudice of today's scholars keeps them from recognizing that Sahagún struggled with the same "intellectual predicament that they are quick to claim for themselves" (32–33). In short, Klor de Alva makes the paradoxical argument that Sahagún is genuinely the father of modern anthropology because he founded an anthropology that was *already* in a state of crisis.

Klor de Alva's central argument rests on at least two erroneous contentions. First, he argues that Sahagún could more easily have adopted the ethnographic and historiographical techniques employed by his Mendicant contemporaries (Alonso de Molina, Diego Durán, Andrés de Olmos). Doing so would have allowed him to highlight the positive attributes of Nahuas and yet remain entirely within the confines of Christian orthodoxy. Klor de Alva argues that Sahagún opted instead for the more difficult and radical technique of applying "confessionlike practices . . . systematically *outside* their sacramental context" (39, my emphasis). Klor de Alva's wording implies several fallacies. For example, even though gathering information the way Sahagún did was not sacramental (why should it be?), there is nothing in Sahagún's work that indicates that he felt he was involved in a nonreligious activity. The Spanish Inquisition, for example, often gathered information in a confessionlike manner outside the context of the confessional, but this information was never perceived as undermining the religiosity of the church in any way. Moreover, if Sahagún considered his contemporaries' methods successful—which he did not—he surely would have saved himself some trouble and imitated them. In fact—as I shall argue in the second part of the book—the failure of Sahagún's contemporaries' methods constituted one of the primary motivations behind Sahagún's peculiar methodological style of using native informants and retaining their words in Nahuatl.

Klor de Alva's second (and related) erroneous contention is that the entire Sahaguntine corpus is written in a combination of tragic, realistic, and ironic modes that facilitated and even encouraged contradictory interpretations by both Europeans and Nahuas of the time.[12] He argues that an ironic reading of the entire corpus is both intended and necessary because the highly realistic description of Nahua mores indirectly demonstrates the "integrity of this culture" and surreptitiously undermines the purported pastoral and linguistic goals that Sahagún laid out in one of his prologues (Klor de Alva, 44–45). Although Sahagún may have a few moments of irony in the prologues of his work, the assumption that Sahagún wished that the entire corpus be read in an ironic mode represents a profound misreading of the *Florentine Codex*.[13] Modern readers may find it ironic that the culture Sahagún depicted could never possibly coalesce with the tenets of a unified Christian cosmology, but, given his missionary intent, Sahagún would never have been able to share in the sly smiles and bitter humor that this kind of irony implies.

The ability to read Sahagún's text ironically must be kept entirely separate from any claim that Sahagún intended an ironic reading of his work, at least until more convincing evidence surfaces.

Sahagún himself recognized a certain lack of cohesion between the text in Nahuatl and its preliminary translation, for, despite its polished appearance, Sahagún considered the *Florentine Codex* to be only a preliminary draft of a later version (*CF* I:"Al sincero lector"). In the reference just given, Sahagún briefly described his plan to compose a three-column version of his work that would bring the Nahuatl text into perfect balance with a Spanish version. Sahagún's intentions are made clear by his "Memoriales con escolios"—part of a larger manuscript known as the *Madrid Codices* housed in the Real Palacio and Academia de la Historia in Madrid. In this text, Sahagún began work numbering, parsing, and glossing the sentences in Nahuatl in order to establish a one-to-one relationship between the two languages. If Sahagún had, in fact, intended an ironic reading of his entire project based on the contrasting Spanish and Nahuatl texts, it is unlikely that he would have gone to the trouble of planning and beginning an elaborate process intended to bring them together.[14]

The most suggestive aspect of Klor de Alva's essay is his allusion to the possible influence on Sahagún's methodology of one of the most important religious practices of the time: the use of confession as a hermeneutic device to elicit and structure information in a form readily comprehensible in terms of the prevailing Catholic orthodoxy. Since the fourteenth-century European "crisis of the Middle Ages"—when such changes as the growth of cities and the transformation of social roles created an increasingly complex definition of what constituted sin—the practice of confession grew to be a carefully orchestrated procedure in which checklists of sins were often employed in an attempt to structure a social custom that no longer seemed self-evident.[15] Like the essay by Keber to which I alluded earlier (1988), this aspect of Klor de Alva's argument could potentially present a more complex picture of how the religious epistemology of the time determined the form—and to a great extent the content—of the indigenous information gathered by Sahagún. For example, not only did Sahagún present the entire *Florentine Codex* as a tool for confessors (*CF* I:"Prologo"), Sahagún interpreted the fact that pre-Hispanic Nahuas confessed once a year as Catholics did as both a useful evangelical tool and proof that the Nahuas had been touched by the wisdom of God "*in lumine natural*" (natural enlightenment; *CF* I:101).

The potential usefulness of Klor de Alva's suggestion of the possible importance of confession in Sahagún's methodology is in direct contrast to his contention that Sahagún "genuinely" is the father of modern anthropology. Whereas Klor de Alva's idea about confession potentially constitutes an attempt to understand Sahagún in the context of his own time, his use of the label "father of modern anthropology" places Sahagún squarely in the midst of an unabashedly redemptive view of history in which a visionary Sahagún seemed to prophesy—and sacrifice himself for—our *current* intellectual dilemmas. In this last scenario, the importance of Sahagún's work can only be interpreted from the vantage point of today's ongoing definitional crisis of modern anthropology.

Whether or not Sahagún can be considered the father of anthropology depends, first, on what is meant by anthropology and, second, on the assumption that the search for the sole progenitor of the discipline of anthropology is a legitimate pursuit. Most scholars who place the origins of anthropology in the sixteenth and seventeenth centuries do not tend to be interested in discovering a close correlation between the scientific paradigms of the Renaissance and today's anthropological paradigms. The most coherent strain in the work of these scholars is their interest in pointing out that the Renaissance invention of a *general* idea of a secular scientific paradigm and its application to the study of humanity constitute the necessary starting point for determining the origins of what are now the human sciences (e.g., del Pino; Hodgen; Rowe). However, when anthropology is characterized by the use of specific paradigms (such as the comparative method), the search for its origins becomes increasingly problematic. An anthropology that is characterized by the use of a specific scientific paradigm can only be as old as the paradigm itself. Furthermore, as Kuhn has demonstrated, the introduction of new scientific paradigms is never an overnight affair and never rests solely on the shoulders of one individual. The very definition of a scientific paradigm presupposes the existence of a community of scientists who, by agreeing on how to articulate and try to solve scientific problems, manifest themselves as adherents of the paradigm.

In the European and Anglo-American context, scholars who search for the founding fathers of an anthropology defined by governing paradigms tend to nominate candidates who lived in either the nineteenth or twentieth centuries since those individuals are more likely to resemble current practitioners of the discipline. In this vein, Auguste Comte and Edward B. Tyler are two of the figures most frequently claimed to be fathers of the discipline. Nevertheless, the more closely their intellectual styles are examined, the more the methods of Comte and Tyler are revealed to be lacking in many of the basic features of current anthropology (Stocking, 27–28, 302). European and Anglo-American scholars have been unable to come to any unanimous conclusion about who founded modern anthropology because the ill-defined, elusive nature of the discipline resists this kind of attribution. I will come back to this point again, but here it is important to note that the struggle to identify the father of the discipline played itself out primarily in nationalistic terms. Moreover, it was nationalism that lent legitimacy to the very question of who founded what—a question whose dispensability is rarely considered. One of the most important side effects of the debate was the exclusion of Latin American candidates from the running even though indigenous Latin Americans constituted one of the discipline's principal objects of study.

The rise of nationalistic sentiments in Latin America coincides with the growing desire on the part of its inhabitants to establish an intellectual foundation separate from Europe or the United States. The increasing frequency with which Sahagún was heralded in the twentieth century as the father of modern anthropology coincided with the growing *political* importance of anthropology in the independent Latin American nations and the increasingly vociferous manner in which Europeans and Anglo-Americans laid claim to the invention of a discipline that developed largely in, and at the expense of, Europe's old colonies. Mexico, arguably the Latin American country with the strongest anthropological tradition, is—not coincidentally—the country that has most consistently made the claim that it was the true site of the birth of modern anthropology.

The arguments of origin-seeking Europeans and Anglo-Americans who used definitions of anthropology characterized by scientific paradigms were countered by Latin Americans who argued that Sahagún employed a modern scientific paradigm in a Latin American context long before anthropology emerged as a discipline in Europe in the nineteenth century. Manuel M. Marzal's frequently cited *Historia de la antropología indigenista: México y Perú*—a relatively recent example of this trend—is the most elaborate attempt to establish a point-by-point connection between Sahagún's methodology and the methodology of a modern-day, thriving, indigenist anthropology. Since Marzal's *Historia* supports Klor de Alva's claim that Sahagún is "genuinely" the father of modern anthropology—a critical discourse that is commonly neglected in the non-Hispanic world—his work merits closer examination.

Marzal's *Historia* is part of a projected three-part history of anthropology in the Western world. Marzal's dedication of the first volume to indigenist anthropology is self-consciously meant to tilt the scales against a "certain Anglo-Saxon ethnocentrism that thinks that anthropology learned to speak in English" (18). Marzal wishes to redress a situation in which the "almost perfect ethnography" of Sahagún is neglected by scholars as a precursor to modern anthropology in favor of nineteenth-century European anthropology (18).

Marzal's history of indigenist anthropology is divided between an analysis of ethnography during the Spanish colonial period and an analysis of latter-day anthropology in Mexico and Peru. Despite the obvious discrepancy in time between the two periods, Marzal hopes to establish the existence of a certain sympathy between these two differing contexts. Sahagún's work is one of the linchpins of Marzal's argument because Marzal believes that Sahagún was the first to use the methods and techniques of a "scientific ethnography" that has been associated with anthropology since the nineteenth century (70). Nevertheless, the fact that Sahagún's methodology "did not found a school"—as one like Bronislaw Malinowski's did, according to Marzal—presents the author with the strange dilemma of claiming that Sahagún is the father of the discipline despite Sahagún's lack of any immediate following (73).

Marzal attempts to circumvent his dilemma by limiting his definition of scientific ethnography to an atemporal combination of the concepts of a "systematic description of cultures" and the use of "the most rigorous techniques" to verify the information gathered. Any sociopolitical or functional aspect of this ethnography is irrelevant as long as it is kept separate (75). Since Marzal believes that Sahagún's work fits this definition, he paradoxically believes that Sahagún should be recognized as the first scientific ethnographer even though ethnography did not begin with him. Moreover, Marzal chooses (in this case) to ignore the social grounding of all scientific disciplines and argues that, had Sahagún's work been published in his day, the birth of ethnography would not have been delayed until the nineteenth century (74). Ironically, Marzal's wishful thinking about Sahagún's legacy runs counter to the spirit of the latter half of his book, where he cogently demonstrates how Mexican and Peruvian anthropology is inextricably meshed—and rightly so—with politics and social problems. It is, in fact, an avowed pride in the political and nationalistic nature of Latin American anthropology that led Marzal—as it has led others—into the paradoxical situation of claiming Sahagún as a founding father for the apparently objective, apolitical side of his work. Despite the openly nationalistic side of arguments like Marzal's, a specious nineteenth-century European definition of science as an entirely objective pursuit stands behind the claim that Sahagún is the true father of modern anthropology.

If Klor de Alva is conscious of arguments like Marzal's, he is equally conscious of the fact that notions of scientific objectivity have been seriously undermined in recent years. Nevertheless, rather than let go of Sahagún as a symbol for a scientifically objective (but politically engaged) Latin American anthropology, Klor de Alva portrays Sahagún as the symbol of an anthropology undergoing a "crisis of representation" in which the urgency of anthropology's political engagement is no longer justifiable or kept separate or secondary by the pretense of an objective methodology.

As Klor de Alva acknowledges, much of the fallout of the "crisis of modern anthropology" is the result of Foucault's *Les mots et les choses: Une archéologie des sciences humaines* ("Sahagún," 31). Klor de Alva cites other authors who helped bring about the "crisis of representation" in the human sciences, but Foucault's work has arguably been the most important catalyst for change, as evidenced in recent histories of the human sciences such as *Victorian Anthropology*, by George W. Stocking, Jr.; *Between Literature and Science: The Rise of Sociology*, by Wolf Lepenies; and the collectively written *La antropología en México: Panorama histórico* (edited by Carlos García Mora).

Foucault's influence on a new wave of historians of the human sciences stems from his demonstration that, not only do the human sciences represent their objects of study, they *constitute* these objects of study in terms of the figurative modes of discourse that they employ.[16] Moreover, the figurative modes of discourse used in the West to determine such concepts as "man," "society," and "culture" have not always been the same. For example, Foucault argues that the "episteme" (the languagelike deep structure that determines both the shape and content of knowledge) governing at the end of the sixteenth century is characterized by an elaborate interplay of resemblances or similitudes between the various objects of study. These resemblances were thought to manifest themselves through clues or markings in the object of study itself, and these markings were then decoded through an elaborate system of interpretation epitomized by the figures of *convenientia, aemulatio,* analogy, and sympathy (*Les mots,* 33–39). What distinguishes this episteme from its medieval predecessor is the fact that it was self-consciously applied by an observing subject who saw hermeneutics as a necessary antidote to a world that then seemed opaque. Unlike a medieval mode of thinking in which an individual's pars pro toto relationship with the cosmos was thought to render objects of knowledge transparent,[17] the early modern episteme is characterized by an exiled observing subject who felt the need to interpret the world from outside. The early-modern advances in artistic perspective, for example, coincided with the sixteenth-century obsession with tables as an interpretive strategy intended to render objects of study transparent through their identification and placement in an ordered form.

Foucault argues that the Enlightenment and the nineteenth century are governed by different epistemes and that these epistemes cannot be understood either as an accumulation of knowledge nor as the teleological outcome of previous epistemes. *Les mots et les choses* is written as a series of descriptions of these epistemes, and Foucault's penchant for undermining teleological or cumulative notions of progress in the human sciences leads him to emphasize the ruptured, discontinuous nature inherent in the replacement of one episteme by another. As White describes it,

epistemes (which function much like Kuhn's "paradigms") do not succeed one another dialectically, nor do they aggregate. They simply appear alongside one another—catastrophically, as it were, without rhyme or reason. Thus, the appearance of a new "human science" does not represent a "revolution" in thought or consciousness. A new science of life, wealth, or language does not rise up against its predecessors; it simply crystallizes alongside of them, filling up the "space" left by the "discourse" of earlier sciences. (234)

Foucault's emphasis on "ruptures" and "discontinuities" in the history of consciousness has led many critics to argue that Foucault's analyses lack an adequate explanation of how transformations from one episteme to another occur. Nevertheless, White's most important contribution in the essay "Foucault Decoded" is his demonstration that an explanation of epistemic change is implicit in Foucault's argumentation.[18]

White's discussion brings to light the fact that, in Foucault's analysis, new epistemes and their accompanying modes of scientific discourse only follow naturally on one another to the extent that they take up residency in the *interstices* left open by their predecessors. Whereas a non-Foucauldian history of a scientific discipline would be similar to the evolution of a single plantlike organism, a Foucauldian history could be characterized as a series of separate, parasitic organisms that move into the ecological niches left open by other organisms. In this sense, the more Foucault's scenario is taken seriously, the more any search for the origins of the human sciences is converted into a complex, discontinuous affair.

Foucault's central critique of the human sciences is that they not only crystallized in the interstices of mathematics, the life sciences, and philosophy, they are pulled in a variety of different directions—toward imitating mathematics' formalism; employing the borrowed models of biology, economics, and linguistics; or adopting philosophy's ontological or metaphysical quests as their own (*Les mots*, 358). The human sciences' lack of any clear identity leads Foucault to the conclusion that they are not sciences at all (*Les mots*, 378).

If something is lost in a Foucault-like critique of the legitimacy of the human sciences, something is also gained. For example, in *Culture and Truth*, Renato Rosaldo, an anthropologist, advocates turning anthropology's nebulous parameters to its own advantage and dismantling the false dichotomy between a "them-oriented" anthropology and an "us-oriented" sociology. Rosaldo argues that social analysis should take advantage of the added perspective of an ad hoc, engaged methodology that incorporates the role of the observer in its application.

In the sphere of intellectual history, George Stocking, Jr., Wolf Lepenies, and the Mexican collective responsible for *La antropología en México* all cite Foucault as one of the determining influences in their development of novel interpretations of the emergence of the interconnected fields of sociology and anthropology in the nineteenth century. For example, Stocking not only demonstrates the unrelated uses in various epochs of the word "culture" (necessary for any definition of anthropology), he demonstrates that, using older paradigms, nineteenth-century scientists increasingly had difficulty explaining the mass of ethnographic data gathered as a result of Europe's overseas expansion. Since biological evolutionary theory had been successful in filling a gap left open by the Bible's inability to account for the age of the Earth and its species, its trappings—in the form of social evolutionism—were also applied as a remedy for the confusion caused by the heightened awareness in the nineteenth century of the diversity of cultures and human behavior. Culture, hence, was reconfigured under the rubric of race, and races were placed at various levels on an evolutionary ladder. The "comparative method"—the technique of using primitive cultures to determine the physiognomy of earlier stages of civilization—became the way in which anthropology helped to solidify its standing in European universities (if only temporarily) as a truly scientific discipline.

In a similar vein, Wolf Lepenies argues that sociology—a discipline whose origins are intertwined with anthropology's[19]—emerged as a field of study as a result of the nineteenth-century split between the natural sciences and literature and the elevation of the *"sciences exactes"* (exact sciences) to the status of *"hautes sciences"* (high sciences; 9). Whereas at the end of the eighteenth century there was no discernible difference between the "modes of production" of literature and the natural sciences, nineteenth-century France, England, and Germany witnessed an ideological struggle between literati and natural scientists to determine who would orient the course of society as a whole. In legitimating itself as a new discipline with grandiose claims about the redemption of society, nineteenth-century sociology was caught in the dilemma of having to choose between imitating the natural sciences and having to follow the hermeneutics of an increasingly nationalistic body of literature.

Lepenies's use of a Foucault-like method, which examines sociology in light of its parasitic stature rather than as the natural

extension of an age-old scientific pursuit, results in at least two
unexpected discoveries. First, Lepenies shows that modern sociology's
skeleton in the closet is its relationship to a nineteenth-century
literature that staged itself as the moral flagship of various European nation-states. Second, and perhaps more interesting, Lepenies's
substitution of a founding-father approach to historiography with
a contextualized analysis of the epistemic tensions underlying the
emergence of sociology as a discipline produces one of his greatest
discoveries: the key role *women* played in the emergence of sociology
in France, England, and Germany. This discovery brings into the
foreground the issue of gender bias in the search for the founding
fathers of any discipline. (If Sahagún is the father of modern anthropology, who is the mother?)

The related historiographical approach of the collective *La antropología en México* stands in closer proximity to the problem of Sahagún's
status as the father of modern anthropology. Like the work of
Stocking and Lepenies, *La antropología en México* is an attempt to
rewrite the history of the emergence of a human science as a field
more grounded in the social and epistemological tensions of its
time than in the visionary insights of any single founder. In his
introduction, Carlos García Mora, the coordinator of *La antropología*,
argues that the confusion of colonial histories like Sahagún's with
the modern practices of anthropology runs the risk of looking for
the origins of anthropology as far back in time as the sources permit. Moreover, García Mora also shies away from the idea that the
more contemporary Manuel Gamio is the true father of anthropology in Mexico since he is thought by some to have instigated the
scientific theories, methods, and techniques that characterize the
twentieth-century Mexican anthropological tradition (1:37).

The entire project intentionally sidesteps the problem of absolute origins in order to analyze the emergence of Mexican anthropology in terms of the epistemological tensions of different time
periods. Rather than arguing that Mexican anthropology is characterized by a smooth, self-propelling evolution over time of anthropological pursuits, the contributors to *La antropología* examine the nature

of anthropological pursuits separately in the numerous contexts of Mexico's fragmented political history. If one thing unifies anthropological pursuits in Mexico, it is their overt relationship to projects intended to fortify the nation. Nevertheless, since Mexico's history is the story of several, different images of itself as a nation, the history of Mexican anthropology is the story of a succession of diverse projects that attempted either to read the indigenous population out of its history or to read it back in in various forms.

By dividing Mexican anthropology up into the different, ruptured contexts of Mexico's political history and by emphasizing the importance at any one point in time of various scientific paradigms and academic or government institutions, García Mora's team successfully traces the emergence of Mexican anthropology as it crystallized alongside clusters of differing social and political tensions. The project as a whole abandons the attempt to demonstrate Mexico's right to the claim that the modern discipline of anthropology began there. Nevertheless, by grounding Mexican anthropology in the particularity of the social conflicts and political upheavals of Mexico's history, the series demonstrates the truly individual character of Mexican anthropology. Whereas the European and Anglo-American traditions of anthropology have disingenuously tended to present their political and social messages as a secondary aspect of their more pure, scientific natures, Mexican anthropology has a much stronger tradition of placing its goal of social praxis in the forefront. In a sense, given the context of post-1968 academics, one could say that the European and Anglo-American anthropological traditions could benefit from the Mexican point of view, in which anthropology is never the detached science of museum curators and armchair pundits.

If, as I believe, Sahagún has no place as the father of modern anthropology, nevertheless, anthropology's ongoing struggle to come to terms with the diversity of cultures and human behavior may still lead to a better understanding of Sahagún. For an anthropology uninterested in founding fathers, the particularity of Sahagún's situation offers an interesting point of comparison for

what happens when two cultures come into contact. Marshall
Sahlins has argued in *Islands of History* that the structures of cultural
"conjunctures" such as those found in "first contacts" between differing peoples are particularly revealing of the different structures
used by cultures to read themselves synchronically and diachron-
ically into history. To the extent that Sahagún's work represents an
extremely elaborate example of cultural conjuncture, it is particularly revealing of the different social structures that were in play at
the time he assembled the *Florentine Codex*. Nevertheless, this aspect
of Sahagún's work is accessible to social analysis only if one is
willing to accept that Sahagún is at least as different from modern
readers as he is similar. Sahagún was neither a positivistic anthropologist approaching the Nahuas with photographic objectivity nor
an anthropologist wrestling with the identity crisis of a modern-
day discipline. Sahagún is the result of the tensions and conflicts of
his own time and circumstances.

The idea that Sahagún was an anthropologist avant la lettre
creates several interpretive blind spots. First of all, contemporary
anthropological thought runs counter to absolutist ideas, morals,
and esthetic judgements. Any all-encompassing, cross-cultural statement will almost inevitably butt heads with the sheer diversity of
anthropological data: "customs, crania, living floors, and lexicons"
(Geertz, "Anti Anti-Relativism," 264). The diversity of anthropological data has led anthropologists to work with a highly polysemous
definition of culture. It has also presented anthropologists with the
ideal, for example, of showing how unfamiliar customs are actually
quite coherent when understood from within the framework of the
culture in question. Sahagún, however, did not employ a plural
definition of culture or of civilization. In fact, anthropologists did
not begin to speak of civilizations in the plural until the nineteenth
century (Stocking, 18). When Sahagún was confronted with the
sheer diversity of cultural data presented by the Nahua world, Sahagún's goal was to *reinscribe* this information into a known, previously
cohesive Christian cosmology. Sahagún validated or condemned
aspects of Nahua culture from the standpoint of the Christian

West. Sahagún was somewhat unsuccessful in his task since the *Florentine Codex* overflows with information that does not fit into the world of the Christian West. Nevertheless, it would be a mistake to interpret this residue as an attempt on Sahagún's part to depict a culture that was valid on its own terms.

The esthetic aspect of Sahagún's work constitutes another blind spot for the anthropological perspective. The superficial division between science and beauty is a fairly recent phenomenon.[20] The misconstrued "cool reason of science" argument that lies at the root of claims that Sahagún's methodology entitles him to the label "father of modern anthropology" does an injustice to the esthetic nature of Sahagún's work. Book XI is ostensibly the most mundane of the *Florentine Codex* since it is part herbal, part bestiary, part lapidary, and so forth, but Sahagún describes it in the following manner: "The knowledge of natural things—in order to give examples and make comparisons—certainly is not the least noble jewel of the coffer, of evangelical preaching" (*CF* XI:"Prologo"). Book XI of Sahagún's evangelical "coffer" is by far the longest of the books and one of the most richly illustrated. For Sahagún—as for all thinkers of the time—knowledge and beauty were not two clearly separate categories. Any attempt to explain Sahagún from within the confines of any single modern discipline—whether it be anthropology, religious studies, art history, or botany—will run up against the fact that Sahagún was attempting to approach his knowledge of the Nahuas in a more totalizing fashion than the specialization of modern disciplines permits.

As my final point, I would like to address the question of why anyone would want or need a founding father figure in the first place and whether or not it is possible simply to do without one. The quest for founding fathers for the modern disciplines and the disputes surrounding these quests have been so widespread that the absolute strangeness of this uniquely human need has been over-looked or forgotten. In general, I believe the search for founding fathers answers a human need to render complex, seemingly indif-ferent social forces comprehensible by anthropomorphizing them.

Identifying historical individuals as founding fathers is a way of interpreting and including certain complex forces of society as members of one's own immediate family—members who, not surprisingly, seem to share a striking resemblance to one's most flattering self-portraits.

Unfortunately, the choice of founding fathers is as socially exclusive as it is inclusive. When different cultural traditions begin to coexist, overlap, and intermingle, the constructed nature of their respective founding fathers comes into the foreground as each cultural group scrutinizes and questions the legitimacy of founding fathers who are unrelated to their own cultural bloodline. This heightened scrutiny leads inevitably to the conclusion that there is nothing genealogical about the paternity of these individuals.

The question remains whether or not it is possible to live without the illusion of such strong, direct ties to a distant cultural past. In my view, I do not think it is necessary to abandon the idea that the cultural past has influenced the present, even if there are no ties on a quasi-genealogical level through the cultural Y-chromosomes of founding fathers. Furthermore, I believe the cultural past can be more fully understood if the pursuit of cultural progenitors is replaced by an appreciation of the multifaceted, eclectic formation of cultures and their manifestations of knowledge. Once the pursuit for founding fathers is abandoned, the myriad contradictory forces that make up any culture can come into view, and previously excluded elements or groups can be recognized as constitutive factors of the culture. A similar view of Sahagún and his time reveals a complex conjunction of a diversity of social and cultural forces and tensions.

2. Humanists

In the widely dispersed anthology *Idea y querella de la Nueva España*, Ramón Xirau gathered together what, in his opinion, were representative texts of "seven humanists of New Spain"—including an excerpt from Bernardino de Sahagún's *Historia universal* (21). In Xirau's view, the seven authors he selected represent two intertwined strands of Spanish humanism that were exported to the New World: a practical and an abstract one. Xirau defines humanism as a "humanitarian" and "charitable" attitude combined with an "attitude of defense of the rights of peoples." Xirau employs this broad definition in order to argue more easily that "men of action," such as Sahagún, were proponents of a "practical humanism" whether or not they were capable of demonstrating their familiarity with the more "abstract" aspects of erudite Christian humanism. In Xirau's eyes, humanism means the pretension of "arriving at a more pure and a more evangelical form of Christianity" and is best exemplified by such thinkers as Lorenzo Valla, Cardinal Francisco Jiménez de Cisneros, and Erasmus (10–12).

In what follows, I will argue against the suitability of definitions of humanism such as Xirau's. Moreover, I will argue against the notion that Renaissance humanism was merely a phenomenon that was *exported* to the New World by such figures as Sahagún. I will employ a very narrow definition of the word "humanism" in my analysis of Sahagún's Spanish- and Nahua-language *Coloquios y doctrina cristiana* in order to show how humanism could be modified—or even galvanized—by the particularity of the New World context.

Unlike many of the terms commonly employed to describe the work of Sahagún, the idea that he was a Renaissance humanist holds the promise of interpreting Sahagún from within the intellectual currents of his time. Nevertheless, in what follows, without disposing of the terms completely, I will argue that critics have stretched the terms humanism and humanist too far in applying them to Sahagún. In most cases, when scholars deem Sahagún a humanist they burden him with a surprising amount of recent cultural baggage. To date, Bustamante García is the only critic of Sahagún's work who has attempted to lend a degree of subtlety to how the term humanist is or should be applied to Sahagún.[21] In many respects my analysis will use Bustamante's example as its starting point, but I will add another layer of interpretive complexity onto Bustamante's through my own approach to Sahagún's *Coloquios y doctrina cristiana*—a text whose dialogue form, because of its strong association with Renaissance humanism, would seem to confirm Sahagún's humanist tendency.[22] If Sahagún truly exhibits humanist features, it should be possible to verify this through an examination of his works on a textual level.

In order to employ the term humanism with a certain degree of precision, I must first define it. In its current usage, the semantic reach of the term humanism is so broad it is often difficult to determine what it is meant to exclude. Of all Renaissance scholars, Paul Oskar Kristeller has done the most to pare down the words "humanism" and "humanist" so that they have the potential to refer to actual, discernible attributes of specific thinkers of the European Renaissance. Kristeller emphasizes the fact that humanism—a term coined at the beginning of the nineteenth century—does not refer to any single Weltanschauung or philosophical system, for humanists not only disagreed with each other a great deal, they also frequently contradicted their own positions. Kristeller points out that "humanist" is too often confused with "humanistic" (as in "human values") and that the term is applied indiscriminately as a "rather elusive label of praise" to a vast array of thinkers (*Renaissance*, 21). Even though humanists frequently staged their writings as more ethical than other texts, any identification there might have been between eloquence and ethics did not lead to any single, discernible system of ethics or philosophy.

Menéndez y Pelayo's coinage of the term "Christian humanism" is perhaps the most deeply rooted misconception of humanism in Hispanic studies. Menéndez y Pelayo attributed to humanism in Spain a moral, "Christian" superiority over Italian humanism and saw the Reformation as a reaction to Protestant historians of northern Europe. These Protestant historians considered the Reformation to be the true Renaissance and disparaged the Italian Renaissance as "pagan." Menéndez y Pelayo's profound influence on many Hispanists has led to the almost ubiquitous confusion between Spanish humanism and a heightened spirituality (Di Camillo, 56).

Kristeller limits his definition of the humanists to the following:

Hence I am inclined to consider the humanists not as philosophers with a curious lack of philosophical ideas and a curious fancy for eloquence and for classical studies, but rather as professional rhetoricians with a new, classicist idea of culture, who tried to assert the importance of their field of learning and to impose their standards upon the other fields of learning and of science, including philosophy. (*Renaissance*, 92)

Kristeller believes that the humanist movement must be understood as a *cultural* and *educational* program of the early modern period—not a philosophy—which placed emphasis on classical antiquity as a worthy model for imitation (*Renaissance*, 22, 87–88).

Even though it is unreasonable to argue that the Renaissance humanists shared any single ethical or philosophical position that distinguished them from other thinkers of the day, many people find it quite difficult to divorce the word "humanism" from its current ethical connotations. Many scholars of literature—especially Renaissance literature—still find it difficult to let go of the idea that literature is or should be the beacon for the other academic disciplines or society as a whole. Humanism carries so many ethical connotations that even Kristeller—who previously eschewed any connection between humanism and a consistent ethical belief system—ends his *Renaissance Thought and Its Sources* with an exaggerated, moralistic diatribe against the recent demise of the rhetorical arts: "I am afraid we are left in chaos, in rhetoric as in other areas of our civilization" (257). Ironically, even though no one agrees on how the rhetorical arts are supposed to improve one's moral fiber, many literature scholars are certain that they do. Although I do not deny the importance of the rhetorical arts, I believe a dose of moderation is in order. In accordance with Kristeller's earlier statements—the ones that pertain specifically to the Renaissance—I think it is nonsensical to associate Renaissance humanism with any coherent (and superior) sense of moral redemption.

In "Retórica, traducción y responsabilidad histórica: Claves humanísticas en la obra de Bernardino de Sahagún," Bustamante

García uses Kristeller's pared-down definition of the humanists as the starting point for his study of Sahagún's humanist features. In light of Kristeller's identification of humanism with a specific educational program, Bustamente points out that Sahagún was educated as a Latinist at the University of Salamanca at a time that humanist classicism was thriving and then began teaching Latin in the Colegio de Santa Cruz in Santiago de Tlaltelolco. The continuity Bustamante establishes between Sahagún's years in Salamanca and his educational role in the Colegio de Santa Cruz is nothing new or startling— Sahagún was qualified to teach Latin because he had been taught Latin—but his definition of Sahagún's humanism is. Bustamante points out that Sahagún's missionary endeavors primarily played themselves out through a "linguistic" project—whether this be his teaching or the philological nature of the *Florentine Codex*[23]—whose roots are to be found in his humanist formation at Salamanca.

Ever since Lorenzo Valla's famous exposure of the Donation of Constantine as a forgery through the use of a comparative, historical, linguistic method, humanist philology has been closely associated with a nascent historical relativism and an early modern emphasis on human agency, which saw the world as something to be acted on rather than succumbed to.[24] One of Bustamante's central arguments is that the close tie between humanist philology and historical relativism determines Sahagún's relatively open-ended sense of history—a sense of history Bustamante feels runs counter to the millenarian beliefs of his brethren. Bustamante associates Sahagún's perspective with the need for individuals to play a role in the shaping of history. Nevertheless, Sahagún's reliance on human agency in his missionary project should not be confused with any particular ethical stance or philosophical system erroneously thought to be emblematic of Renaissance humanism. Not all humanist thinkers interpreted the role of human agency in the production of knowledge in the same way. For example, even though the well-known Renaissance notion of the "dignity of man" found a place in the moral systems of many humanists, it was strongly opposed by numerous others (Kristeller, *Renaissance*, 169–81).

Bustamante is the first to study in any depth the influence of humanist philology on Sahagún's missionary mind-set and unique outlook on the Nahuas, but he is not alone in his approach. In "Sprachbeherrschung und Weltherrschaft. Sprache und Sprach-wissenschaft in der europäischen Expansion," Wolfgang Reinhard underscores the importance humanist philology had in determining the manner in which the American indigenous population was proselytized. Unlike many other religious traditions of the time, European Christian learning was dependent on translations of its sacred texts. With Renaissance humanism there was even more emphasis placed on translation as an art as more texts—especially classical texts—were translated and well-known texts such as the Bible were reexamined in light of an increased awareness of differences between the translation and the original. During the Renaissance, European Christianity came to define itself more than ever as multilingual, and this multilingualism led to the establishment of norms for translation.[25] Although, as Reinhard points out, this multilingualism did not make European Christianity any less ethnocentric than other traditions, it does explain in part the manner in which Europe was able to expand so quickly. Unlike other traditions that considered "barbarous" tongues unworthy of study, the European missionaries were quick to study these languages and use them to their own advantage. This is evidenced by the numerous grammars and dictionaries these missionaries wrote as practical manuals for proselytizing. These manuals were mostly modeled after the Latin, Greek, and vernacular language studies associated with early Renaissance humanism, but they took on their own shape in the context of the New World.

Both Bustamante and Reinhard strip Renaissance humanism of any unique ethical (i.e., "humane") or philosophical connotations in order to demonstrate the important role it played on a philological level in colonialism and colonial texts. Sahagún was not a humanist because he was "humane" or brought some so-called humanist philosophy to bear on his missionary endeavors; he was a missionary whose linguistic, humanist formation became one of the important features of how he carried out his work. In this very limited sense of the word, "humanism" does not appear to be an inappropriate term to use for Sahagún.[26] Both Bustamante's and Reinhard's treatments of the issue of humanism in the New World represent serious advances over the way the subject is normally handled. Both Reinhard and Bustamante are careful to interpret humanism as a transatlantic phenomenon that was in some measure spurred on in Europe by the particular circumstances of the New World and transformed in the New World context once it was brought over. In what follows, I would like to take this aspect of their work a step further.

My primary objection to the way in which the term Renaissance humanist is applied to Sahagún lies in the tendency of many scholars to interpret humanism principally as a European phenomenon that was exported to the New World rather than as a phenomenon that developed in and was shaped by the context of colonial America.

I do not believe that Eurocentrism is at the root of this misunderstanding—although that is certainly the form it takes in the context of colonial studies. Rather, it is the way humanism is interpreted in general. The underlying notion in most studies of Renaissance humanism is that humanism is exclusively a *cause* of a change in the early modern Weltanschauung rather than also a *symptom* or result of it. Francisco Rico's scholarly *El sueño del humanismo: De Petrarca a Erasmo*, an otherwise commendable book, might be cited as an example of what I mean. Rico avoids the usual pitfalls of studies of humanism by avoiding the so-called constants of the movement and concentrating on humanism as a succession of evolving influences over time and across Europe. In essence, Rico delineates his subject matter by treating humanism as the story of a collective protagonist whose journey through time and space is only unified by a "dream" in which humanism serves as the vehicle for a literary and linguistic culture that shapes all facets of life, from philosophy down to dice throwing (Rico, 60–61, 125).

According to Rico, humanism's greatest legacy was the introduction of a relative historical perspective:

In that direction undoubtedly lies the greatest achievement of the *studia humanitatis*, as soon as we look for the deepest conceptual foundation of their uncountable contributions. To humanism, as a matter of fact, we continue to owe the discovery that our dimension is history, that man lives in history—that is, in variation, in the diversity of surroundings and experiences, in relativism. . . . But, in that direction also lies hope. Because that vision of reality and temporality implies a program of action: it implies that it is possible to change life, that the restitution of ancient culture opens up new perspectives, that the world is corrigible as one corrects a text or a style. (43–44)

If Rico is right, however, he is only half right. If historical and cultural relativism are the result of humanism, it can just as easily be argued that humanism is the result of an increasing awareness of historical and cultural relativism. Through an analysis of the *Coloquios y doctrina cristiana*, I will show that Sahagún's humanism—to the extent that this is a useful term—must be understood in this sense. Sahagún arrived in New Spain with an education in the classics, but it was the variegated, turbulent context of the New World that prompted his works to take on certain features associated with humanism and provided them with a relevance they would not have had otherwise. Not only is Sahagún's philological—humanist—enterprise an outgrowth of his years at Salamanca, it is his response to the growing suspicion amongst the missionaries of the time that a deep epistemological chasm separated the Nahuas from the Spaniards. Sahagún's elaborately constructed philological works represent his attempt to bridge this chasm. Sahagún hoped to *remedy* this inchoate relativism through his philological enterprise, not increase or produce relativism through philology, as a statement like Rico's might imply if it were applied to the context of the New World.[27]

In her book-length study of Sahagún's *Coloquios*, Ana de Zaballa Beascoechea places herself among several scholars who have emphasized—in her own words—Sahagún's "extraordinary humanistic baggage" (9). This perspective has led Zaballa Beascoechea to point out the dual origin of the dialogue form employed in Sahagún's *Coloquios*. First, and obviously, the *Coloquios* are in dialogue form because they are meant to be a reconstruction of an actual conversation or debate the first twelve Franciscan missionaries in New Spain held with leaders of the indigenous population at the prompting of Hernán Cortés.[28] Second, the dialogue form of the *Coloquios*—actually written in 1564—coincides with the growing popularity of the form among European humanists, who appropriated it from the classical tradition (77). Although rarely philosophical in content, the dialogues of Renaissance humanists were often moralistic tracts whose only common denominator other than the dialectic form seems to be an emphasis on *eloquentia* (eloquence). As Kristeller has aptly noted, the dialogues of the humanists were "purely literary" texts "written from the start to be read." Kristeller explains their popularity as a result of a predilection for "personal, subjective expression, as well as by the admiration for famous ancient examples" (*Medieval,* 13).

Sahagún had a few New World precedents when, in his missionary context, he chose the dialogue form to depict the debate of 1524 (Duverger, 63n.1). On both sides of the Atlantic in the sixteenth century, the form grew in popularity as a literary endeavor, although it is possible that Sahagún intended his dialogue for staging as well as for reading. Sahagún's concern for style in the *Coloquios* has led Ángel María Garibay K. to note that Sahagún's "work is literature much more than history" (Garibay K., 2:241). Nevertheless, it is necessary to remember that the divorce between a so-called ornamental literary style and supposedly objective scientific prose is a fairly recent phenomenon.[29] In fact, style in Sahagún's *Coloquios* must be analyzed as one way in which he establishes the authority of his text and the veracity of his message. Moreover, not only is Sahagún's dialogue a carefully wrought piece of stylistic persuasion, the protagonists—both Spanish and Nahua—explicitly refer to the importance of style at several junctures.[30]

The problem of authority lies at the heart of Sahagún's *Coloquios,* and I would like to argue that Sahagún's use of a characteristically humanist emphasis on style and the popular dialogue form is a serious critical *response* to the particular circumstances of his missionary endeavor in New Spain rather than a haphazard use of literary ornamentation. If the conversion of the Nahuas had been smooth and unproblematic, as the missionaries initially believed, then Sahagún would probably never have resorted to writing the *Coloquios*.

The *Coloquios*, as the full title indicates, were composed to aid in the ongoing conversion of the Nahua population. Under the pretense of preserving history, Sahagún intended the *Coloquios*—which depict the quick, successful conversion of a group of indigenous religious leaders—to serve as a model for subsequent conversions. In order to ensure that the didactic aspect of the work would be noted, in his prologue Sahagún analyzes the method—divided into *"fundamentos"* (foundations)—that the twelve Franciscans supposedly used to convert the group of Nahua leaders. These are the four fundamentos: (1) the friars are messengers of God and the Pope and have come to save the Nahuas' souls; (2) the Pope is only motivated by the Nahuas' salvation; (3) the doctrine they the friars teach is divine, not human; and (4) God's kingdom is in Heaven, and the Pope represents him on Earth through the church. Subsequently, Sahagún declares, "To a great extent, these fundamentals are efficacious in persuading to the holy Catholic faith people unfamiliar with any knowledge of divine things and, to a large extent, disabled in the knowledge of human things" (*Coloquios*, 74). Emphasizing the importance in his eyes of rhetorical rules, Sahagún ends his prologue with the statement that these fundamentos must be presented in "a clear and plain style, well measured and proportioned to the abilities of the listeners, as will become apparent in the work that follows" (*Coloquios* 74).

Sahagún composed the *Coloquios* in 1564—that is, forty years after the event he depicts. The composition of the *Coloquios* coincided with Sahagún's most prolific period, and like virtually all of Sahagún's works, it represents an attempt to address the recently perceived failure of the mission in New Spain. Unlike the first missionaries in New Spain, who initially believed conversion had been swift and complete, Sahagún was obsessed with his recognition of the superficial nature of the conversion.[31] This is perhaps clearest in Sahagún's Arte adivinatoria, where he argues—in what is obviously a thinly veiled critique of his predecessors—that the first twelve Franciscan missionaries failed to perceive the superficial nature of the conversion:

They did not forget in their preaching the warning the Redeemer gave his disciples and apostles when he told them: *Estote prudentes sicut serpentes et simplices sicut columbae*: Be prudent like snakes and simple like doves; and even though they proceeded with caution in the second, in the first they were wanting, and even the same idolaters fell in that they were lacking some of that serpentine prudence, and hence with their sly humility they offered very quickly to receive the faith that was being preached to them. But they remained underhanded in that they did not detest nor renounce all of their gods with all of their rites, and hence they were baptized not as perfect believers as they pretended, but as pretenders who received that faith without giving up the false one of many gods that they had. This palliation was not noticed at first, and the very strong cause of it was the opinion that the aforementioned preachers held in perfect faith, and hence they affirmed it to all of the ministers of the Gospel that came over to preach to this people. (García Icazbalceta, 382)

In light of these statements, Sahagún's depiction of the rapid conversion of the Nahuas in his *Coloquios* must be understood as an idealized or archetypal version of the events. There has been a long, heated debate about the historicity of the *Coloquios* that I believe has finally been put to rest by Klor de Alva in his "La historicidad de los 'Coloquios' de Sahagún." Although it is possible that Sahagún— as he claims—loosely based his dialogue on some *"papeles y memorias"* (papers and memoirs) that he came across (*Coloquios*, 75), the work must really be understood as that of Sahagún and his Nahua students. Moreover, one should not be disconcerted by Sahagún's lack of concern for the fact that his rendering of the event is not a literal transcription. As is often the case with humanist dialogues, the authority or legitimacy of the text is not established through any close proximity it is purported to have with a real conversation. For example, in Juan de Valdés's *Diálogo de la lengua* there is supposedly a hidden scribe who writes down the words of the ongoing discussion, but the scribe only begins his work several pages into the text (130–31).

Nevertheless, the issue of textual authority is more relevant in the *Coloquios* than it might have been in a different, nonmissionary context. The conversion of the indigenous New World population presented colonial era evangelists with a previously unheard-of predicament. Since the Nahuas of New Spain had never been exposed to Christianity, Sahagún could not hold them accountable for their sins against Christianity. The Nahuas' ignorance of the Christian faith seemed to place them *outside* of a previously all-encompassing Christian cosmology, but this was theologically unacceptable at the time. Previously, this problem had only been dealt with in the West in relationship to the pre-Christian past, and Christianity resolved this problem through ample use of *figura*. For Christians, every important event was "prefigured" in a past event whose historical culmination was fulfilled only with the advent of Christianity. Not only were New Testament events and personages prefigured in the Old Testament, subsequent elements of church history were thought to be prefigured as well (Auerbach, *Scenes*, 11–76). In a similar vein, Christianity dealt with the thorny problem of a pre-Christian redemption only with particularly important biblical figures. For example, in a work renown for its depiction of a carefully ordered, self-enclosed Christian cosmology, the *Inferno* of Dante's *Divine Comedy*, Vergil alludes to Christ's harrowing of Hell in order to save a few pre-Christian figures such as Adam, Eve, Noah, and Moses (1:38).

Sahagún resolves the dilemma in a somewhat contradictory fashion. On the one hand, the Nahuas deserved their overthrow by the Spaniards because their idolatrous practices offended God:

Indeed, many things, by night, by day, you do by which you cause Him an injured heart, by which you live in His anger, His ire, very much by your

account, by the injuries of your heart. Because of it He sent them hither,
these who came before, His subjects the Spaniards, these who conquered
you, these who grieved you, these who afflicted you with tormenting
sorrow, by which you were punished so that you ceased these not few
injuries to His precious heart, these in which you are living.[32] ("Aztec-
Spanish Dialogues," 71)

On the other hand, the fact that the Nahuas had no previous
knowledge of Scripture seemed partially to exonerate them:

Because, indeed, you never heard it, the precious word of God. You did
not guard it, the divine book, the divine word. It never came to reach you,
His precious breath, His precious word, this one of the Possessor of
Heaven, the Possessor of Earth. And, then, you are blind, you are deaf, as
if in darkness, in gloom you live. On account of this your faults are,
furthermore, not very great. But now, if you do not desire to hear it, the
precious breath, the precious word of God (this one He gives to you), you
will be in much danger. And God, Who has commenced your destruction,
will conclude it, you will be completely lost. ("Aztec-Spanish Dialogues,"
131–32)

Since Sahagún is aware that the Nahuas never received Christianity's message, he realizes that the authority with which the missionaries justify their conversion and deliver their message must be
established from the ground up—at least from the perspective of
the Nahuas. Sahagún's suspicion of the profound epistemological
rift separating the Nahuas from the Spaniards prompts him to
devise novel ways in which to establish the authority of the twelve
Franciscan missionaries in their dialogue with the Nahuas. In short,
the awareness of cultural relativism serves as a catalyst for the
adoption of new techniques of legitimization, and many of these
techniques crystallize as *rhetorical* devices—including, as I shall show,
the choice of the dialogue form.
    The structure of the *Coloquios* is surprisingly complex. It begins—
as do several of its chapters—with a narrative embedding which

both sets the stage for the dialogue to follow and conjures up a long indigenous reading/speaking tradition in which only designated leaders were given the privilege of speaking the community's most valuable words. *Tlatoani*, for example, in Nahuatl means both "ruler" and "the one who regularly speaks." The scribe/painter (*tlahcuiloh*) and the reader of books (*amoxpohuani*) were important figures in Nahua culture who were associated with certain gods and calendar days and were responsible for safeguarding the Nahua store of knowledge. Preconquest Nahua "reading" was partially an oral discourse in which the reader based the recounting of an event on pictures depicted in a book. At the beginning of each chapter of the *Coloquios* Sahagún mimics the oral element of this process. In these moments, the narrator seems to be pointing to the book as a traditional Nahua reader would: "Here begins the word which instructs" ("Aztec-Spanish Dialogues," 56); "There it is told how they recounted something" (57); "There it is told, from where it came, from where it appeared" (73); "There it is told who He is" (79); and so forth.[33] Although it is possible that the "book" the narrator seems to be pointing to is Sahagún's Spanish version of the events that is given on the reverse side of the folios, the reading process is nevertheless inscribed in a Nahua tradition in which readers of books were considered to be among the wisest members of the community.

Sahagún's use of Nahua rhetorical devices is more than a case of convenience. Sahagún dedicated the second largest book of the *Florentine Codex* to a study of Nahua rhetoric. Sahagún argues in the prologue to this book that all nations—"however barbarous and of low metal they have been"—look to the wise and powerful among them "to persuade" (*CF* VI:iv). Sahagún felt that the Nahuas were particularly gifted speakers and considered his book on Nahua rhetoric to be his finest accomplishment (*CF* VI:3v).

Sahagún's desire to persuade with a style "proportioned to the abilities of the listeners" leads him to direct the message of the twelve friars to the "hearts" of the Nahuas. The European association of the heart with love and feeling is coupled with the more

cognitive connotations of the Nahuatl word *"yolli."*[34] The twelve
Franciscans hope to persuade the Nahuas' "hearts" through their
own presence in New Spain ("Aztec-Spanish Dialogues," 58), but
since they consider themselves to be only "messengers" of God, they
must go to great lengths to establish the authority of their words.
They begin by saying they are common men like the Nahuas and
then proceed to read a letter from the Pope (58–59). The Pope, in
turn, refers to the words of Charles V—which are delivered in the
first person through the voice of the emperor—and then proceeds
to explain how he made the decision to send the first twelve Franciscans to New Spain by meeting with other authorities: namely, his
cardinals (61–63). Sahagún uses this complicated layering of narra-
tional embeddings and cross-references—in which each one defers
to another one's authority in a circular fashion—to establish the
irrefutability of the divine wisdom of a mortal man whom the
Nahuas have never seen and probably never will see. Sahagún is
sensitive to the somewhat tenuous nature of this process, for he is
careful to have the twelve Franciscans explain to the Nahuas that
they never need to worry about seeing the Pope because the friars
are his representatives (111).

The somewhat lengthy process by which the twelve Franciscans
establish the authority of the Pope is followed with an equally
elaborate attempt to convince the Nahuas of the authority of God's
word as it is recorded in Scripture. This process is primarily accomplished through the frequent use of rhetorical questions and by
putting words in the Nahuas' mouths that make the dialectic nature
of the text almost a pure fiction. Here are only two examples: "But,
perhaps, you ask, now, perhaps, you say, this one, the divine word
you mention you mention with reverence, where did it come from?"
(74). "And, perhaps, you say, our beloved: What is the name of your
God, the One you came to show us?" (92).

The rhetorical questions of the twelve Franciscans are supplemented with questions from the Nahuas that—from the point of
view of the missionaries—are extremely apropos. At one point, the
Nahuas concede that their gods are false and ask what they really

are. This leads into a long description of the fall of Lucifer and the origin of devils. This discussion is crucial to Sahagún's endeavor because the false gods enable him to reinscribe the Nahua past into the Christian cosmology. Even though they just arrived in New Spain, Sahagún's twelve Franciscans talk about the false gods, who are identified as fallen angels, with the utmost confidence—a confidence that arises from their familiarity with the Bible and the idea that it is the utmost spiritual authority:

Indeed, we know it well, who they are, those whom you regard as gods, these whom you have continually implored; where, and in what manner they began, they commenced, who they were, beyond there, at first; and of what sort is their being, their heart, their function, their will, and from where they came. (129)

Even though, as I mentioned before, Sahagún was not convinced that the Nahuas had been successfully converted, the Nahuas in the *Coloquios* are quickly and easily persuaded that their gods are false. The twelve Franciscans are partially able to convince the Nahuas that their gods are false through the idea that the gods did not come to the Nahuas' aid during the conquest. At one point, the Nahua leaders are quick to acknowledge this and announce, "Oh, indeed, let us perish, since, indeed, the gods have died!" (119). Furthermore, in the heading for one of the latter chapters of the dialogue, the Nahuas announce that they have been successfully persuaded (*Coloquios*, 77).[35] In the context of the dialogues, this conversion does not seem too surprising, for the Nahuas are depicted as a fairly malleable group from the start.

Sahagún adds another dimension to the might-makes-right argument in order to bolster the way in which the twelve missionaries established their authority. Not only is one group of Nahuas successfully converted, the converted group is, not coincidentally, composed of superiors to whom other, lesser Nahuas previously deferred. At one point in the proceedings, the Nahuas who were first addressed claim they lack the necessary authority to make important religious decisions and recess to talk with their leaders. After a long discussion among themselves, the first Nahuas bring their leaders into the debate ("Aztec-Spanish Dialogues," 111). The message clearly is that each and every Nahua—no matter how low in station—should defer to the example of the wise leaders. In fact, Sahagún is careful to point out that the Nahuas are conscious of throwing away a long, ancient tradition of idolatry whose authority had been established partly through its sheer durability (107).

What I hope to have shown by now is that Sahagún employed extremely elaborate means of establishing the authority of the missionary process in New Spain as depicted in the initial encounter between the first twelve Franciscans and a group of Nahua leaders. Much of this authority is self-consciously established through rhetorical devices from the Western and Nahua traditions that make the *Coloquios* seem—to the modern reader—more literary than historically objective. The dialogue form itself is my final case in point, and brings the discussion back to the problem of Sahagún's humanism.

Sahagún employs the dialogue form in order to be able to embed acquiescent and interactive Nahuas into his text in a manner that is less possible with mere historical narration. The Nahuas in the *Coloquios* are, finally, not convinced because Scripture has revealed the light to them in one fell swoop but because *they arrived at their own conclusions* after zigzagging through their discussion with the friars. This, at least, is what the dialogue would suggest if one were to accept it at face value.

Throughout the Middle Ages, Scripture and the church were the only authorities necessary to arrive at the knowledge of what was felt truly to be worth knowing, but Sahagún ensconces these authorities in a rhetorical scaffolding that comes close to overshadowing them. In an almost paradoxical fashion, the divine revelation or illumination the friars promise to shed on the Nahuas (70) is entangled in an elaborate rhetorical web that seems to contradict the spontaneity often associated with revealed truth. Since the Nahuas had no reason to accept the authority of Scripture or the church except through coercion, Sahagún could not assume their authority as a given (as was typically the case in the Middle Ages) and was required to bolster it with arts of persuasion that he invented or that are associated with the Renaissance humanists and the Nahua oral tradition. Faced with the novel problem of converting people (the Nahuas) who had no compelling reason to accept Christianity on its own authority, the dialogue form enabled Sahagún to reason his way back to the authority of Scripture and the church.

To the extent that Sahagún's rhetorical acrobatics and use of classical models qualify him as a humanist, his humanism must be defined in the narrow terms that I laid out earlier. Sahagún's humanism is neither a philosophy nor a positively charged ethical or humane position unique to humanism. It is less the inevitable result of "humanistic baggage" brought over from Europe than a mode of discourse that was galvanized or propelled into motion by the particular circumstances of sixteenth-century New Spain.

3. Medievalists

Several scholars have identified medieval European influences on Sahagún's works. The works of these scholars merit some scrutiny because they provide one of the few coherent critical backdrops for future research on Sahagún. This, as I hope I have made clear, is not the case for the other two prevalent understandings of Sahagún's mind-set. The claim that Sahagún is the first modern anthropologist is, at worst, an irresponsible anachronism and, at best, a hollow statement that in reality says nothing substantial about his work. In order usefully to apply the term humanism to Sahagún, it must first be stripped of its weighty, positively charged moral connotations. Next, the origins of Sahagún's humanism must be recognized in the particular missionary circumstances of New Spain that provided the true stimulus for its emergence in his work. Sahagún's humanism is not of that of European origin—which is normally what people have in mind when they talk about humanism.

Those scholars who have attempted to show the influence of medieval thought on Sahagún's work are on much firmer ground.

Until very recently, most of these scholars have been content merely to identify medieval models Sahagún used in his work, but it is now becoming clear that the implications of these medieval influences reach much further than has previously been appreciated. There is nothing simple or obvious about what happens when indigenous culture is pressed into the currents of medieval thought. Nor are the motives behind such a bizarre grafting of cultures entirely transparent. In what follows, I would like to allude briefly to the work of a few scholars who have laid the foundation for the arguments I will pursue in the second part of the book.

As Anthony Grafton, April Shelford, and Nancy Siraisi note in *New Worlds, Ancient Texts*, around 1500 European books assumed that a basically complete and accurate body of knowledge already existed, and readers had a particular predilection for encyclopedic books of various proportions that summed up this knowledge (13). The pithy *Margarita philosophica* (1503)—Gregor Reisch's history of the world since creation—for example, "reveals no sense that either the world or knowledge has changed dramatically since ancient times" (16). Grafton, Shelford, and Siraisi note that authoritative texts of the time were presented as comprehensive wholes: these texts were generally printed in large print surrounded by commentaries that could "allegorize away" superficially uncomfortable texts such as the Song of Solomon (26).

In the middle of the sixteenth century, however, the pristine world of European book-bound knowledge started to come apart at the seams as less and less about what was being learned about the world fit into the earlier, static model of knowledge. According to Grafton, Shelford, and Siraisi, "between 1550 and 1650 Western thinkers ceased to believe that they could find all important truths in ancient books" (1).

New Worlds, Ancient Texts is a study of how knowledge of the New World helped to loosen and transform over a long period of time a medieval model of knowledge in which wisdom was thought of as a timeless, unchanging entity—much like an insect fossilized in amber. For my purposes, the analysis of Sahagún's work is particularly interesting. Grafton, Shelford, and Siraisi point out that "Sahagún's enterprise as a whole *imposed* the Western form of an encyclopedic, canonical text on a culture that had had no such texts and could never have conceived of such an enterprise" (145, my emphasis). Further, Sahagún

freeze-dried the multiple, protean ingredients of their [the Nahuas'] cultural tradition, producing a solid and immobile text and commentary, unchanging if readily accessible in form, and as divergent in character from its oral sources as its illustrations—which reflected Western techniques of construction and drawing—differed from those of pre-Conquest codices. (146)

What Grafton, Shelford, and Siraisi allude to—but do not develop further—is that there is something extremely unnatural and forced about the way in which Sahagún gathered and organized knowledge about Nahua culture. Nahua culture did not fall easily into a European schema. Sahagún had to do a good deal of pushing, pulling, and pruning in order to present Nahua culture as compatible enough with European culture to describe it according to European norms. Unlike most critics who have assumed that Sahagún's elaborate editing process simply represented a desire to authenticate and verify his sources,[36] Grafton, Shelford, and Siraisi are the first to emphasize that Sahagún "freeze-dried" or homogenized a vast array of extremely complex and contradictory cultural information. In other words, they are the first to depart from the view that Sahagún was doing nothing more than *passively* seeing Nahua culture through European lenses.

Ever since Donald Robertson's groundbreaking studies in the 1950s and 1960s, Sahagún scholars have been aware of the fact that Sahagún structured his *Florentine Codex* according to the precepts of such medieval "encyclopedias" as Isidore of Seville's *Etymologies* and Bartholomaeus Anglicus's *De Propietatibus Rerum*. Robertson noted that the twelve books of the *Florentine Codex* are organized in a hierarchical order of divine, human, and mundane things as are the works of Isidore of Seville and Bartholomaeus Anglicus (Mexican, 169; "Sixteenth," 622). Robertson also shows that patterns extracted from *De Propietatibus Rerum* actually affect the content of Sahagún's material. For example, a

> pattern of contrasting good and evil persons of the various classes, relationships and occupations occurs in Book VI [of *De Propietatibus Rerum*]; in Sahagún's work it is found in Book X. One of the most quoted examples from Sahagún is the description of the good artist, where the contrast is, on the face of internal evidence, European not native. ("Sixteenth," 624–25)

Despite Robertson's recognition that the European structure Sahagún employed affected the content of his material, he does not seem to find it out of the ordinary that Sahagún would use this schema in the first place. The assumption seems to be that Sahagún was simply unaware that he was imposing his worldview on the world of the Nahuas. The fact that Sahagún went to such great lengths to force the diversity of Nahua culture into a preconceived and static medieval hierarchy of knowledge produces surprisingly few waves in Robertson's analyses. The issue here is whether Sahagún passively received knowledge about the Nahuas according to his own preexisting modes of thought, or whether he sensed certain fundamental discrepancies between the European and Nahua worlds and *actively* tried to make the worlds coalesce by engaging and imposing certain structural tenets of the medieval system of knowledge.

Since Robertson, several critics have identified more European patterns and structures that govern both the form and content of Sahagún's enterprise. Working in Robertson's wake, Ellen Baird signals in *The Drawings of Sahagún's "Primeros Memoriales"* the transformation of indigenous painting as a *source* for discourse to its later, European-influenced role in Sahagún's work as *illustration* of discourse. In one interesting discussion, Baird shows that an apparently indigenous drawing of a seated, introspective man with a beard in the *Primeros memoriales* is, on closer examination, derived from a common prototype of European book illustration (35–36). Baird's study is rich in this kind of detail and lays the foundation for analyzing the far-reaching import or implications of a situation in which medieval European patterns were transforming the content of "indigenous" information.[37]

Luis Weckmann's comprehensive *La herencia medieval de México* also traces medieval elements in Sahagún at several junctures of his argument. Weckmann, however, points to medieval commonplaces in Sahagún's interpretation of the Nahua world without trying to explain why Sahagún felt compelled to explain facets of Nahua culture in such a highly contrived fashion. Why, for example, did Sahagún feel it was necessary to identify Lucifer with a *specific* Nahua deity, Tezcatlipoca (242)?

Debra Hassig's article "Transplanted Medicine: Colonial Mexican Herbals of the Sixteenth Century" offers a partial answer to the question of why Nahua culture was increasingly Europeanized in general in sixteenth-century European texts. Hassig notes that throughout the sixteenth century, New World herbals increasingly came to resemble their medieval Old World predecessors until there was little except the origin of the plants to distinguish them: "Taken together, the colonial Mexican herbals mark progressive steps toward the European appropriation of New World resources and medical information for use in the Old World" (53). Hassig notes that the last stage of this process—herbals entirely produced in Europe—is characterized by a complete lack of concern with the indigenous culture of Mexico (53).

According to Hassig, Sahagún modeled the illustrations in his herbal after the fairly unrealistic illustrations of southern European *tacuinum sanitatis* manuscripts, which "were contemporary health manuals that were popular beginning in late fourteenth-century Italy" (44). Hassig compares Sahagún's work to two other New World herbals: the Badianus manuscript, a New World herbal authored and illustrated by Nahuas but influenced by the European theory of the four humors; and Francisco Hernández's *Historia natural*, a text whose indigenous medicinal information was carefully filtered through the skeptical vision of its European author. Hassig characterizes the evolution of New World herbals as a process in which herbals with a strong indigenous influence, such as Sahagún's, gave way to works like Hernández's, and finally to European herbals containing New World plants without any apparent reference to indigenous culture or influence (51–53). In general, this process took indigenous knowledge and made it palatable to European tastes by sloughing off what did not fit into the preexisting categories of European humoral medical theory. The important implication of Hassig's argument is that there is nothing direct, immediate, or automatic about how the particular knowledge system of one culture appropriates knowledge from another culture. Implicit in arguments like Hassig's is something that now should be brought into the foreground of Sahagún studies in a more systematic fashion.

The time has come to ponder why someone like Sahagún took such extreme pains to cull information from the Nahuas and press it into a European model like the *tacuinum sanitatis*. The sheer amount of raw energy that Sahagún exerted to accomplish his task defies the notion that there was anything natural or inevitable about what he did. Historical hindsight makes it seem obvious that Sahagún would want to compose a kind of *pagan summa*[38] or encyclopedia, but, if one pauses for moment to think about it, there is nothing obvious about Sahagún's desire to reinscribe the world of the Nahuas into the categories of Western knowledge if it did not already present itself as a comfortable fit. Sahagún did much more than see the New World through European eyes: he labored intensely—if not entirely successfully—to make all that jarred with a Western schema fit into a preexisting perspective. Sahagún spent the latter half of his ninety-year life span gathering, sifting, cutting, and pasting information on the Nahuas in order to produce what can only be understood as a highly orchestrated text. And he did all of this against great odds.

The first question medievalists ask—or should ask—themselves when approaching a preprinting era manuscript for the first time is why at all the scribes or authors felt it was important enough to write down what they did. In a time of disposable paperbacks, e-mail, photocopying, and shredding machines, the paramount importance of this simple question is easily overlooked. Even if the discussion is limited to the copying of "unoriginal" works,[39] the production of medieval manuscripts required countless hours of grueling physical labor and a substantial monetary investment that rendered the final product a veritable treasure.

Although there were printing presses in New Spain from 1539 on, Sahagún's *Historia universal de las cosas de la Nueva España* was produced—albeit with its clear, essential indigenous influence—according to the standards of European medieval scriptoria.[40] Sahagún's *Historia* was an extremely time-consuming and expensive project. Not only did the project dominate the second half of Sahagún's life, it required the cooperation of paid scribes and expensive writing materials. Moreover, any time Sahagún spent on his *Historia* took time away from the other duties meted out to a Franciscan missionary in a volatile colonial context. For this reason, Sahagún scholars should be asking themselves the same questions medievalists ideally do about the *physical*, media-oriented—and not just ethereally semantic—constitution of the text.

Much has been made of the apparently unreasonable Franciscans who tried to stop Sahagún's project. One critic even goes as far as depicting Sahagún as a persecuted Christ figure who suffered a "scientific Calvary" (Ballesteros Gaibrois, 75–98). Today, the value of Sahagún's work seems clear enough, so why would anyone—especially one of Sahagún's companions—want to stand in its way? In one of his prologues, Sahagún complains bitterly about the fellow Franciscans who impeded his work on grounds that its cost—all the "*tomines*" (monies) spent on scribes—was not in accord with the Franciscan vows of poverty. Sahagún's provincial, Fray Alonso de Escalona, dispersed his materials throughout the province so he could not work, and the governing members of a chapter meeting left the shaky-handed author without monies to pay for scribes (*CF* II:2r).

Nevertheless, the actions of Sahagún's intramural opponents, although unfortunate, are not as unreasonable as is commonly assumed. From the beginning, the history of the Franciscan order engaged in heated debates over what role—if any—books and learning should play in the daily life of the friars. Saint Francis himself was opposed to study and erudition—much to the consternation of his more learned followers (Moorman, 53–54). According to Le Goff, "St Francis was very distrustful towards intellectual culture because he always considered it to be a treasure and because the economic value of books seemed to him to be in contradiction with the practice of poverty which he wanted for his brothers" (*Medieval Civilization*, 345). Since Sahagún referred to his work as a "treasure" (*CF* I:"Al sincero lector"), it is not surprising that it would be met with some opposition. Moreover, when the value of Sahagún's work was being debated by his companions, it did not exist in the impressive, pristine form now known as the *Florentine Codex*. What Sahagún's companions probably saw was the sixteenth-century equivalent of a runaway expense account and an incomprehensible collection of papers written only in Nahuatl whose value was not readily apparent to the less linguistically gifted Spanish friars.

Sahagún meticulously records the objections of his companions and his struggle to obtain patrons and supporters in order to highlight the obstacles he had to overcome. He states, "All of the above said serves the purpose of making clear that this work has been examined and purified by many and over many years and with much labor and misfortune until it was put in the state it is now in" (*CF* II:2r). Sahagún also emphasizes more than once the "extreme cost and amount of work" that his work entailed along with the fact that he considers it to be still unfinished (*CF* XI:"Prologo," I:"Al sincero lector"). Nothing simply fell into place for Sahagún. Sahagún was doing more than seeing the Nahua world according to the precepts of his European background. He was going against the grain of some well-established Franciscan principles and expending great financial resources and labor to push Nahua culture into a European manuscript tradition.

Simply put, recent Sahagún scholarship has opened up the possibility of a new type of question. Given the cost, labor, and orchestration involved, the question is no longer just *which* medieval models Sahagún used in the completion of his work, but *why* Sahagún went to the lengths he did in the first place. The question is no longer so much why his companions tried to stop his work, but why he was so driven to overcome the physical and financial obstacles placed in his path—obstacles whose existence modern scholars should not be so surprised, let alone outraged, to discern. Finally, what was happening in mid-sixteenth-century New Spain that so strongly compelled Sahagún to go to the lengths he did in writing his *Historia universal de las cosas de la Nueva España?*

PART 2

SAHAGÚN AND HIS WORLDS

3

WHEN WORLDS COLLIDE

Crisis and Structure in Sahagún's Historia universal

1. Crisis

Indeed, the main thrust of the historical endeavors of medieval Christian
thinkers consisted in trying to bring history to a stop or to complete it.
(Le Goff, *Medieval Civilization*, 173)

Sahagún arrived in New Spain in 1529 at the age of twenty-nine
or thirty, and he never returned to Europe. It was quite uncommon
for anyone at that time to live as long as Sahagún did—ninety years.
The older Sahagún grew, the more energy he expended on his written
legacy. In spite of debilitating illnesses that impeded his ability to
write in his own hand (requiring that he employ scribes), Sahagún
pressed on in his determination to finish his *Historia universal*. Old
age, however, was not Sahagún's only obstacle. Although, as I argue
in the first chapter, Sahagún was not a victim of a personally directed "conspiracy" orchestrated by the government of Philip II, he
did fall victim to the inner politics of his order in New Spain. For
example, in 1570, when Sahagún tried to go over the heads of his
immediate superiors in order to secure the right to continue his
work with the help of scribes, the Provincial Fray Alonso de Escalona
retaliated by scattering his papers across the province. Fortunately,
Sahagún was able to retrieve them (*CF* II:2r).

As I argued in the last chapter, the sheer amount of time and
energy that were necessary to compose the *Historia universal* and its

final manifestation, the *Florentine Codex*—coupled with the personal and intramural obstacles placed in Sahagún's path—should do away with any possible notion that Sahagún pursued his work during his leisure hours like a disinterested gentleman scholar or hobbyist. Some strong force or forces compelled Sahagún to undertake his task, and these forces came into play at the midpoint of Sahagún's long life. In what follows, I will argue that Sahagún's work was driven by a sense of crisis and that this crisis had more dimensions than first meet the modern reader's eye.

One of Sahagún's forerunners in New Spain, Fray Toribio de Benavente o Motolinía, could still believe in 1542, when the manuscript of his *Historia de los indios de la Nueva España* was sent to Spain, that the religious conversion of the indigenous population had been both profound and complete. In a passage that Motolinía initially placed in the final pages of his history, he declares, "Because where the doctrine and word of Christ has arrived, nothing [of idolatry] remains that is known nor that needs to be taken into account" (254). Motolinía makes this claim as a response to Spaniards who claimed that the Nahuas never gave up their idolatrous practices and kept their idols and celebrations well-hidden. Motolinía counters that the Nahuas were completely disinterested in the idols they had buried until the Spaniards started digging them up in the hopes of finding gold and jewels. In fact, Motolinía argues, the innocent Nahuas were so persecuted by Spaniards outside the orders that they took the extreme measure of fabricating new idols in the hopes of squelching the Spaniards' greed (255). Arguing from the standpoint of his *"harta experiencia"* (vast experience), Motolinía claims that the real deceit (*"engaño"*) was in the camp of Spaniards who hoped to take advantage of the Nahuas (256). The following quotation is possibly Motolinía's strongest encomium of what he interpreted as the pure hearts of the Nahuas:

Oh Mexico, such mountains encircle and crown you! Now with reason your fame will take flight, because in you the faith and gospel of Jesus

Christ shine! You who were before teacher of sins, now you are an instructor of truths; and you who were before in darkness and obscurity, now you gleam with doctrine and Christianity. . . . Before you were a Babylon, full of confusions and evils; now you are another Jerusalem, mother of provinces and kingdoms. (314)

Motolinía's claim that the conversion of the Nahuas had been entirely successful might seem politically expedient. But, initially at least, the first twelve Franciscan missionaries sincerely believed that they had wrought profound changes on the moral landscape of New Spain. This self-confidence was passed on to the second group of missionaries that arrived in New Spain, and Sahagún, who was in the second group, complains bitterly in his *Arte adivinatoria* (1585) of the gullibility of his predecessors and the precious time that was lost in listening to their advice (quoted in García Icazbalceta, 382).

Sahagún's *Arte adivinatoria* is the clearest statement that exists of his pessimism and despair concerning the mission in New Spain. After over fifty-five years in New Spain, Sahagún was convinced that the church in New Spain was rotten to the core because its foundations were never properly laid. Sahagún accuses the Nahuas of duplicity when, for example, they concealed their idolatry under a falsely expurgated calendar: "There is another trick very harmful to the Catholic faith, that these lake-dwellers invented, very difficult to uproot, and it is that those who silently guard the cult of many gods made a calendar in which they ingested this Art of Divining" (García Izcabalceta, 383). Sahagún is haunted by the recent discovery of an internal Nahua psyche that does not coalesce with outward shows of Christianity and concludes—in a kind of run-on chain reaction—that everything about their conversion is false:

Having set forth these two great unsuitable aspects of the foundation of this new church, it is clear that everything is false because, since they were all baptized as adults, and since children continue to be baptized, and their parents continue to catechize them in their faked faith and take them all out into public in order to receive the sacraments and celebrate the

Christian holidays, in their interior they have not left off holding their gods as gods, nor rendering them services, offerings, and celebrations on the sly, and hence this affair suffers by being secret. (383)

The interiority Sahagún refers to—the vast, unfathomable world of the Nahua psyche—did not exist at first for Motolinía. For reasons I will examine in detail further along, initially Motolinía and the other early missionaries simply lacked the conceptual framework that would have been necessary to perceive the superficiality of the Nahuas' conversion. Sahagún was so frustrated with Motolinía's inability to perceive the duplicity of the Nahuas and their calendar that, at the late date of 1572, he denounced him to the Inquisition (Baudot, "Fray Toribio"). For Sahagún, the Nahua *tonalpohualli*, or soothsaying calendar, was a diabolical mockery of the Christian religious calendar, but the blindness of the friars ran so deep Sahagún still felt compelled to write his *Arte adivinatoria* decades after most of the missionaries—including Motolinía—had abandoned once and for all their utopian dreams for the Nahuas of New Spain.

What Sahagún perceived as the duplicity of the Nahuas was at least partially the result of misunderstanding. In "Some Nahua Concepts in Postconquest Guise," James Lockhart introduces the useful concept of "double mistaken identity": "each side of the cultural exchange presumes that a given form or concept is operating in the way familiar within its own tradition and is unaware of or unimpressed by the other side's interpretation" (477). Lockhart is primarily concerned with the curious fusion of Spanish and indigenous forms of government and economy in New Spain, but he is quick to point out that what initially seemed like the success of the first missionaries was primarily due to the striking superficial resemblance between European and Nahua religious practices:

It was because of such things as their own crafts and writing systems, their tradition of sumptuous temples as the symbol of the state and the ethnic group, their well-developed calendar of religious festivities and processions, their relatively high degree of nucleation of settlement, that they could quickly take to similar aspects of the Spanish heritage. (467)

The missionaries were quick to latch on to indigenous practices and turn them to their own advantage, but these very same practices were often the undoing of any true, complete conversion. For example, the Nahuas had a form of confession before the arrival of the Spaniards, but it did not play the same role in their culture as it did in the Christian faith. The friars were perplexed by the fact that the Nahuas often presented themselves for confession without any sign of remorse. Following a practice from their own culture, the Nahuas often used confession as a way to exonerate themselves from crimes and frequently asked the priests for a note proving they had confessed. Subsequently, they would repeat the offense without any scruples. Moreover, the Nahuas assessed the proportions (or lack thereof) of sinning in a manner that was quite alien to Christianity: they quickly agreed to whatever number was suggested to them when they were asked how many times they had committed a particular sin. The friars were torn between attributing this apparent confusion on the Nahuas' part to faulty memory and questioning their overall sincerity. In the early stages of the mission, the faulty-memory explanation prevailed (Ricard, 117–20).[1]

Sahagún was among those friars who were worried by the degree of similarity and difference between precolonial and Christian confessional practices. Book I of the *Florentine Codex*, for instance, includes a lengthy description of precolonial Nahua confessional practices in Nahuatl and loose Spanish translation. Sahagún adds to the Spanish translation an extremely interesting passage that signals the inappropriate survival of indigenous practices in poorly administered confessions in Christian New Spain:

In what concerns the above said we know that even after here, in Christendom, they persisted in carrying it forward in what concerns doing penance and confessing grave and public sins such as homicide, adultery, and so forth, thinking that, as was the case in the past for the confessions

and acts of penance they performed, they were pardoned for those sins in
the judicial forum. Even now when someone kills or commits adultery
he/she takes refuge in our houses and monasteries, and remaining silent
about what they did, they say they want to do penance, and they dig in the
orchard and sweep in the house and do what they are told, and after a few
days they confess and then declare their sin and the reason why they came
to do penance. Having finished their confession, they ask the confessor
for a signed document in order to show it to those who rule—the
governor and mayors—so they know that they have done penance and
confessed and that justice now has nothing against them. Almost none of
the monks or clerics understands where the trick is headed because they
are ignorant of the ancient custom they had as is described above, but
think that they ask for the document in order to show that they have
confessed that year. (*CF* I:9v)

The final part of this passage is perhaps the most telling. Sahagún
describes the survival of indigenous customs as an *"embuste"* (trick)
and points out that most of the priests have been blind to the
implications of this cultural residue.

Sahagún provides another example. In one of the most famous
passages of the *Florentine Codex*, Sahagún describes the demise of the
Colegio de Santa Cruz de Tlaltelolco. He tells how the Franciscans
who founded the colegio took advantage of a preexisting indigenous
educational institution (the *calmecac*) to found their own school. The
colegio was originally founded with the hope of creating an indigenous clergy, but this dream soon gave way to less lofty goals until,
finally, the Franciscans lost all confidence in the project, and the
school was abandoned. In his lengthy description of the colegio's
history, Sahagún ascribes the downfall of the colegio to its inability
to rein in the inherent corporeal appetites of the Nahuas as effec-
tively as the old indigenous schools did (*CF* X:70v-84r). The initial
perception of strong similarities between preexisting indigenous
educational institutions and Catholic seminaries gave way to the
notion that European and indigenous students were educationally
incompatible because of differing physiological makeups. I will

return to the issue of the Nahuas' sensuality in chapter 5 since it merits further comment, but suffice it to say for now that Sahagún's analysis reveals his burgeoning awareness that superficially similar concepts and institutions can mean entirely different things in different cultures.

Today, in the abstract, it is taken for granted that each culture will respond to and interpret novel concepts and situations according to the limitations and contours of its own preexisting structure. Furthermore, even though one need never abandon one's own belief system in the process, it is generally recognized that cultural artifacts, beliefs, and so forth must be understood (to the extent it is possible) from within the cultural context in which they developed if they are to be appreciated to any degree. These points may seem obvious today, but they were anything but obvious in the Middle Ages or at the very beginning of the early modern period. Even in early modernity, such relatively extreme cases of cultural relativism as Michel de Montaigne's essay "Des cannibales" are fairly infrequent and normally appear when an author is operating from what could be called a safe distance.[2] The groundwork of cultural relativism really was laid in the nineteenth century, when European imperialist expansion was accompanied by a vast accumulation of cultural data that—because of its sheer volume—defied a facile European conceptualization.[3]

Sahagún's realization that a shared concept or practice could mean something entirely different to the Nahuas than it meant to the Spaniards resulted in the strong, reactionary charges of deceit and duplicity in his *Arte adivinatoria*. Sahagún simply could not admit to himself that Nahua customs made sense in a manner that had nothing to do with the Christian West or God's divine plan. Nevertheless, much as nineteenth-century Europe was overwhelmed by the quantity and diversity of ethnographic data, Sahagún was faced with a vast array of indigenous cultural information that did not easily fit into a preexisting Western schema. Once Sahagún noticed what lay beneath the superficial compatibility of a few Christian and indigenous practices, *everything* was subject to reinterpretation.

Hence, Sahagún called his history *"universal"* in order to highlight his desire to comprehend the entirety of Nahua culture. In short, the crisis that drives all of Sahagún's work is his realization that the easy fit between Christian and Nahua customs, as reported by Motolinía and the rest of the first twelve Franciscans, was nothing more than a dream.

Sahagún was in a privileged position to observe the nature of this case of religious double mistaken identity, but this position was not shared by all of his European contemporaries who were residing in the New World. Most Spaniards in sixteenth-century New Spain were not overly concerned with the true conversion of the Nahuas unless it somehow played into their more worldly objectives. In fact, contact between Spaniards and Nahuas outside of Tenochtitlán in the sixteenth century was often minimal in spite of the economic ties established through such measures as the appropriation of the indigenous tribute system.[4] Cases of both cultural and political double mistaken identity were widespread because most Spaniards only concerned themselves with the internal affairs of Nahua communities when they felt they had to. This was not the case for the most zealous members of the regular clergy. The missionaries from the Mendicant orders had more direct contact with the Nahuas than any other group of Europeans and were thus more likely over time to grow to understand the differences that existed between the two worlds.

Sahagún was considered to be one of the foremost European speakers of Nahuatl (Mendieta, 663) and therefore had entrée into the world of the Nahuas that was shared by relatively few other Europeans. Much of the purported missionary success of the earlier twelve missionaries is probably attributable in part to the language gap. Once the missionaries acquired enough Nahuatl to recognize nuances, they were in a better position to discern discrepancies between Nahua and European interpretations of superficially similar ideas. The more the Mendicant friars acquired knowledge of the indigenous languages (and not all did), the more they became obsessed with the misinterpretation of Scripture and doctrine.

Motolinía's eulogistic words on the Nahuas' conversion—dating from 1536, but still endorsed in 1542—represent the swan song of unadulterated missionary optimism. From the middle of the sixteenth century on, the work of conversion took on an increasingly pessimistic and inquisitorial nature.

When it comes to suspicions concerning the efficacy of missionary practices in New Spain, 1555 was a watershed year. In this year—according to Robert Ricard—all sermons written in an indigenous language were ordered to be seized (57); the ordination of mestizos, Negroes, and Indians was forbidden (230); and, suspecting the survival of pagan rites, the ecclesiastic authorities attempted to instigate the careful regulation of indigenous displays of their Christian faith such as the "*areitos*" or "*mitotes*" (celebrations/ dances) held in honor of the patron saints of villages (186–87). Although these decisions were not effective in every case, they represent the growing conviction that the early success of the first Franciscans was actually an out-and-out failure. The growing discouragement of the missionaries also can be deduced from Philip II's order in 1561 that the monasteries of New Spain be built at greater distances from each other. Apparently, by this time the missionaries preferred to live close together in cities and away from the rural populations, who were previously felt to be the ones in greatest need of conversion (Ricard, 81). By 1570, Ricard notes, "a violent antinative reaction may be observed among the Franciscans" (35).

Despite Sahagún's professed admiration for many aspects of Nahua culture, he was not immune to this trend. In his analysis of the strongly worded *Arte adivinatoria*, Bustamante García expresses Sahagún's attitude toward the "*conspiración*" (conspiracy) of the Nahuas quite succinctly: "Sahagún, undoubtedly, is an extremely fine observer and excellent authority on traditional indigenous culture, but here, with more clarity than in other parts, his fundamental point of view is apparent: he is not an ethnologist, he is an inquisitor" (*Fray Bernardino*, 376).

Sahagún shared with his brethren the feeling that they had been duped by the "deceitful" Nahuas, but Sahagún did not react to this

crisis in entirely the same way his companions did. Despite his pessimism, Sahagún set about elaborately and systematically cataloguing
Nahua culture on a grand scale in order to extirpate idolatrous
practices more efficiently. Around 1547, Sahagún began work on the
"Rhetoric, Moral Philosophy, and Theology of the Mexican
People"—the earliest part of the *Florentine Codex* (*CF* VI: 215v). In
1558, Sahagún was officially charged with writing his history by his
prelate, Fray Francisco Toral. This last date is a further indication of
the friars' growing awareness in the mid-sixteenth century that there
was more to the world of the Nahuas than met the eye. This official
endorsement followed in the wake of a similar one in 1553 for the
now missing work of Fray Andrés de Olmos (Nicolau d'Olwer, 28).

Since the unique scope of the Sahaguntine corpus is a direct result
of how the author personally experienced the crisis, it is worthwhile
to contrast his views in a somewhat more detailed fashion with the
mind-set of the Franciscan missionaries when they first arrived in
New Spain in 1524.

Fray Martín de Valencia and the "Twelve Apostles" (as they
called themselves) arrived in Mexico in 1524, driven by the belief
that their mission would fulfill expectations of the coming end of
the world.[5] The first Franciscans to arrive in New Spain were
Observants who partook in the fifteenth- and sixteenth-century
revitalization in Spain of the apocalyptic belief that a thousand-
year reign of Christ on earth was at hand. They believed that the
history of the world was divided into three complementary ages:
the time from Creation to the death of Christ; the age of the church;
and the coming, final age in which Christ would return to rule a
kingdom of absolute peace.

The Twelve Apostles interpreted the discovery of the New
World—and particularly the conquest of Mexico—as a sign that
the millennium was looming on the horizon and only the task of
quickly and "miraculously" converting the New World's population
stood in the way of its pending arrival. The millennium the Twelve
Apostles envisioned was to be characterized by the contemplative
life, for, as the present age was the age of priests and the church, the

coming age was to be the age of the friars. On the eve of their departure to the New World, the minister general of the Franciscan order who was bidding the twelve farewell described their eleventh-hour mission as a final battle against the forces of evil. The subtext is clearly drawn from Revelation:

To you, then, o sons of mine, I, unworthy father, cry out as the last end of the century approaches and grows old, and I move and awaken your wills in order that you defend the squadron of the High King that moves as if vanquished and almost fleeing the enemies; and that, undertaking the victorious struggle of the Sovereign Triumpher, you preach to the enemies with words and works. (quoted in Mendieta, 204)

Despite the fact that the friars were entering into the unknown, the minister general who spoke these words was careful to inscribe their mission into a preestablished historical trajectory. For example, the minister general chose a prelate and twelve "apostles" to go to New Spain precisely because of the precedents set by Christ and Saint Francis (Mendieta, 201). Throughout the entire speech, the minister general entreats the twelve to follow the example of Christ and Saint Francis else they deviate from their path. Interestingly, the minister general refers to the friars' journey as a "pilgrimage"—implying the preestablished and closed-ended nature of their spiritual, historical, and geographical trajectory (200).

John Leddy Phelan's *The Millennial Kingdom of the Franciscans in the New World* and Georges Baudot's *Utopía e historia en México* have been perhaps the greatest contributions to date to the identification of apocalyptic or millennial elements in the sixteenth-century Franciscan evangelization of New Spain. Relying also on the work of Reinhart Koselleck, I will draw out certain features of the Franciscan millennial movement that distinguish it from modern-day conceptualization of history. This distinction is important for an understanding of Sahagún's own position.

The millennialism of New Spain represents a last vestige of a predominantly medieval conception of history. In general, this conception of history slowly came to disintegrate in Europe over the course of the sixteenth century. The initial stages of its undoing in New Spain, however, occurred at the midpoint of Sahagún's life in a somewhat more rapid and dramatic fashion than in Europe.

In "Modernity and the Planes of History," included in the volume *Futures Past: On the Semantics of Historical Time*, Reinhart Koselleck argues that, in the medieval conceptualization of history, the present and past were enclosed within a common historical plane and the perception of temporal difference in general was virtually nonexistent (4). The minister general's speech to the twelve friars on the eve of their departure is symptomatic of this phenomenon. The friars did not embark on their journey expecting to encounter and live through entirely unforeseen historical events. They left with the expectation that whatever they encountered would make sense in terms of an already existing, self-enclosed vision of history. Koselleck points out that until well into the sixteenth century, the history of the Christian world is a history of expectations: an oscillation between the anticipations of the end of the world and the continual deferment of this end (6). The continuously deferred end of the world had been constituted by the church and then projected in the form of a *static* time capable of being experienced as a tradition (17). Only when the signs of the apocalypse are applied to concrete events or instances does the church's eschatological vision of history show signs of erosion (8). Until the sixteenth century, however, the failure of any single apocalyptic prediction could always be displaced onto the future.

Koselleck argues that the modern "temporalization" of history began in the sixteenth century, when the Reformation underscored the "failure" of a unified church or Christian empire and when modern politics emerged in the recently opened gap between the maintenance of "peace" and "religious duty." Beginning in the sixteenth century, religious wars no longer heralded the final judgment, and the modern absolutist state came to define itself through its struggle *against* eschatological predictions (8–10).

Koselleck argues that the main difference between the medieval and modern conceptualizations of history is the distinction between prophecy and prognosis: "Prognosis produces the time within which and out of which it weaves, whereas apocalyptic prophecy destroys time through its fixation on the End" (14). Lacking the security of absolutes that a medieval eschatological reading of history provided, the modern politician was forced to make relativized moral judgements according to greater or lesser evils. The modern perception that the Christian empire had failed in its task to follow an eschatologically preestablished historical path forced the modern politician to make predictions about an open-ended future rather than prophecies about a closed one. Koselleck points out that the advent of prediction or prognosis as a political tool helped to usher in the modern concept of progress. For the modern period in general, the future is characterized by its uncertainty and the increasing speed with which it seems to approach us (17).

Koselleck's analysis provides a useful framework for examining how the Franciscan millennial dream played itself out in sixteenth-century New Spain, and, in turn, Sahagún's position vis-à-vis the millennial movement. When the Franciscan missionaries recognized their failure in the mid-sixteenth century, they inevitably had to readjust their expectations about the role of the mission in the larger framework of the apocalypse. The recognition of the stubborn survival of non-Christian modes of thought was the most important factor in the missionary crisis, but it was exacerbated by the dramatic decrease in the Nahua population due to plagues. In 1545, for example, there was a major epidemic in which Sahagún himself fell ill:

After the plague of 1520 and after the Spaniards had won New Spain and were keeping it peaceful and preaching of the Gospel was being exercised with much prosperity, in the year 1545 there was a great and universal plague where in New Spain the greater part of the population who lived here died. And at the time of this plague I found myself in this city of Mexico in Tlaltelolco, and I buried more than 10,000 corpses, and at the end of the plague I, myself, fell ill and almost died. (*CF* XI:238r)

The epidemics and the ensuing deaths of the Nahuas became the most visible indication of the plight of the Franciscans' mission. Simply put, with the indigenous population being taken to its grave in droves, there was little hope left for the large-scale conversion and reign of peace that the Franciscans had originally envisioned. Motolinía's reaction to these epidemics is quite telling. Motolinía never abandoned his apocalyptic interpretation of the role of the Franciscans, but he seriously modified it. In 1555 he wrote a letter to Charles V that is, in essence, a diatribe against Fray Bartolomé de Las Casas's defense of the rights of the indigenous population. Motolinía turns his back on the interests of the Nahuas and sides with the Spanish colonists whom Las Casas had so often accused of mistreating the indigenous population. In this letter, Motolinía proffers his own explanation (while claiming not to) of the large-scale deaths of the Nahuas. The manner in which Motolinía reads his newly acquired coldheartedness into the greater Christian eschatological scheme merits the lengthy quotation that follows:

[A]nd everyday these natives are being diminished; whatever the cause is, God knows because his judgments are many and hidden from us. If the great sins and idolatries that were in this land cause it, I do not know, but I see that the promised land that those seven idolatrous generations possessed by God's commandment was destroyed by Joshua, and afterwards it was populated by the children of Israel in such a way that, when David counted the people, he found in the ten tribes just [in counting] the strong men of war 800,000. And in Judah and Benjamin's tribe 500,000, and afterwards in the time of king Asa of the tribes in the battle that Sarah gave to the king of the Ethiopians 580,000 men of war were found, and it was so populated that land that it is read that the city of Jerusalem alone more than 150,000 residents, and now in all those kingdoms there are not so many residents as there used to be in Jerusalem—not even half. The cause of that destruction and that of this land and islands, God knows, for all the means and remedies that Your Mercy and the Catholic Kings of holy memory humanely could provide, you provided, and it is not enough, nor have counsel and human might been enough to remedy it. ("Carta" in *Memoriales e Historia*, 342)

Motolinía is able to salvage an eschatological, apocalyptic reading of recent events by redefining his relationship with the Nahuas since the time he wrote his *Historia*. Motolinía's position throughout this letter is that the Nahuas received their due and Charles V is the legitimate standard-bearer, in both a spiritual and temporal sense, for God's peregrinating religious empire ("Carta," 339).

Sahagún's interpretation of the events of the mid-sixteenth century and the historical role of the Franciscans in New Spain is more complex than Motolinía's. Baudot believes that Sahagún was part and parcel of the millennial movement (*Utopía*, 17). Phelan categorically denies that Sahagún was associated with the apocalyptic thinking of his companions and argues that Sahagún formulated a novel "geohistorical law that Christianity is being continuously replaced from east to west," which Sahagún called "the peregrination of the Church" (27). Despite their opposing views, both Baudot and Phelan are only half right about Sahagún's interpretation of the historical role of the mission in New Spain. Sahagún's understanding is only a slight *modification* or alteration of a staple of medieval historical thinking. Moreover, it is incomprehensible without the conceptual backdrop of the millennial beliefs of his companions.

Sahagún's recognition of the superficiality of the conversion of the Nahuas coupled with their decimation forced him—as Phelan argues—to formulate a new explanation of the role of New Spain in the history of the church. This explanation, however, is not as novel as Phelan believes. The notions of *translatio imperii* and *translatio studii* are commonplaces in medieval historical thinking. Medieval historians believed that both power and culture in the guise of the Christian church and empire were following a carefully scripted trajectory from their beginning in the east to their terminus in the west. Le Goff cites the following examples in his *Medieval Civilization*:

Otto of Freising wrote: "all human power or learning had its origin in the east, but is coming to an end in the west", and Hugh of St Victor wrote, "Divine Providence has ordained that the universal government, which at the beginning of the world was in the east, has gradually, as the time approaches for its end, moved itself to the west to warn us that the end of the world is coming, for the course of events has already reached the edge of the universe." (172)

When Sahagún subscribes to the notion of a peregrinating church, he is not advancing anything that any medieval thinker would have trouble accepting.

What is new in Sahagún, however, is the notion that the church has passed New Spain by and gone on to another stopping point further west:

It seems to me that already God our Lord is opening a way for the Catholic faith to enter into the kingdoms of China where there are extremely able people of great refinement and great knowledge. As the church enters into those kingdoms, I believe that it will last for many years in that mansion because throughout the islands and New Spain and Peru, it has done nothing more than pass by on its way and even to make a way in order to be able to converse with those peoples of the regions of China. (*CF* XI:240r–v)

Recalling Koselleck's analysis of medieval and modern conceptualizations of history, one can see in Sahagún the initial symptoms of the erosion of a self-enclosed medieval, eschatological understanding of history. Like his medieval predecessors, Sahagún understands history as a monolithic, preordained temporality conjoined with a divinely inspired geographical trajectory, but he is careful not to provide the church with any specific terminus. Sahagún's statement that the church "will last a long time" in China seems to imply that it might one day move on to yet greener pastures. As Sahagún's church circles the globe in a westerly direction, it could conceivably return to its point of departure in the "east," although Sahagún does not speculate on this point.

Sahagún's vision of the future is slightly open-ended, but not in the sense that Koselleck suggests. The modern substitution of prognosis for prophecy and of progress for expectation was a long, drawn-out process that lasted until the end of the eighteenth century. A truly modern conceptualization of history was not available to Sahagún because of the sheer rapidity with which his circumstances changed. Instead of rushing headlong into a notion of history epitomized by the ideals of the European Enlightenment, Sahagún did what one might expect: he made do with the conceptual framework he had. His life-is-elsewhere approach to the mission in New Spain enabled him to explain to himself the failure of the project. It also resulted in his profound pessimism. Since the church had passed Sahagún and his brethren by, their status as the moral vanguard was replaced with the necessary, but less appealing, task of cleanup duty.

The rigid, simplistic, apocalyptic game plan of the first friars in New Spain fell away, leaving little that was coherent to replace it. Since Sahagún was not content to abandon the surviving Nahuas to their idolatrous fate or to the wiles of the Spanish colonists, he needed something to explain the veritable messiness of the mission in New Spain—a messiness that stood in marked contrast to the single-minded, idealistic expectations of his youth. Sahagún's real crisis was his struggle to make the unforeseen events of the New World coalesce with the universalizing schemata of his medieval Christian heritage. It is not a coincidence that Sahagún began work on his *Historia universal* at precisely the same time that the more astute friars began to question the efficacy of their evangelization of the Nahuas. The meticulousness with which Sahagún produced and organized his *Historia universal* was as much for his own sake as the sake of the mission. Through the careful study of details, Sahagún hoped to make sense of what had eaten away at the foundation of a unified Christian cosmology that, when first transplanted to New Spain, not only included the Nahuas, but saw their conversion as its greatest achievement. All in all, Sahagún's crisis was defined by his attempt on a conceptual level to control the centrifugal forces of a worldview that was rapidly splintering into a multiplicity of contradictory interpretive planes and diverging historical trajectories.

2. Structure

Late medieval works are confined within a definite frame, socially, geographically, cosmologically, religiously, and ethically; they present but one aspect of things at a time; where they have to deal with a multiplicity of things and aspects, they attempt to force them into the definite frame of a general order. (Auerbach, *Mimesis*, 275)

Any true understanding of Sahagún's enormous written output will ultimately be based on the work that he himself considered to be his most important—the opus that consumed the second half of his life. In approaching this work, the title is an obvious place to begin—but this is more complicated than one might think. Unfortunately, the title normally used to refer to Sahagún's magnum opus—*Historia general de las cosas de Nueva España*—is incorrect. Bustamante García has demonstrated that Sahagún intended his work to be entitled *Historia universal de las cosas de la Nueva España*, for this is the only title that appears in a manuscript directly under the stewardship of the author (*Fray Bernardino*, 249).

Carlos María de Bustamante's 1829–30 edition of Sahagún's history—the first to bring Sahagún to a wider public—was based on the Tolosa manuscript. The sixteenth-century title page of the Tolosa manuscript is badly mutilated, and the word "Vniversal" is only discernible as "V . . . sal." At the end of the Tolosa manuscript, the copier refers to the work in the following manner: "Fin dela Historia general compuesta Por / El Muy Rdo. Pe. fray bernardino de sahagun / [adorno]" (quoted in Bustamante García, *Fray Bernardino*, 334). The title of the 1829–30 edition was apparently derived from the copier's careless appendage to Sahagún's work.

Only recently has it become incontrovertibly clear that the Tolosa manuscript is a copy someone made of the *Florentine Codex* once it had left Sahagún's hands and arrived in Spain.[6] Moreover, the incorrect title has survived over the years because the *Florentine Codex*—the most polished (but, nonetheless, incomplete) version of the *Historia*—is missing its title page. The correct title can be found, however, in Sahagún's "Memoriales en español"—which, in part, is a draft of the loose Spanish translation of Book I of the history (*Historia de las cosas* VII: 401).

The word "universal" in the title *Historia universal de las cosas de la Nueva España* merits further examination since Sahagún intended it to be the reader's first indication of the scope and nature of the work. In the sixteenth century, scholars made a distinction between the words "universal" and "general"—even though a universal history might sometimes be subsumed under the rubric of a general history. By "universal history," sixteenth-century historians meant a complete history that begins with the Creation (Mignolo, "Cartas," 78). Sebastián de Cobarruvias's definitions of "general," "universo," and "universal" from his dictionary of 1611 are worth noting even though they were published over two decades after Sahagún's death:

GENERAL. That which is common to many and ordinary, speaking simply and outside of the terminology of scholarship.

UNIVERSE. Means the entirety, without excluding anything; and hence it is often seen as the making/edifice [*fábrica*] of the world. Universal, that which is common and includes everyone. . . .

UNIVERSAL. That which reports on many different things and speaks about them scientifically. (986)

Even though the definitions overlap some, Sahagún's use of the word "universal" rather than "general" places his work in a different light. As I shall show, Sahagún sought to produce an inclusive history that dealt with the overall "*fábrica*"[7]—the origins and makeup—of the Nahua world. He hoped to locate all the particulars of this world in a totalizing or universal schema. Sahagún's use of the word "universal" is indicative of a much more ambitious—and scholarly—project than any general or potentially incomplete history. In this section I will analyze the relationship between the structure of the *Historia* universal and the tensions of the particular epistemological backdrop that both defines and motivates Sahagún's thinking.

In many respects, Sahagún's *Historia universal* is an eclectic mix of many diverse types of materials. The twelve books of the history range from the descriptions of the gods in Book I to descriptions of plants in Book XI, from the "rhetoric and moral philosophy" of Book VI to the mercantile practices described in Book IX, from an explanation of the Nahua calendar in Book II to the genealogy of lords and kings in Book VIII. Only the Spanish part of Book XII—which is concerned with the conquest of New Spain by Hernán Cortés—is properly a narrative history in line with post-Enlightenment definitions of historiography. Sahagún's catalogue of Nahua culture is so diverse and so extensive, it is no wonder that his work is the most frequently cited reference in books and articles that treat colonial and precolonial Nahuas.

The heterogeneous nature of Sahagún's work is unified in part by its overarching linguistic concerns.[8] No matter what Sahagún was talking about, he always returned (or planned to return) to the semantic level of the individual words and morphemes that made up his descriptions of Nahua culture. Sahagún's history is universal in reach and minutely particular in practice.

In the previous section I argued that Sahagún discovered profound incongruities between the Nahua and the European worldviews as he grew more and more familiar with Nahua thinking through his unparalleled acquisition of Nahuatl. This discovery led to his sense that the mission in New Spain was an overall failure, since he discovered that such foundational elements of Christianity as baptism and confession were counted among the vast quantity of European concepts misunderstood by the Nahuas. Sahagún's sense that the mission had failed forced him to readjust his sense of history, since the mission's failure did not correspond to his and his companions' tightly woven eschatological expectations. The significance of this movement—the movement from the particularity of

semantic inconsistencies between languages (problems of translation) to a more generalized revision of a historical worldview—is
easily overlooked by present-day scholars. I must make some general
points about the long and rich tradition of medieval sign theory in
order to understand the true magnitude of Sahagún's predicament
and how it played itself out in his *Historia*.

Modern linguistic theory holds that much, if not most, of language is arbitrary, conventional, or instinctively determined.[9] This
view stands in direct contradiction to the medieval view that all
meaningful words or statements—regardless of language—referred
back to a universal *significatio*, or an essential, transcendental meaning.
The medieval doctrine of significatio held that

a word's actual meaning (its meaning on a particular occasion of its use)
ultimately is, or can be reduced to its fundamental "significance" (*significatio*), which as the word's natural property constitutes its essence or form
(*essentia, forma*), in virtue of which it is at the root of every actual meaning
of that word. (Kretzmann, Kenny, and Pinborg, 162)

It was not so much that medieval linguists were unwilling to abandon the doctrine of significatio and the related notion of a universal language; the doctrine was simply never in question.[10] Medieval
linguists took significatio for granted (since only God could provide all original meaning) and set about the arduous task of trying
to determine how significatio related to the more idiosyncratic and
contextually influenced meanings that crop up in ordinary usage.

For example, medieval scholars were fascinated by the apparent
self-referentiality of *insolubilia* ("insolubles," or semantic paradoxes),
such as the "liar paradox" ("What I am now saying is false"), but
they "did not seem to have any 'crisis mentality' about these paradoxes" (Kretzmann, Kenny, and Pinborg, 253). The unquestioned
validity of the doctrine of significatio led medieval scholars to the
conclusion that insolubilia said nothing fundamental about the
nature and expressive capacity of language. Language, ultimately,
was neither arbitrary nor a mere human attribute; rather it always—

if only elusively—referred back to universal meanings established through divine ordinance. Medieval thinkers believed that whether one used the words "man," "hombre," "homo," "Mensch," or what have you, one was always pointing back to a universal definition of man.[11]

If one keeps this legacy of metalinguistic universals in mind, it is easy to see why Sahagún should find the flagrant lack of correspondence between Nahua and European concepts so disconcerting. The discovery that the Nahuas were not at all talking about the same thing when they used superficially similar ideas threw a wrench into the medieval Euro-Christian system of unified meaning. Much of the semantic level of Nahuatl proved menacing—and even demonic—to Sahagún, since it clashed with his inherited views on the ultimate unity of all semantic content. Faced with this dilemma, Sahagún had three (hypothetical) choices: (1) do nothing, (2) accept that linguistic meaning is often contextually and arbitrarily determined, and hence not derivative of God, or (3) prove that Nahuatl and European languages share a semantic substratum. Sahagún chose the third option.

Sahagún's modern-day readers are most familiar with the version of the *Historia universal* preserved in the *Florentine Codex*. The folios of the *Florentine Codex* are principally divided into two columns—one in Spanish, one in Nahuatl. Most readers, however, are unaware that Sahagún had planned that a third column of scholia would constitute an integral part of his history. Sahagún alludes to these scholia in the first prologue of the *Florentine Codex*: "A clean copy of these twelve books with the appended grammar and vocabulary was finished this year of 1569. It has not been possible yet to put them in Spanish and provide the scholia according to the outline of the work" (*CF* I:"Prologo," 1r). And more explicitly:

These twelve books are planned such that each page has three columns: the first, in the Spanish language; the second, in the Mexican language; the third, the declaration [clarification] of the Mexican words, signaled with numbers in both parts. A clean copy of the Mexican language part in all

twelve books is finished. The Spanish language part and the scholia are
not done, because of not being able to do more, because of a lack of help
and favor. If I were given the necessary help, in a year, or a little more, I
could finish everything. (*CF* I:"Al sincero lector")

Sahagún's original intent is clearest in the drafts of his history
preserved in the "Memoriales con escolios."[12] The example shown
in the diagram below—selected somewhat randomly—is a segment
on the nature of good and bad great-grandfathers.[13] This same text
appears in the *Florentine Codex*, but without the scholia or right-hand
column (*CF* X:4r,v).[14] Sahagún apparently did not choose to include
the scholia in the *Florentine Codex* because they were still in prepara-
tion, although it is clear that he had every intention of doing so at
some further date.

The system of correspondences that Sahagún establishes between
the two columns to the right follows the scholastic distinction
between "categorematic" and "syncategorematic" terms. Categorematic terms are those that "have meaning in their own right." Syncategorematic terms are only meaningful when joined to categorematic terms (Kretzmann, Kenny, and Pinborg, 162). For example, in
the selection presented in the diagram, Sahagún does not bother to
provide glosses for the Nahuatl article "in." Sahagún's intention
throughout his history was to establish a one-on-one correspondence between the meaningful terms—the terms that corresponded
to a transcendent and universal language—of both Spanish and
Nahuatl. Sahagún hoped that by establishing a single referential
frame for both Nahuatl and Spanish, it could be shown that their
respective worldviews were representative of a single—albeit distorted, in the Nahuas' case[15]—cosmos.

In the selected passage, there is an example of the type of general
movement from particulars to universals that Sahagún hoped to
establish throughout his work. In the right-hand column, Sahagún
translates the Nahuatl phrase of someone "worthy of murmurs in
his absence" quite conservatively, but in the left-hand column, this
"absence" is given a specific location in the Christian cosmos: Hell.

DIAGRAM 1

Sahagún's Original Plan for the Structure of the *Historia universal*

Visabuelo

❡ El bisabuelo es decrepito es otra vez niño, *po* bisabuelo que tiene buen seso es hombre de buen exemplo y de buena dotrina, de buena fama, de buena nombradia, dexa obras de buena memoria en vida en haziendo, en generacion escritas: como un libro.

❡ Achtontli[1], aoc [2]quimati veue oppa[3] piltontli, ❡ yn qualli achtontli tlillo[4] tlapolo teyo[5] tocaye necauhcayo[6] amoxtli tlacuilolli tenevalo[7] ytollo, tzotecoacocuiua[8], xiyutl[9] octacatl quitecavilia.

1. bisabuelo. 2. decrepito. ca haoc quimati noueuetcauh. 3. dos vezes niño 4. persona de buen ex*e*plo. 5. persona de buena fama o de buena nombradia. 6. persona que dexa obras honrrosas escritas como un libro. 7. ser tenido nombrado o estimado. *pf.*° onitenevaloc onitoloc. 8. renovar la memoria de los muertos en buena parte o mala. *pf.*° onitzoteconacocuiuac. 9. dexar buen exemplo o buena dotrina. *pf.*° onictecauili /.

❡ El bisabuelo malo es como moradal como rincon como escuridad, digno de ser menospreciado, digno de ser reprehendido o reñido, digno de ser escarnecido digno que los biuen le murmuren donde esta en el infierno le escarnecen y escopan a todos dapena o enojo su memoria o su vista. / .

❡ Achtontli[10] tlaueliloc, xomolli[11], caltechtli, tlayoualli[12], telchiualoni[13] hayoni[14], yca tlatelchiualoni[15], mictlapa[16] ontelicçaloni, teputzcomoniloni[17], yca tlatelchivalo[18], chicalo[19] tlaqualania[20].

❡ El biasabuelo malo. 11. Cosa menospreciada o sozia. ca. noxomol nocaltech 12. cosa escura o escuridad ca. notlayoual. 13. cosa de ser tenida en poco. 14. Cosa digna de ser reprehendida o abominada. 15. Cosa digna de ser escarnecida. 16. *p*sona que dexa de si mala memoria que los biuos hablan mal della despues de muerto 17. persona digna de ser murmurada en su ausencia. 18. ser escarnecido o infamado 19. ser scopido. *pf.*° onichichaloc 20. dar pena o enojo o ser mohino. *p*. onittaqualani. / .

(*Historia de las cosas* VI:207)

As I said in the last chapter, several scholars—most notably Donald Robertson—have shown that Sahagún's entire collection of aspects of Nahua culture is ordered according to a medieval hierarchy of knowledge found in such works as Bartholomaeus Anglicus's *De Propietatibus Rerum*. Sahagún's work follows a medieval pattern that begins with the divine and ends with the mundane. This overall structure is one way in which Sahagún attempts to organize the particular correspondences between Nahuatl and Spanish (the universal significations) in the larger framework of a unified ordering with cosmological implications. As the clumsy leap from "absence" to "Hell" in diagram 1 shows, there was no simple way to bridge the gap separating the two cultures—no simple way to locate the world of the Nahuas in the preexisting medieval *ordo* (a spiritual and temporal ordering of people and things). The appeal—or even the necessity—of medieval structuring devices lay in their promise to reinsert the perceived messiness of Nahua culture into a general order—a Euro-Christian order that Sahagún, as a European man of the cloth, could understand.

There is a name for the characteristic technique or overall guiding principle of Sahagún's endeavor to reinsert the Nahua world into a Euro-Christian order: *manifestatio.* In a pithy book entitled *Gothic Architecture and Scholasticism: An Inquiry into the Analogy of the Arts, Philosophy, and Religion in the Middle Ages*, Erwin Panofsky first set forth the idea that high medieval thought in general is characterized by a particular spatialization of thought, which he labels "manifestatio." Manifestatio means elucidation or clarification, and Panofsky's use of the term refers to the high medieval need to elucidate the very process of reasoning:

Manifestatio, then, elucidation or clarification, is what I would call the first controlling principle of Early and High Scholasticism. But in order to put this principle into operation on the highest possible plane—elucidation of faith by reason—it had to be applied to reason itself: if faith had to be "manifested" through a system of thought complete and self-sufficient within its own limits yet setting itself apart from the realm of revelation, it became necessary to "manifest" the completeness, self-sufficiency, and limitedness of the system of thought. And this could only be done by a scheme of literary presentation that would elucidate the very processes of reasoning to the reader's imagination just as reasoning was supposed to elucidate the very nature of faith to his intellect. (30–31)

Manifestatio—a term Panofsky takes from Saint Thomas Aquinas's *Summa Theologica* (29)—grew out of the separation in the High Middle Ages between faith and reason. In the twelfth and thirteenth centuries medieval people came to believe that not only was the existence of God something to be accepted a priori—it was also demonstrable in his creation through the use of reason (7).[16] Panofsky's most brilliant observation is his contention that the principle of manifestatio was not limited to the verbal realm of scholasticism. Manifestatio is something closer to an epistemic feature that determines the shape of knowledge even when it is in the form of medieval architecture.[17] Panofsky demonstrates that the Gothic cathedral serves the same purpose and follows the same principle of manifestatio that scholasticism does in that both point to God *and* clarify how they point to God through systematic steps that any observer can retrace: "the membrification of the edifice permitted [the medieval observer] to re-experience the very processes of architectural composition just as the membrification of the *Summa* permitted him to re-experience the very processes of cogitation" (59).[18]

Sahagún's *Historia universal* shares what Panofsky (31) describes as the three requirements of both the classic *Summa*, which were medieval summations of knowledge, and Gothic architecture: (1) totality (sufficient enumeration), (2) arrangement according to a system of homologous parts and parts of parts (sufficient articulation), and (3) distinctness and deductive cogency (sufficient interrelation). Sahagún's attempt to cover the gamut between the divine and mundane poles of the Nahua world in a systematic fashion easily fulfills the first requirement. The second requirement is fulfilled by the almost obsessive persistence with which Sahagún cut up, shuffled, edited, and pasted together the information he gathered from the Nahuas over the course of several decades. Sahagún's history went through so many structural transformations that several critics have dedicated countless hours to retracing the evolution of his ordering.[19] This fact, coupled with the fact that Sahagún used questionnaires that shaped the nature of the information he gathered in the first place,[20] precludes the possibility that his work follows a natural, indigenous pattern—despite the fact that he worked with Nahua aides.[21] The systematic arrangement of the parts to the whole of the *Historia universal* is homologous because Sahagún made it that way. As I have mentioned, the third requirement is fulfilled by Sahagún's plan to include a column of scholia. In a kind of "visible logic," this column would enable the reader both to isolate the individual elements of Nahuatl and to see them as part of an "indiscerptible whole" both through the relationship of Nahuatl to universal significations and through the place of these elements in an overall depiction of the Nahua cosmos.[22]

Panofsky points out that one of the consequences of manifestatio and its emphasis on systematization was the introduction of elements that were completely unnecessary on a functional level but that provided overall symmetry (35). Sahagún, in general, makes no bones about the highly artificial construct of his work because he felt that it did not interfere with its overall veracity. On the contrary, the more systematic and symmetrical the work could be, the more valuable it would be. Sahagún describes his history as a *"red barredera"* (dragnet; *CF* I:"Prologo") and, more important, as a *"cedaço"* (sieve), which he says was emended and supplemented at various stages (*CF* II:1r–2v). The idea that the information was adjusted and filtered did not undermine its authenticity. The dubious relevance of much of the material gathered in the history to actual evangelical practice[23] can be explained in terms of Sahagún's desire to create an intellectual edifice whose totality represented a systematic, transparent, and harmonious whole.

This desire also explains why Sahagún included information that was so quotidian or so obvious that it is a wonder that it was included at all. At various points of the history, Sahagún does not bother to translate the Nahuatl into Spanish because he thinks the information is too obvious to merit reiteration in Spanish. For example, in Book XI Sahagún states, "In these words the types of corn are treated, and because it is something clear, it occurred to me to put in this place" (*CF* XI:246r). Even so, Sahagún includes the text in Nahuatl when he might have simply omitted it. Its inclusion seems to imply that Sahagún felt the work would somehow be incomplete without it.

C. S. Lewis has noted in *The Discarded Image* that sometimes "medieval people, like Professor Tolkien's Hobbits, enjoyed books which told them what they already knew" (200) and the medieval "writer feels everything to be so interesting in itself that there is no need for him to make it so" (204). Perhaps there is something of this in Sahagún, but most of the information in the history was alien enough to European eyes to demand another explanation for its format. C. S. Lewis states:

At his most characteristic, medieval man was not a dreamer nor a wanderer. He was an organizer, a codifier, a builder of systems. He wanted "a place for everything and everything in the right place". . . . There was nothing which medieval people liked better, or did better, than sorting out and tidying up. Of all our modern inventions I suspect that they would most have admired the card index.

This impulse is equally at work in what seem to us their silliest pedantries and in their most sublime achievements. In the latter we see the tranquil, indefatigable, exultant energy of passionately systematic minds bringing huge masses of heterogeneous material into unity.[24] (10)

It is my contention that it was to this type of a "tranquil" state of mind that Sahagún hoped to return. Sahagún's somewhat desperate need to systematically catalogue Nahua culture represents his desire to return to a world where there was a place for everything and everything was in its right place. Sahagún wanted to return to the state of what Lewis calls the "clerkly" nature of the medieval person, who had no greater delight than in contemplating how each and every fact or story fit into the greater, unified scheme of things—what Lewis refers to throughout his work as the "Model." This is why it is appropriate to say that Sahagún was trying to write a summa of Nahua culture. The days of summae, however, were drawing to an end.

A need to seek the presence of structure normally emerges when it is felt that an object or a phenomenon's structure is not transparent.

A need to impose structure emerges when it is felt that something is lacking structure all together. The methods or structuring principles of scholasticism emerged in the twelfth and thirteenth centuries as a result of the division between faith and reason. No one doubted God's existence in the thirteenth century; they just felt the need to make his existence transparent. Sahagún, however, seems driven by the fear that the Nahua world is entirely lacking in any kind of structure that would conform to the European Model. For Sahagún, the appeal of scholastic methods lay in their success for medieval scholars who answered God's opacity or mysterious ways with visible demonstrations of his coherent plan.

The appeal to scholastic methods—rather than to textual sources—was especially important to Sahagún because he was acutely aware of the fact that the Nahua world simply lacked *auctores*:

All writers work to authorize /legitimate their writings the best they can: some with reliable witnesses, others with other writers who have written before them and whose statements are held to be certain, others with the testimony of Sacred Scripture. I have lacked all of these foundations in order to authorize what I have written in these twelve books, except placing here the relation of my diligence in trying to know the truth of everything that I have written in these books. (*CF* II:iv)

Sahagún points to both a lack of reliable witnesses or sources and a lack of patently useful references in Scripture. It was this lack of reliability—in Sahagún's eyes—that drove him to embark on the elaborate editing (sifting) process to which I alluded earlier once he had gathered the information from the elders of Tepepulco. Since Sahagún—as he states—places scant faith in his sources, the unimpeachable nature of his methodology must legitimate his project instead.

Scholasticism—through such *auctores* as Saint Thomas Aquinas—provides Sahagún with a way to put credence in method. As I mentioned before, Panofsky first opted for the term manifestatio when he came across it in the *Summa Theologica* (29). Since Sahagún,

himself, was—as is to be expected—familiar with the work of
Aquinas (*Psalmodia*, 79–83), Aquinas's words are worth looking at.
Part I, question I, article 8 of the *Summa* is concerned with whether
or not sacred doctrine should even be a matter of argument. The
second objection states that, if it is, it is either from authority or
from reason. Aquinas responds by saying that "faith rests upon
infallible truth, and since the contrary of a truth can never be demonstrated, it is clear that the arguments brought against faith cannot
be demonstrations, but are difficulties that can be answered" (5).
Aquinas then goes on to say that authority based on human reason is
weaker than authority based on revelation and therefore should not
be used to prove faith but "to make clear [*manifestare*] other things
that are put forward in this doctrine" (5–6).

In the *Historia universal*, there is no systematic attempt to prove
(through logic, for example) that the world of the Nahuas has a
place in God's divine plan. Sahagún admits that he is uncertain
about why God kept Christianity hidden from the Nahuas for so
long: "It is certainly a thing of great admiration that God our Lord
has kept hidden for so many centuries a forest of so many idolatrous peoples, whose abundant fruits only the devil has gathered
and holds as treasures in the infernal fire" (*CF* I:"Prologo"). In the
Historia universal, there is only an extremely intricate—architectonic—
scaffolding set up that is designed to clarify that—or, better, how—
the Nahuas and Europeans share the same referential plane in a
single unified cosmos. Like sacred doctrine, it is an article of faith
that they do.

3. Interpretation

For the Middle Ages, all discovery of truth was first reception of traditional
authorities, then later—in the thirteenth century—rational reconciliation
of authoritative texts. A comprehension of the world was not regarded as a
creative function but as an assimilation and retracing of given facts; the
symbolic expression of this being reading. The goal and the accomplish-

ment of the thinker is to connect all these facts together in the form of the "summa." (Curtius, 326)

Toward the end of the last section, I quoted a passage in which Sahagún laments his lack of both reliable witnesses and traditional authorities. In order to produce his history, Sahagún is forced to rely on his own experience—an experience that he falls back on when he reports on surviving idolatrous practices and an experience he *self-consciously* produces by seeking Nahua elders who can report on the more nebulous contours of times past. For the modern observer, it seems natural enough that Sahagún would want to rely on experience, but—as the passage clearly states—experience would not have been his historical method of first choice. Sahagún saw his methodology more as a concession than an innovation.

During the Middle Ages, there were three—deceptively familiar— ways of knowing something. In hierarchical order, they were: authority, reason, and experience. Medieval people had a hard time believing anything an ancient *auctor* said was simply untrue, and so reason was more often than not unabashedly relegated to the secondary status of reconciling or clarifying the contradictions of authoritative texts. Somewhat tongue in cheek, C. S. Lewis describes the tertiary role empiricism played in medieval thought: "We learn by experience that oysters do or do not agree with us" (189).

As the Middle Ages slowly gave way to the modern period, this hierarchy would reverse itself—and even bifurcate —as reason and experience vied for primacy according to whatever the specialized discipline in question was. In general, medieval and modern her- meneutics can be differentiated in the following manner: medieval hermeneutics tended to rely on the assumption that knowledge was a divinely ordained, preexisting entity, and it was the role of medi- eval interpreters to make manifest (*manifestare*) this knowledge and preserve it against the eroding forces of time[25]; modern hermeneutics is distinguished by the roles the human subject is thought to play in the *production* of knowledge. The medieval interpreter ultimately reduces all knowledge of the cosmos to divine revelation.²⁶ The modern interpreter sees himself or herself as an observer who is eccentric to, or at a distance from, the world and, therefore, as someone who must actively participate in the production of knowledge by heavily relying on such human—and, hence, idiosyncratic—tools as reason and experience.²⁷

The modern hermeneutic recognition that the human subject is a constitutive element in the production of knowledge is most discernible when one contrasts examples from the medieval historiographical tradition. In the prologue to his *Primera crónica general de España*, for example, Alfonso X states that the wise men of the first times "found" (*"fallaron"*) knowledge—including knowledge of the future—only to discover that its "memory" (*"remenbrança"*) was threatened by the mortality and vices of human beings. The wise men looked, therefore, and "found" (fallaron) letters which they in succession put together into syllables, parts, and, finally, "reason" (*"razon"*). Writing allowed people to preserve a preexisting body of knowledge that was "found," not produced—a body of knowledge that people would have a difficult time "finding" again if they had to: "For if there were no writings, what knowledge or ingenuity of man could be remembered from all past things, even without finding them anew which is a very serious thing?" (3). Unfortunately, much knowledge of "Spain" was lost when books were destroyed during military setbacks (4). Alfonso X's history of Spain presents itself as a *salvaging* mission in which every real or imagined reference to Spain from a myriad of textual sources was gathered up and spliced together to tell the story of a single Spain "from the time of Noah to ours" (4).

Sahagún's professed inability to rely on reliable witnesses or *auctores* forces him to confront the limitations of medieval hermeneutics without the consolation of an immediately accessible, viable alternative. The transition to the Age of Reason did not happen all at once. In the last section I discussed Sahagún's efforts to get around this problem by applying the scholastic principle of *manifestatio* to his overall linguistic plan of linking Nahuatl and

Spanish to a common referential substratum. The fact that Sahagún felt he could finish this process of *clarification* within a year or so if he were given help seems to indicate that he felt he had achieved a certain degree of success—that somehow the disparate worlds of the Nahuas and the Europeans were compatible in a single cosmological plan (*CF* I:"Al sincero lector"). In the final section of this chapter, I would like to analyze two parts of the *Historia universal* that indicate the contrary notion that Sahagún was not entirely successful in warding off the erosion of the medieval hermeneutic system. I will turn first to his section on corn and subsequently to the role his numerous prologues and appendages play in the overall contextualization of his work.

In the Middle Ages—and long into the modern period—there were three principal ways in which theology was taught on a formal or institutional level: through lectures, through preaching, and through disputations. The third of these—the medieval disputation, or *disputatio*—was characteristically divided into three parts: (1) an argument for or against something (*et arguitur* [*videtur*] *quod sic/non*); (2) a statement to the contrary that sums up the preferred view (*sed contra*); and (3) a section that gives a fuller response countering the initial argument (*respondeo*).[28] Panofsky notes that part of what distinguishes the dialectic of medieval disputation from the modern Hegelian pattern of thesis, antithesis, and synthesis is its sheer pervasiveness and its conscious application. Panofsky argues, for example, that "the principle, *videtur quod, sed contra, respondeo dicendum*, seems to have been applied with perfect consciousness" to High Gothic architecture (*Gothic*, 86–87). Another distinguishing feature of the medieval disputation is that the argument was often resolved—and acceptably so—by simply citing authorities without further elaboration (Kretzmann, Kenny, and Pinborg, 31).

Sahagún undoubtedly became imbued with the pervasive structure of disputation while at the University of Salamanca.[29] While at Salamanca, however, he never would have had to confront the possibility of a disputation without even indirect recourse to authorities, since the whole of medieval disputation evolved in the first place as a way to reconcile contradictory *auctores*. It is interesting to see what happens to this disputational structure when it is subjected to a situation like the Nahua historical past which—as Sahagún claimed above—lacks reliable or relevant European or indigenous *auctores*.

The Nahuatl text of the first two paragraphs of chapter 13, Book XI of the *Florentine Codex* describes the use of corn in Nahua culture. Sahagún felt the description was obvious, so in place of the usual Spanish translation, he offers the reader a curious, contradictory text about whether or not the Nahuas had had contact with Christians before the arrival of the Spaniards. The text is structured like a dialectic disputation in which a reconciliation of opposing views is attempted. Strangely enough, however, Sahagún puts himself in the position of arguing for both sides. There is no actual dialogue—only an author who seems to be trying on arguments until he finds the one that fits.

In what I will refer to as his first argument, Sahagún claims that there was no contact between Nahuas and Europeans before the arrival of the Spaniards. He argues that the lack of wheat, barley, chickens, horses, and so forth in the New World indicates "that these lands have only been discovered in these times and not before" (*CF* XI:246v). He concludes his "first argument" with the following unequivocal statement:

As to preaching of the Gospel in these parts, there has been much doubt about whether or not there was any before now. And I have always held the opinion that they have never been preached the Gospel because I have never found anything that alludes to the Catholic faith, rather everything is so to the contrary and everything so idolatrous that I cannot believe they have ever at any time been preached the Gospel. (246v)

Sahagún seems to change his mind midsentence, however, because—with no discernible pause or punctuation—he entirely changes course and begins to present the opposing view as his own. Sahagún slips into his "second argument" with the example of two "trustworthy" friars who assured him that they had seen remnants of precolonial Christian worship. Sahagún endorses these findings and attributes them to precolonial preaching: "This seems to me to allude to our Lady and her two sisters, and to our crucified Redeemer—which they must have had from previous preaching" (247r). His second argument then goes on, surprisingly, to contradict the views on Nahua confession Sahagún set forth earlier in Book I: "In the above said, there is more than a little foundation to argue that these Indians of New Spain were obligated to confess once during life, and this *in lumine natural* without having knowledge of the things of the Faith" (*CF* I:10r). Sahagún now—in the second argument of the corn section—resolutely claims that preconquest confession is an indication that the Nahuas had previously been proselytized (247r–v).

Sahagún's second argument moves on to cite further examples of precolonial Christianity, but his thought is interrupted by some lingering doubts: "But I am surprised that we have not found more traces of what I said above in these parts of Mexico" (247v). Sahagún therefore sets forth a watered-down conclusion in which he states that "it may well have been" (247v) and "concluding that it is possible" (248r) that the Nahuas had previously been proselytized but they returned to their idolatrous practices. This leads him to conclude that God sent the Spaniards so that the Nahuas would always have ministers of the faith to keep them from falling back into idolatry.

The corn section ends with Sahagún's contention that the Nahuas are dying off, and that this has been seen both through prophecy and experience (248v). As with the previous arguments, Sahagún starts out with firm opinions and then offers a watered-down conclusion. The prophecy was not biblical in origin but the vision of a Dominican friar in the New World. Sahagún quickly backs off from any unqualified credence he might have lent to the prophecy: "And even though I do not give credence to this prophecy, the things that happen, and those past, seem to indicate its truthfulness.

It is not to be believed, however, that this people is dying out in as brief a time as the prophecy says, because if this were the case, the land would be desolate" (249r). His final statement is that there will always be a number of Nahuas in New Spain, despite the prophecy's more apocalyptic outlook (249v).

The arguments I have outlined above operate like an internal monologue in which Sahagún tries to make up his mind about what he thinks. They resemble the dialectical structure of the disputation, but they are unable to sustain themselves. Sahagún seems to lack faith in his powers of logic, and he ultimately steps back from the only semiauthoritative and nonlogical explanation he offers: the prophecy. Unlike Motolinía, who ensconced his firm opinions in pseudohesitant eschatological readings of history, Sahagún seems to be genuinely uncertain about his own opinions. The colloquial term "waffling" is the most appropriate way to describe Sahagún's reasoning in this section. When medieval hermeneutics is stripped of its auctores, it begins to topple. When Sahagún is stripped of authorities on the New World, his system of interpretation loses all sense of direction: it takes him first one way and then another. His internalized, auctor-less *videtur quod, sed contra, responde dicendum* resolves nothing. In the end, it is unclear what Sahagún thought the place of the Nahuas was in the cosmological and historical order because it is unclear whether he ever resolved this problem for himself.

Sahagún's (medieval) hermeneutics were breaking down in other ways. The most notable thing about Sahagún's prologues is their quantity. Sahagún did not believe that his main text was self-explanatory or transparent enough, so he added numerous prologues and appendices to his work in what appears to be an almost obsessive need to explain himself. Each of the twelve books has at least one prologue, but sometimes there are further addresses to the reader. It is easy to imagine that Sahagún would have added more prologues and appendices to the history if he had been able to continue.[30]

Sahagún's almost obsessive need for prologues marks the dramatic end of an era in which books were understood to exist in a relatively natural or obvious relationship with the world, the author, and the reader—an era in which the book was one of the most potent symbols for the cosmos itself (Gellrich, 29–30). Sahagún's prologues imply that a new kind of hermeneutic space has opened up between the text, the author, the reader, and the world—a space, as I shall show, that shifts the hermeneutic weight off of the shoulders of tradition and onto those of human agency.

In "Eccentricities: On Prologues in Some Fourteenth-Century Castilian Texts," Gumbrecht points out the paradoxical eccentricity of prologues in general and ties their functional evolution to the emergence of subjectivity that medievalists argue took place between the thirteenth and sixteenth centuries. Prologues are paradoxical because they are intrinsic commentaries on the text that nevertheless require that the author assume a point of view that is external to the text:

Today, we normally conceive of the prologue as a space where authors position themselves in relation to a text, to an audience, and to the world as horizon of their communication. Such a definition not only presupposes the existence of "authorship" as an institution but also a relation of mutual eccentricity among author, text, audience, and world. Indeed, one might argue that, without this fourfold eccentricity, "prologuing" cannot take place. (891)

Gumbrecht sets up a typological contrast between prologues from the twelfth and from the late fifteenth centuries in order to situate the strange anomaly of double prologues in fourteenth-century Castilian texts at a halfway point between "two clearly different cultural paradigms" (892). Gumbrecht argues that, by the end of the fifteenth century, authors came to believe more and more that their texts needed to be embedded in a specific "hermeneutic space" in order to guarantee a coincidence between the author's intentions and the reader's understanding. Moreover, Gumbrecht argues that this preoccupation is tied to the growing conviction on the part of many late medieval authors that the world was an increasingly sinful and chaotic place: "Seen from the perspective of fifteenth-century prologues, the aspect of a chaotic and sinful world leads different readers of individual texts to different interpretations, thus making it necessary for the authors to occupy a position of self-reflexiveness from which they articulate their intentions" (895). He goes on to say that one of the results of the author's self-conscious need to express his or her intentions is the splitting of the text into a secondary surface level and a more profound level of authorial intentionality (895).

Gumbrecht contrasts the late-medieval "network of eccentricities among author (intention), readers (understanding), (double-leveled) text, and (chaotic) world" to the function of prologues in the twelfth and thirteenth centuries (895–96). High medieval prologues, he argues, tend to play the role of inscribing texts in a "genealogy of knowledge" or tradition simply so they will not be forgotten: "whatever elements may be considered to justify the importance of a text do not depend on an author's intention but have 'always been there' as a substantial part of the tradition" (896). Nor do these prologues try to ward off misunderstandings on the part of the readers or guide them through a chaotic world: "their fulfillment is not seen as directed 'against' the world but rather as being 'a part of the cosmological order'" (897).

Gumbrecht goes on to analyze the functions of several fourteenth-century prologues and argues that the preponderance of double prologues in fourteenth-century Castilian texts was a response to a situation in which the world was suddenly perceived as opaque and complex. Multiple prologues were used to patch up the "hermeneutic space" that opened up when the relationship of texts to an increasingly complex world was no longer a clear given.[31]

The transition from a medieval situation, in which writers, readers, signs, and things were inseparable and "it was God's privilege to be *auctor* of the Creation" (904), to the modern situation, in which meaning is produced by the human mind, was neither simultaneous nor uniform. I am not arguing that fourteenth-century double prologues in Castile set a precedent for Sahagún; I simply argue that there are certain parallels between the late-medieval framework Gumbrecht outlines and Sahagún's difficulty in inscribing his textual representation of the world of the Nahuas into a pre-existing cosmological order. In general, the preponderance of prologues in both contexts was a result of an unstable interpretive situation.

If fourteenth-century Castilian texts are notable for their profusion of double prologues, Sahagún's *Historia universal* is notable for its veritable avalanche of prologues. Since a few of Sahagún's prologues take up where others left off, it is not inconceivable that Sahagún could have combined several or all of them into a single, lengthy prologue at the beginning of the work. The prologue to Book II, for example, could have been combined with the first prologue without changing much of anything since it refers to the work as a whole. Sahagún does not even directly refer to the text of Book II in its prologue. He leaves that for the "Al sincero lector," which follows the prologue to Book II. The interspersion of the various prologues and addresses to the readers throughout the work seems to indicate that Sahagún is driven by a need to renegotiate the hermeneutic space to which I alluded above at several junctures—as if the reader might lose track of the author's intentions along the way. Each book begins with one or more efforts to reground the reader's understanding of the text in a single, commonly accessible European frame. What is curious about these regroundings is the way Sahagún often tailors them to specific, differentiated aspects of European culture.

In the prologue to Book I, Sahagún sets forth his more general purpose of identifying idolatrous practices so that the Nahuas can be cured of their spiritual "illness," establishing a compendium of Nahua culture through the study of its language, and demonstrating that they are a people worthy of being brought into the fold of European and Christian civilization. These themes resurface throughout the other prologues and addresses to the reader, but they often transform themselves according to the content of the book at hand or according to what—for one reason or another—seems to be occupying Sahagún's thoughts at the time. The prologue to Book II, for example, begins with the problem of auctores discussed above. The prologue to Book III—the book on the origin of the gods—offers the reader a European parallel in the sixth book of Augustine's *City of God*, in case he or she should question the relevance of the section. In the prologue to Book VI—the book, Sahagún says, that is on the "rhetoric and moral philosophy" of the Nahuas—Sahagún appeals to European notions of civilization and barbarism and then argues that the content of his book demonstrates the Nahuas' degree of advancement. In the prologue to Book X, Sahagún appeals to European notions of virtue and vice and claims that his study of the virtues and vices of the various generic persons that make up Nahua society will specifically help preachers trying to teach Catholic values. I could go on listing examples in this fashion, but I believe the point is well taken. Sahagún's prologues go about establishing various interpretive contexts with a wide array of functionally distinguishable arguments.

Sahagún's multifarious use of prologues exhibits a preoccupation with the reader's understanding of his text and intentions at the start of each new division in his work. His prologues work both to gain the reader's sympathy, by continuously reminding the reader of the text's multifaceted relationship to European culture, and to secure specific readings that will coincide with his intentions. This penchant for continuously re-embedding his text in specific interpretive frames can only be explained by the sheer alienness and complexity of the information Sahagún had gathered about the Nahuas. Sahagún set about gathering and organizing Nahuatl texts that would—in a sense—speak for themselves and demonstrate their relationship to Christian culture. As I have shown, Sahagún intended to elucidate (manifestare) this relationship through careful linguistic analysis. Sahagún's extensive use of prologues as a way to cover the newly opened hermeneutic space between authors, readers, signs, and things, however, belies the notion that he felt he had achieved complete success in his endeavor. Sahagún wanted a work that would speak for itself once the scholastic principle of manifestatio was applied, but it is clear from his plethora of functionally differentiated prologues that he ultimately had lost faith in the ability of medieval hermeneutics to provide this. With a barrage of prologues to bolster the text, authorial intentionality begins to bear the structural weight of the edifice of knowledge—a weight that can no longer be sustained by a system of hermeneutics that sees knowledge almost exclusively as (revealed) tradition.

4

PROBLEMS OF
MIMESIS AND EXEMPLARITY
IN SAHAGÚN'S WORK

It must be borne in mind that neither mimetic powers nor mimetic objects remain the same in the course of thousands of years. (Benjamin, 333)

Walter Benjamin argues that the mimetic faculty has an evolutionary history in both the phylogenetic and ontogenetic sense (333). In Benjamin's world, the modern mimetic faculty is in a state of advanced atrophy, where there are "only minimal residues of the magical correspondences and analogies that were familiar to ancient peoples" (334).

More recently, Luiz Costa Lima has argued that the transition from the Middle Ages to modernity corresponds to a dramatic shift in the understanding of the mimetic faculty. Mimesis in general presupposes a dense dialectic between assimilation and differentiation. On the one hand, the individual, through the use of the mimetic faculty, becomes similar to someone or something. On the other hand, the individual emerges from this identifying process also bearing the mark of his or her difference or autonomy. Because of structural limitations, the mimetic faculty never can and never will produce a perfect, identical copy. Costa Lima argues, however, that since the Renaissance rediscovery of Aristotle's *Poetics*, mimesis has been understood as pure *imitatio* (imitation). From early modernity on, he points out, what was once a potentially acceptable difference in the "mimic" became something intolerable or less than adequate (*Control*, 3–53).

Benjamin's and Costa Lima's arguments indicate that both the constitution and the understanding of mimesis have an evolving history that is specific to various peoples, times, and places. For Costa Lima, there is a marked contrast between medieval and early modern conceptualizations of mimesis. For Benjamin, there is a marked contrast between the "magical" mimetic capacities of children and "ancient" peoples and the more atrophied ones of adults and "moderns." In the first section of this chapter I argue that Sahagún stands on the threshold between the medieval and early modern conceptualizations of mimesis, or—more precisely—that Sahagún must contend with the problematic implications of a medieval European conceptualization of mimesis in the novel context of New Spain. In order to situate Sahagún on this mimetic threshold, I compare his conceptualization of mimesis with the earlier one present in Motolinía's work and then briefly with the later one in the work of the seventeenth-century Franciscan criollo, Agustín de Vetancurt.

In the second section of this chapter I explore the notion of mimesis that Benjamin first alluded to in his four-page essay "On the Mimetic Faculty." Over the past few decades, several scholars have begun to study mimesis as a cognitive form of "Othering," or making the Other one's own. I would like to examine this scholarly phenomenon from three disciplinary directions—a philosophical, a biological, and an anthropological one—in order to determine some of the implications for current and future work in Sahagún studies.

In the third section, I approach the topic of mimesis indirectly, through the problem of exemplarity in Sahagún's work. I argue that Sahagún's work is symptomatic in some respects of the phenomenon several scholars have called early modern Europe's "crisis of exemplarity." On one level, exemplarity, or the use of examples, is related to mimesis as a didactics of imitation: "Be like that; don't be like that." On a more basic level, however, the use of examples "is a way of taking our beliefs about reality and reframing them into something that suits the direction of the text"—or discourse (Lyons, ix). An example overtly establishes a referential link between the exterior world and the internal structure of any communicative action: an "inside" and "outside" to language (Lyons, 3). Exemplarity is often understood in explicitly rhetorical terms, because in their everyday usage, examples are more often than not self-consciously labeled as such. When the taken-for-grantedness of the medieval worldview clashed with the recently glimpsed, unfathomable depths of the Nahua psyche, Sahagún the spiritual instructor was forced to undergo his own crisis of exemplarity.

1. Mimesis and Modernity

And, why would God not give to those He formed in His image, His grace and glory—they being as well disposed as we? (Motolinía, *Historia*, 188)

Almost all of the *autos sacramentales*[1] performed by Nahuas in sixteenth-century New Spain were organized by the Franciscans (Ricard, 205–6). For Fray Toribio de Motolinía, these *autos* were visible proof of the devotion and sincerity of the recently converted Nahuas. The longest chapter of his *Historia de los indios de la Nueva España* is a glowing description of several of the representations put on by the Nahuas in their own language. Even though Motolinía's descriptions betray a propagandistic intent, his enthusiasm comes across as amazingly naive to the modern reader. The autos are riddled with remnants of pre-Christian Nahua rituals that could potentially interfere with orthodox Christian views.

It is easy to see why Motolinía might fail to perceive the significance of a few of these remnants, but the sheer amount of distinctly Nahua ways of honoring the Christian God would probably lead the modern observer to suspect that the autos held important non-Christian meanings for the Nahuas. For instance, Motolinía is deeply impressed by the abundant and elaborate use of flowers in the autos. For Motolinía, these flowers are simply one of God's gifts and a way for the impoverished Nahuas to honor God without jewels, which they did not possess (192). Flowers, however—as a modern observer might suspect—held specific religious meanings for the Nahuas before the arrival of the Spaniards. They were primarily associated with the deities Xochipilli, Macuilxochitl, and Xochiquetzal—"all of whom serve[d] as patrons of beauty, pleasure, and the arts" (Miller and Taube, 88). Flowers were often "sacrificed" in lieu of human flesh, and the Nahuas referred to battles specifically instigated to capture sacrificial victims as "wars of flowers." Motolinía could not be expected to know all this, but a modern reader might wonder why the emphasis placed on flowers combined with other uniquely Nahua features of the autos did not make him suspicious: the Nahuas' peculiar dances (192), their emphasis on reproducing *"todo lo natural"* (live animals, fruits, and so forth) in their stagings (194), and, most important, their inclusion of completely extraneous subject matter such as camouflaged archers hidden in "mountains" constructed along the procession route of the Holy Eucharist (194–95).

Motolinía enthusiastically describes several other scenes that a modern observer might have more trouble reconciling with orthodox Christian views. In an auto representing the Fall of Adam and Eve, Motolinía delights in describing a boy dressed as a lion tearing apart and devouring a real deer on top of a fake rock (201). In another auto performed for Corpus Christi in Tlaxcala, Nahuas were dressed in their traditional warrior garb of feathers and shields as they reconquered Jerusalem. Other Nahuas were dressed as Moors, Jews, Spaniards, other Europeans, angels, and even the Pope. At the end of the auto, the "great Sultan of Babilonia and *Tlatoani* of Jerusalem" sees the error of his ways and succumbs to the Nahuas playing Christian soldiers (203–12). Throughout the description, Motolinía seems to have no inkling of the possibility that the recently converted Nahuas might have trouble appreciating the long-standing significance in Europe of crusades to the Holy Land. A modern observer would immediately assume that the Nahuas interpreted this auto/war-game in terms of the mores of their own bellicose culture.

Motolinía failed to perceive the discrepancy between his spiritual reality and the Nahuas' because he was operating entirely within the framework of two important medieval conceptualizations: first, that of alterity; second, that of mimesis. Alterity in the Middle Ages was always understood in relation to a single frame of reference: a unified Christian cosmology. Anything outside of this cosmological order was inevitably understood in terms of the solitary perspective of this ordo. In discussing medieval heresy in *The Writing of History*, for example, Michel de Certeau states:

> Alterity was hence eliminated, effaced, or integrated, not only for a lack of strong political or social bases, but just as much—or more—for lack of a capacity for being shown to differ in respect to the system of reference, for lack of situating its practice within a code other than the highly doctrinal one it had called into question. (150)

Alterity in the Middle Ages did not present itself as a deep, unknowable domain of experience. Bronislaw Geremek has pointed out that the social condition of individuals in the Middle Ages was assumed to be indicated through *exterior* signs. He also notes that infidels are characterized through simplistic stereotypes and marginalized individuals are rarely mentioned explicitly in documents that reflect the collective conscience of the Middle Ages (381–413). Medieval people tended simply to dismiss as a fabrication any form of alterity that ran counter to the prevailing stereotypes. The early reception of Marco Polo's *Travels* is a well-known case in point. Throughout the Middle Ages, Marco Polo was referred to as "Marco of the millions" because of the large distances covered and varieties of people encountered in his so-called fabrication. Soon after his death, Marco Polo began to be depicted at every Venetian carnival as a clown full of gross, comic exaggerations (Polo, xxii). According to Gumbrecht, medieval people normally could not distinguish between lying and unintentional errors because both were perceived simply as different modes of missing one's predetermined place in the world (*Geschichte*, 45–46).[2]

For Motolinía, the extremely enthusiastic participation of the Nahuas in the autos preempted the notion that they were lying or erring. Le Goff notes in *Medieval Civilization* the preeminent role gestures play in medieval culture. The body was such a pivotal determinant of expression and meaning in medieval society that even churches were perceived as divine "gestures in stone" (357). Like most medieval people, Motolinía did not think of the body as a mask likely to hide internal, contrary thoughts. The tears the Nahuas shed in profusion for the Fall of Adam (202) and the horror they expressed when confronted with a representation of Hell—even though "they knew no one was burning" (215)—are offered as genuine proof of the Nahuas' sincerity. Modern theater-goers, however—steeped as they are in the ideas surrounding Aristotle's *Poetics*—would distinguish between the feelings evoked in representations and those evoked in real-life situations. Autos, nevertheless, were not considered fictional representations in the modern sense of the word. They were just one more way in which medieval people affirmed their existence as dwellers within the single frame of the cosmological ordo. The act of Holy Communion that ended every auto was, and is, visible proof of the seriousness and devotion that accompanied these representations. Because of a simple lack of any contrasting frame of reference, Motolinía neglected to see any profound form of alterity and assumed that the Nahua participation in the autos affirmed their own place in the Christian cosmological order.

Motolinía's failure to perceive any profound form of alterity in the Nahuas' behavior was compounded by his medieval sense of the nature of mimesis. Before Renaissance thinkers of the sixteenth and seventeenth centuries subjugated mimesis to the yoke of Aristotle's definition of imitatio in the recently discovered *Poetics*, absolute verisimilitude was not the criterion used to evaluate any particular copy of a model (Costa Lima, *Control*, 3–53).[3] Moreover, copies were not denigrated as secondary, imperfect by-products of an original the way they are now in the modern era of copyright infringement, plagiarism, and "derivative" art. The word "*copia*," in fact, was associated in the Middle Ages (as in antiquity) with abundance, copiousness, fullness, and even wealth and power. The mere fact that the Nahuas' mimetic enactment of various biblical scenes differed in some respects from European models was not in itself cause for alarm because, throughout the medieval period, mimesis was understood as "copy-with-a-difference."

The religious scenes depicted in the autos sacramentales are part of a rich iconographic tradition that is better known now through the pictorial icons that have survived from the Middle Ages. To the modern eye, most religious icons from this time seem extremely unrealistic. In part, this is because religious icons adhered to a sacred type (*typos hieros*) or invisible spiritual reality that was alluded to through an intricate and deliberate use of unnatural styles. Medieval thinkers felt that naturalistic icons would obscure the spiritual truth of a general type or image and perhaps lead to the prohibited worship of the actual image-object. John of Damascus (ca. 680–749), "the first theologian of images," made this distinction official when he insisted that "the image is a likeness that expresses the archetype in such a way that there is always a difference between the two" (quoted in Belting, 145). This view survived the iconoclasts, and as Hans Belting has shown in his thorough study *Likeness and Presence*, it goes a long way toward explaining the enormous amount of variation tolerated—and even encouraged—in what were meant to be authentic depictions of holy figures and scenes. Like the autos (and often as part of them), religious icons were invariably linked to the liturgical calendar and the local traditions of specific places of worship. Given this fact, it is not surprising that Motolinía would *expect* the Nahuas' depictions of religious scenes to take on an air of their own culture. For Motolinía, the differences between Nahua and European representations of religious scenes simply ensured that spiritual truths or archetypes were being invoked rather than everyday physical realities.

The medieval inability to distinguish between lies and unintentional errors explains the strong, reactionary response many mission-

aries displayed when they discovered problems in the Nahua conversion: "deceit" (engaño) became the operative word in most friars'
subsequent writings. The discovery that the Nahua conversion was
superficial caused a cognitive "decentering" in which the friars no
longer knew where to ground hermeneutically their understanding
of the situation in New Spain and the role they should play. As I
argued in chapter 3, the friars responded to this novel situation in
different ways. Sahagún, in particular, responded by trying to work
his way back to the common ground between the Nahuas and the
Europeans via his universalizing cultural and linguistic project, the
Historia universal. I also argued in chapter 3 that Sahagún's novel
approach to the situation did not entirely quell his doubts about the
roles of the friars and the Nahuas in the greater, eschatologically
defined scheme of things. Sahagún's uncertainties about how to interpret, and hence respond to, all facets of the unsuccessful conversion
of the Nahuas led him to react simultaneously with several quite
different evangelical tactics. The *Historia universal,* of course, is the
most celebrated of these tactics, but the extant Sahaguntine corpus—all of which is evangelical in nature[4]—also consists of numerous native-language texts such as sermons, the *Colloquios* dialogue,
and the canticles of the *Psalmodia christiana.* It also contains three texts
called *Addiciones a la Postilla, Apéndiz a la Postilla,* and *Exercicio quotidiano.*[5]
The most interesting thing about these latter texts in the context of
this chapter is their tendency to proselytize with an extremely
pared-down set of religious ideas that defy easy visualization.

It might be tempting to attribute the relative lack of a visual
component in the *Addiciones, Apéndiz,* and *Exercicio* to an internalized,
Erasmian spirituality in the wake of Marcel Bataillon's work, but
this approach overlooks the specific missionary situation of New
Spain as Sahagún experienced it.[6] Sahagún's texts in general display
a distrust of visual manifestations of religiosity that is primarily
attributable to his contention that pagan rites lurk just below the
surface of the superficially Christian behavior of the Nahuas. His
condemnation of shrines set up for the deity Tonantzin in the guise
of the Virgin of Guadalupe or for the deity Toci in the guise of

Saint Anne are well-known examples (*CF* XI:233r–36v). All of Sahagún's texts constitute various attempts to sort out and respond to the mimetic "residue" that was inevitably produced when the Nahuas were encouraged or coerced into assimilating Christian culture.

Once Sahagún suspected that conversion had been superficial (or even false), the mimetic differences that Motolinía had previously interpreted as irrelevant in light of a higher spiritual reality quickly came into the foreground as visible symptoms of a mimetically *mis*appropriated Christian faith. In section three of this chapter I argue that part of Sahagún's work is an attempt to redirect the mimetic process of spiritual *imitatio* through a careful delineation of good and bad examples. The *Addiciones, Apéndiz,* and *Exercicio,* however, constitute Sahagún's minimalist approach to dealing with the problem. In these works, Sahagún attempts to strip Nahua Christianity down to its bare essentials rather than build up an elaborate network of good and bad examples.

Sahagún defines his *Addiciones* as a discourse on the theological virtues of faith, hope, and divine charity, "[w]hich *alone* are enough to make one a perfect Christian" (2, my emphasis).[7] The *Addiciones* were not meant to be used directly by the Nahuas. Rather, they are a statement of the bare minimum of knowledge necessary to be a good Christian for preachers to use as a native-language guide in verbally instructing Nahuas. As a whole, the *Addiciones* wrestle with the problem of explaining spiritual truths that are inaccessible to the physical senses without recurring to misleading tangible or visible comparisons. The difficulty Sahagún has in achieving this goal is apparent in a passage where he seems to offer all the arguments necessary for *not* believing in an invisible God:

You who are a Christian should know in your heart that what you believe as a Christian exceeds in certainty everything that your eyes see. Your eyes can see that the sun exists, that the moon exists, that the stars exist. Your eyes can see them; your heart is satisfied, because it is certain that the sun, the moon, and the stars exist. And if someone were to tell you that it is not true that the sun, moon, and stars exist, then you would say: It is true you lie, for my eyes see that the sun, the moon, and the stars truly exist. What your eyes see is not absolutely determined, because many times the eyes are deceived. What is most certain is that there is only one deity, God, the Lord of all parts of the world, and He is the Father, the Son, and the Holy Spirit, three Persons but one sole God. (15)

This argument is Sahagún's attempt to explain to the Nahuas the tautological doctrinal statement *"Dubius in fide, infidelis est"*[8]—a statement that loses its logical coherence in the context of New Spain because it precludes any alternative, exterior, non-Christian viewpoint from which to understand it.

Sahagún's battle with the world of appearances takes an extreme turn when he warns the Nahuas not to sin even if angels, saints, and priests implore them:

Listen, oh Christian! Your obligation and your vow are that you will love your God, your Lord, with all of your heart, with all of your soul. There is nothing in the entire world that you are to love in this manner. That is to say that, even if all of the angels, saints, ancient priests, emperors, kings, wise men, and learned men of Scripture, if all of them entreated you to commit a mortal sin, in no sense is it necessary that you consent; you must not obey them. (37)

This passage—which borders on the heretical—rings out as a desperate appeal to adhere only to a spiritual truth that is not necessarily present in the everyday visible world.

The fragmentary *Apéndiz* originally had the form of seven warnings (*"amonestaciones"*), which are punctuated with threats of severe punishment. It denounces several pre-Hispanic beliefs, and offers several directives for everyday comportment. In one interesting passage, Sahagún attempts to reconcile the differences between Nahuas and secular Spaniards. He compares the Spaniards to lions and the Nahuas to rabbits, and argues that each group is simply incompatible on the level of everyday, worldly interaction. The two groups, however, are unified through Christianity: "But even though your beings and the beings of the Spaniards proceed separately, the Christian life unifies your souls and the souls of Spaniards. As a Christian the latter will become a lamb, and the Indian, as a Christian, will also become a lamb" (113). The context of this passage was the growing pressure on the Mendicant orders in the mid-sixteenth century to "Hispanicize" the Nahuas. A royal letter from 1550, for example, ordered "that the Indians be instructed in our Castilian speech and accept our social organizations and good customs" (quoted in Ricard, 52). Sahagún, however, specifically tells the Nahuas *not* to imitate the Spaniards in his *Apéndiz* (112–14). Sahagún attempts to hold out a spiritual model (the "lamb") that transcends the worldly models of both the Nahuas (the "rabbits") and the Spaniards (the "lions"). The "lamb," in short, is the invisible, spiritual side of human existence that is capable of explaining cultural difference as it self-consciously relegates it to a secondary status. Sahagún's animals bear a superficial resemblance to the allegorical animal fables of the Middle Ages, but they are, in reality, metaphors that are too abstract to qualify as examples.

The most interesting aspect of the *Exercicio quotidiano* is the manner in which it converts the visual devotional images of collective medieval masses, autos, and icons into mental images for internal contemplation. The exercises are divided into seven "*meditaciones*"— one for each day of the week. On Tuesday, for example, the pious Nahua is asked to contemplate a Nativity scene (157–63). By rendering these scenes into Nahuatl in the form of "spiritual exercises," Sahagún (and perhaps the friar who wrote the original version) found a way to forego completely the mimetic confusion produced by indigenous attempts to represent religious images in icons or autos. Simply put, the *Exercicio* was ostensibly a way of sidestepping the deceits of the visible world by concentrating on verbally conjured truisms.

Over the course of the sixteenth century and the later colonial period, it is possible to distinguish three different positions or mentalities vis-à-vis mimesis and the mimetic difference or residue the

Nahuas inevitably displayed when they appropriated aspects of European culture. Motolinía represents the first mentality in which the mimetic difference of the Nahuas—their externally visible alterity—was considered inconsequential. Sahagún represents the second mentality. Extremely mistrustful of any form of mimetic residue but unwilling to concede the absolute alterity of the Nahuas, Sahagún responds in two ways. On the one hand, he attempts to construct a systematic determination of the nature of each and every facet of Nahua culture in the *Historia universal* so the bad mimetic residue can be "sifted" (his metaphor) from the good. Sahagún is willing to tolerate worldly differences between Nahuas and Europeans as long as these differences do not represent remnants of idolatry. On the other hand, Sahagún's suspicions surrounding the mimetic residues of the Nahuas lead him to attempt to articulate and emphasize the fundamentals of the faith in a nonvisual way. Texts such as the *Addiciones*, *Apéndiz*, and *Exercicio* represent Sahagún's attempt to fortify the Nahuas with the internal and invisible side of Christianity.

The third discernible mentality in colonial New Spain is the growing intolerance of any mimetic residue in the Nahua population whatsoever. This position is first visible in the Spanish colonialists' demands that the Nahuas be thoroughly Hispanicized—against the express wishes of the early regular clergy. This conceptualization of mimesis holds out an impossible task for the Nahuas: reinvent yourselves as perfect imitations of the Spaniards or suffer the consequences. Obviously, this latter view contains no tolerance of alterity. Unfortunately, it was the view that prevailed as the relatively idealistic regular clergy lost its political hold on the indigenous population over the course of Mexico's colonial period.

Some of the ramifications of the three mentalities vis-à-vis the mimetic residue of Nahuas can be glimpsed through the infamous problem of postconquest indigenous drinking. In one of the *autos* Motolinía describes in his *Historia*, a drunk Nahua stumbles into a scene in which Saint Francis is giving a sermon. Saint Francis warns him to stop his drunken singing or he will go to Hell. The drunk

Nahua ignores him, and demons emerge to drag him into the mouth of an artificially constructed Hell (214–15). The light, almost slapstick tone of this episode indicates how quickly Motolinía thought an acute problem for the Nahuas could be reincorporated into the general order of the premodern Christian worldview.

In his *Addiciones*, Sahagún treats the same problem of indigenous drunkenness in a more serious tone and gives it a little bit more moral structure and direction. After extolling the virtues of caring for one's body, he states:

Do not follow the example of those who eat too much, who are unreasonable in their eating, who get drunk, who dress strangely, who dress pompously, who live luxuriously, who live amusing themselves in carnal delights, who live vainly, who live getting drunk and with knavishness. All of them are headed down the road to the region of the dead. (49)

Sahagún's rules of behavior cover a wide gamut[9] and are meant to direct the acculturation of the Nahuas *without* using the Spaniards as models. The Nahuas are told, for example, to pray in their own language (104) and wear "moderately good, moderately apt, moderately durable" indigenous clothing (108).

Spaniards who expected the Nahuas to imitate them in every respect ran into serious ethical problems when it came to the growing problem of indigenous drinking in New Spain. Many Spaniards chose to interpret indigenous drunkenness as an inherent deficiency: colonial Spaniards saw the Nahuas as "perpetual minors" or "moral weaklings who were easily led astray" when it came to holding their liquor (Taylor, 42). In an interesting text from 1692, a friar named Antonio de Escaray holds out Spanish drinking as a model the Nahuas would do well to imitate if only they were capable: "If the Indians drank pulque the way Spaniards drink wine (which is not the case, nor has it been, nor is there any hope of their ever doing so) it could be permitted. . . . but these are Indians and it is proven that their custom is to get drunk, and it is for that reason that they drink" (quoted in Taylor, 42). Nevertheless, Escaray's words bear traces of protesting too much. What bothered Spaniards most about indigenous drinking was the feeling that their hands were not entirely clean—that they were at least partly responsible for the problem in the first place. Indigenous drunkenness was perceived as a flagrant parody or mockery of the Spaniards' supposed moderation because it brought to the fore the inherent absurdity of offering Spaniards as absolute, worthy models for Nahua imitation in the first place.

A polemical tract by the seventeenth-century Franciscan Agustín de Vetancurt makes this problem quite explicit. Vetancurt wrote in the context of a burgeoning criollismo. In the seventeenth century the criollos of New Spain noted that they had culturally grown apart from the peninsula and sought ways—for reasons of political leverage—to legitimate their separate identity. Since Europeans could always claim a closer tie to a Roman past, criollo scholars in New Spain set about locating their origins in a fictitious, reconstructed Nahua past. As Benjamin Keen has noted, Vetancurt's major work—the *Teatro mexicano*—is obsessed with those monarchical and aristocratic features of Nahua society that provide New Spain "with a suitably dignified and heroic past" (Keen, 188–89). One immediate result of this ideological context was the perception of a profound disparity between the glorious, idealized Nahuas of the past and the contemporary "drunken," "ill-clad" Nahuas Vetancurt discusses in the excursus called "Manifest of the zeal of a religious minister of the natives concerning the state of the Republic of the Indians in regard to the pulque they drink and their perdition."

After describing a highly idealized portrait of preconquest drinking practices, Vetancurt directly attributes the current problem to the Spaniards and the introduction of Castilian wine (95). Like many religious figures of the day, Vetancurt attributes virtually all of the Nahuas' physical, social, and spiritual woes to the problem of excessive drinking (96). He argues that the Spaniards are partly to blame because they fail to see the Nahuas as members of the same spiritual family (97). The Spaniards in general fail to hold themselves out as worthy examples—especially in what pertains to their lucrative involvement in the sale of pulque to the Nahuas (98). According to Vetancurt, the problem of being bad role models is especially acute because "the Indians have no more understanding than their eyes—they believe more what they see than what they hear. . . . How are they to be brought back to a state of grace and make retribution if they see that drunkenness is tolerated and that such a detestable sin that threatens lamentable damnation is not prohibited?" (98). Vetancurt's tract highlights one of the consequences of the now firmly entrenched notion of mimesis as pure imitatio. Whether the Nahuas' failure to drink in moderation, supposedly like the Spaniards, is attributed to inherent Nahua deficiencies or to the shortcomings of Spaniards as role models, the result is the same: Nahuas are now clearly expected to embody the Spanish experience thoroughly or be relegated to second-class status. Somewhere over the course of the sixteenth and seventeenth centuries, Motolinía's simplistic and Sahagún's complex notion of mimetically ascribing to some ethereal, spiritual model of perfection gave way to the impossible demand for Nahuas to deny themselves in their entirety and live as Spaniards—as mimics in the modern, pejorative sense that critics of colonialism have come to denounce as an absurd, but all too real, double standard.[10]

2. Mimesis as Othering

Nature creates similarities. One need only think of mimicry. The highest capacity for producing similarities, however, is man's. His gift of seeing resemblances is nothing other than a rudiment of the powerful compulsion in former times to become and behave like something else. Perhaps there is none of his higher functions in which his mimetic faculty does not play a decisive role. (Benjamin, 333)

When Donald Robertson published *Mexican Manuscript Painting of the Early Colonial Period: The Metropolitan Schools* in 1959, indigenous Mexican art was hardly considered art at all. Robertson's book irreversibly turned this situation around by applying, whenever possible, the hermeneutic tools of contemporary European and American art history. The pursuit of "artistic personality" proved futile, for example, so Robertson analyzed indigenous Mexican art in terms of stylistic schools—an approach that was meant to surpass the then current approach to manuscripts as mere repositories of iconographic information (4). Robertson can be credited with almost single-handedly bringing colonial indigenous painting into its own, and it is not surprising that much of the work of subsequent art historians in this area has been concerned with using the techniques of Western art history to valorize works that were previously considered unworthy of aesthetic attention. In this process of cross-cultural absorption, the limits of the referential framework of art history have inevitably been stretched and modified to the point where it is now possible to question the very necessity of using Western standards to evaluate indigenous works of art. Art historians lent legitimacy to colonial indigenous art only to be faced with the question of what privilege allows their discipline to bestow this kind of legitimacy in the first place.

This question is not as isolated as it might seem. Art historians in general have begun to explore the limitations of applying the standards of art history to art that existed before the advent of the discipline in the nineteenth century and even the advent in the early modern period of the idea of art as a fundamentally *human* endeavor. The experience of "art for art's sake" and the primacy of the individual artist's intentions in the modern period, for example, called for a hermeneutics of art that would have been entirely foreign to the Middle Ages. As Belting has ably demonstrated in *Likeness and Presence*, this situation necessitates the systematic problematization of post hoc applications of modern art history to the Middle Ages. In short, contemporary art history must now contend with the recognition that it is just one way among others of knowing and experiencing art. The recent problematization of one's own hermeneutic limitations—the positing or awareness of alternative meaning systems without possession of the ability to decode them—is not confined to the field of art history. In his introduction to *Local Knowledge*, Geertz offers the following syntactic tour de force:

> To see ourselves as others see us can be eye-opening. To see others as sharing a nature with ourselves is the merest decency. But it is from the far more difficult achievement of seeing ourselves amongst others, as a local example of the forms of human life has locally taken, a case among cases, a world among worlds, that the largeness of mind, without which objectivity is self-congratulation and tolerance a sham, comes. (16)

Geertz argues that it is the role of interpretive anthropology to keep teaching this "fugitive truth," but his insight could conceivably be applied to other areas of knowledge. To see oneself as "a case among cases" does not mean that one should, or can, have a bird's-eye view of a diverse terrain of mutually exclusive, relativized fields of knowledge. It means that one must approach other spheres of knowledge by groping along the outer reaches of one's own cognitive, cultural, and historical boundaries. When this tenet is applied to the concrete case of Sahagún's work, it suggests the need for reining in one's own thought processes each and every time one is on the verge of explaining (away) the Nahuas' point of view. Taken to extremes, this precaution could cripple all discussion; but taken in a mild dose, it could conceivably redirect critical attention to interpretive matters that have been overlooked in the frantic race to get from point A to point B—from the point of good intentions to a sympathy, cohesion, or even collusion with the Other.

Art historians have documented the increased Europeanization of the indigenous artwork in Sahagún's early and late versions of the *Historia universal*: the *Primeros memoriales* and the *Florentine Codex.*[11] This Europeanization can be explained in part through the growing amount of contact over time between indigenous artists and the European missionaries, but this process was perhaps not as inevitable or teleological as is commonly thought. On more careful examination, the so-called Europeanization of Nahua artistry betrays defining, constitutive features that are not European at all. Perhaps the import of these features will never be completely understood, but they do indicate that the Western way of seeing is just "a case among cases." In this section I argue that the mimesis involved in the Nahuas' so-called Europeanization was different from a Western one. I also explain why the current epistemological situation allows recognition of this difference even though modern viewers of the Nahuas' world are excluded from the possibility of any thorough analysis.

Part way through the *Primeros memoriales*, just above an unrelated column of writing, there is a line drawing of a man seated on a *petate*, a reed mat (*Historia de las cosas*, 6:142). The most curious thing about this man is that he is clearly a hybrid of indigenous and European features. On the one hand, he is wearing indigenous clothing and is seated on the petate—a typical symbol of authority throughout Mesoamerica. On the other hand, he is bearded like a European and has—as Baird has astutely noted—his face turned toward the viewer in a decidedly non-pre-Hispanic fashion. Baird has shown that this element combined with his location above an unrelated text and his contemplative or melancholy expression place him in an old European artistic tradition. According to Baird, this tradition runs from classical images of resting Herakles and pensive philosophers to disconsolate Adams, thoughtful evangelists, and "sorrowing Josephs" (*Drawings*, 36).

One's first impression of this hybrid figure might be that it is a crude, naive, or inept attempt to imitate a European model. But there are elements in this drawing that contradict the notion that the indigenous artist was trying to exact an identical copy of a European type. For one thing, the artist intentionally dresses the figure in indigenous clothing when anyone at the time would know that Europeans did not dress in this fashion. Moreover, the man, while dressed in indigenous clothing, has a beard that gives him a Spanish appearance. Is this a subversive parody of European authority—a depiction of a wolf in sheep's clothing?

That might be one's second response to this figure, but this interpretation, too, proves inadequate or overly simplistic. The appearance of beards in pre-Hispanic painting is rare or non-existent. Donald Robertson even contends that the presence of beards can be used as a way of dating indigenous codices after the 1540s (*Mexican Manuscript*, 195). As the centuries progressed, the increasing appearance of beards could merely be indicative of the growing *mestizaje* (mixed-blood population), but early on they seem to hold a fascination for some indigenous artists that is hard to interpret. For example, Moteuczomah II (Montezuma) was known to have an uncommon, slight beard.[12] Not all artists of the colonial period chose to depict Moteuczomah's beard,[13] but in the *Florentine Codex*, Moteuczomah is depicted ("realistically"), with a relatively sparse beard (*CF* II:32r). Other indigenous artists, however, have been known to accentuate Moteuczomah's beard to such a degree that he looks like a veritable Spaniard dressed in Nahua attire.[14] It is hard to determine the purpose of such Hispanicized depictions of Moteuczomah, but perhaps the answer lies somewhere in the growing use in the sixteenth century of familial ties to Moteuczomah as a way to legitimate hereditary claims in the eyes of the Spaniards. The bearded figure from the *Primeros memoriales* may or may not be a depiction of Moteuczomah; in any case, he seems to represent some kind of amalgam of indigenous and European authority figures, although the artist's final purpose in producing such a hybrid remains unclear.

The two interpretations of naiveté and parody are suggestive initially, but I believe both are untenable in the end. It is clear that a strange interplay of authority is being depicted, but it is unclear for what reason. If it is naive, why the petate and indigenous clothing? If it is subversively parodic—a mockery of European types—why does the man seem so unthreatening—so passive?

I will not try to resolve this conundrum. The drawing engages the Western gaze and then—intentionally or unintentionally—excludes it. Ironically, this exclusion is the result of the uncanny inclusion of one of the West's most potent male archetypes: the thinker. A man from the West can imagine he sees someone who looks like himself in the drawing without having any idea what he is supposed to be looking at. I believe this drawing is more interesting if it is left hermeneutically open-ended. In that way, it brings to light some of the limitations of a hermeneutic system the West has come to take for granted. It is a reminder that one's own way of knowing is only one among many.

The bearded figure in the *Primeros memoriales* signals the existence of an alternative, alien form of mimesis without defining it. The composite structure of the drawing undermines the notion that it is meant faithfully to imitate exactly any one thing in particular. It seems, rather, to be more a case of mimetic exuberance than mimetic exactitude. Writers from the early colonial period delighted in pointing out the heightened mimetic capacities of the Nahuas without ever really understanding them. Motolinía wrote in his *Historia*, for example, that the Nahuas "go around observing like monkeys in order to imitate everything they see—even with skilled jobs, by only watching without putting their hand to it, they become masters" (195). This type of mimetic exuberance is what Benjamin was referring to when he claimed in "On the Mimetic Faculty" that "ancient" peoples see and are a part of the "magical correspondences and analogies" that exist throughout the cosmos—"magical" connections that the "modern" adult does not perceive because of the "atrophied" state of his or her mimetic faculty. According to Benjamin, the potent mimetic faculty of "ancients" not only allowed them to imitate the cosmos through dance, it allowed them to manipulate similarity itself—establishing meaningful, but now elusive, ties between persons and objects that he refers to as "nonsensuous similarity" (334).

Benjamin's notion of a fertile, ancient mimetic faculty will seem alien or cryptic until one realizes that he is trying to describe something that can only be glimpsed from within the confines of the modern mimetic faculty. Benjamin's brief essay is self-consciously riddled with assumptions about the existence of a premodern mimetic faculty; and he treats contemporary language like an archeological site, where only scattered, fragmentary remnants of the old mimesis can be discerned, and only then with much care. He cites as one example of such an archeological artifact the belief that graphology can reveal an unconsciously produced, hidden imprint of the psyche in an individual's handwriting (335).[15]

In the last two or three decades there has been an increase in scholarship that, like Benjamin's, attempts to reformulate a sense of a premodern or alternative mimesis from within the limitations of the contemporary intellectual scaffolding. The modern, dualistic notion of mimesis as original/copy (or imitatio, in Costa Lima) is so ingrained in present-day cognitive functions that it is nearly impossible to conceptualize the products of mimesis in nonhierarchical terms—to sense the "magical" primacy of mimicry, as Benjamin would see it. Before returning to an examination of indigenous artwork in the Sahaguntine corpus, I would like briefly to set forth three examples of scholarship interested in avoiding original/copy conceptualizations of mimesis. The most interesting aspect of this scholarship is the fact that it is emerging in the context of very diverse disciplines. This seems to indicate that different scholars are trying to respond to a novel predicament of culture or "sign of the times" with the analytical tools of their respective fields.

In "Plato and the Simulacrum," Gilles Deleuze attempts to grapple with the limitations of modern mimesis by historicizing it within—and perhaps even outside of—the Western philosophical tradition. Deleuze argues that Plato established the terms for understanding mimesis, which Christianity adopted and which permeated the philosophical tradition until the advent of Nietzschean thought, the objective of which was "to reverse Platonism." He argues that Platonism makes a dialectical distinction between a transcendental "Idea" (essence) and its appearance in the human world. This differentiation is understood to distinguish "the 'thing' itself from its images, the original from the copy, the model from the simulacrum" (253). Deleuze, however, shows that these expressions are not equivalent. The distinction between the Idea (Justice, for example) and its mimetic offshoots (the quality of being just; a just person) is not, as might be assumed, a neutral taxonomic distinction: it does not take the form of the division of a genus into species. Rather, the Idea and its mimetic copies are hierarchically organized along a receding line, like pretenders to a throne. At the far end, farthest away from the Idea, lies the simulacrum: the "copy of the copy," "the false copy," the "infinitely degraded icon," "the image without resemblance," the "impure" and "inauthentic" pretender to the throne. The true throne, or Idea, according to Deleuze, is *always* founded in the circular structure of a myth (255).

The simulacrum must be subjected to the naturalized hierarchy of a pretender-to-the-throne schema because it consistently threatens to disrupt the notion that there is really a difference between a copy (the "secondary possessor" of the throne) and the throne itself. Deleuze describes it this way:

Let us consider the two formulas: "only that which resembles differs" and "only differences can resemble each other." These are two distinct readings of the world: one invites us to think difference from the standpoint of a previous similitude or identity; whereas the other invites us to think similitude and even identity as the product of a deep disparity. The first reading precisely defines the world of copies or representations; it posits the world as icon. The second, contrary to the first, defines the world of simulacra; it posits the world itself as phantasm. . . . The simulacrum is not a degraded copy. It harbors a positive power which denies *the original and the copy, the model and the reproduction.* At least two divergent series are internalized in the simulacrum—neither can be assigned as the original, neither as the copy. (261–62)

In light of Deleuze's arguments, the bearded man in Sahagún's *Primeros memoriales* is a simulacrum. He stands both between and beyond being a copy and being an original. In order to be properly perceived, he cannot be subjected to genealogical criteria that set him far down the road from a European Idea or model. In the words of Deleuze, if our bearded man has a model at all, "it is another model, a model of the Other (*l'Autre*) from which there flows an internalized dissemblance" (258).

In *Autopoiesis and Cognition* and *The Tree of Knowledge*, Humberto Maturana and Francisco Varela set forth interrelated definitions of life (living systems) and cognition that are distinguishable from the cause/effect explanations that an *outside* observer can give to the operations of living organisms. The authors, both biologists, coin the term "autopoiesis" to describe the creative autonomy of living systems and to break out of the linguistic confines of a scientific discourse that conflates biological processes (including cognition) with the observation of them—a discourse that inevitably characterizes living systems on the actual level of operations with notions of purpose and function (*Autopoiesis*, xiii, xvii).

This is not the place to describe in detail their complex arguments,[16] but a few points relative to the discussion might be made. Maturana and Varela demonstrate that it is possible to give a biological explanation for cognition that precludes intentionality except from the vantage point of the observer. They use the term "autopoietic organizations" to describe enclosed, autonomous living systems in which outside stimuli (the environment) can only *resonate* in or *trigger* structural changes in the internally determined activity of living systems. Autopoietic systems do not recognize an "inside" and "outside" of themselves, and only an observer can extraneously make such distinctions. Maturana and Varela show how their model of autopoiesis can be extended from the level of the cell to other levels of human activity such as knowledge. Although they do not use the word, a novel understanding of mimesis can be extrapolated from their arguments: "mimesis" is another word commonly used to describe one level of autopoietic activity in human beings. Through mimesis, human beings make the Other (the environment) their own, but in the framework of Maturana and Varela's arguments, they can only do so according to the preexisting relational limitations of the human state in question. In short, they offer a biological explanation for why a cognitive process like mimesis can *never* be a form of pure imitatio. When autopoietic systems like human knowledge undergo an actual structural change, the change is not *directed, determined,* or *specified* by an external cause—or Idea (as Deleuze puts it).

In the context of colonial contact, this means that there are
sound, biologically rooted cognitive reasons why Nahuas—*like anyone
else*—inevitably apprehended European cultural features according
to the internally determined parameters of their own dispositions.
The expectation that Nahuas should or could simply reinvent
themselves in the image of Spaniards on all levels of their being is
an expectational or purposive fallacy set forth by the West's traditional inability to delineate properly the relationship between the
autonomy of certain cognitive and biological phenomena and their
secondary observation—or, as Geertz might put it, objectivity as
"self-congratulation."

Michael Taussig's *Mimesis and Alterity* is more explicitly concerned
with cross-cultural mimetic interchanges in colonial situations.
Taussig defines the mimetic faculty as "the nature that culture uses
to create second nature, the faculty to copy, to imitate, make models,
explore difference, yield into and become Other" (xiii). Mimesis is
normally associated with similarity, and alterity is normally associated with difference, but Taussig shows with an astounding array
of anthropological examples (both Western and non-Western) that
the two are inextricably meshed. Taussig's definition places mimesis
at a crossroads between essentialist and constructionist views of the
world, for mimesis is the ability to experience as real the "really
made-up" (xvii).

Taussig builds on the work of Benjamin, Theodor Adorno, and
Max Horkheimer in order to argue that modernity has permitted a
resurgence of the mimetic faculty in the West. Modern techniques
like slow-motion in film facilitate the cognitive apprehension of
previously unknown domains of the world as they simultaneously
destabilize representational security. Discourses like advertising
force one to reassess or experience in a new way the "objectness" of
the object. This "retooling" of the modern individual's atrophied
mimetic faculty has been accompanied by a breakdown in the mind/
body distinction: modernity's reinvigoration of mimesis allows one
to experience (anew) the *tactility* that governs vision as a cognitive
operation (20–26). This resurgence of mimesis and representational

insecurity enables one to look back on moments of cross-cultural contact and perceive for the first time the existence of alternative forms of mimesis—forms of mimesis that nevertheless remain just outside one's reach.

Taussig is particularly interested in examples of European cultural traits mimetically reproduced by so-called primitive peoples for unknown reasons. In these examples, ideas about subversion or parody will not explain why it is that when Westerners sometimes look into what may considered primitive cultures, they see themselves represented there. In colonial situations, the colonizer and the colonized mimetically feed off of each other as they "naturalize" the Other's world as part of their own. However, it can no longer be assumed that this happens on both sides of the equation for the same reasons—or that the reasons of the so-called primitives are even accessible to people outside their culture.

I have made this somewhat digressive foray into the works of Deleuze, Maturana and Varela, and Taussig in order to establish the type of novel critical backdrop that I believe is now both necessary and possible for looking at the kind of colonial indigenous artwork found in the Sahaguntine corpus. The opacity of colonial indigenous artwork cannot fully be appreciated without first pressing hard on current assumptions about mimesis—a feature of hermeneutics that is so embedded that pictures are often thought to "speak for themselves." If Deleuze, Maturana and Varela, and Taussig suggest anything, it is that vision and human understanding cannot be described on any level in terms of a thing-versus-image schematics.

With this in mind, I would like to return to the artwork in the Sahaguntine corpus. In "Deity Images and Texts in the *Primeros Memoriales* and *Florentine Codex*," Eloise Quiñones Keber succinctly describes the increased European character of the deity images in the *Florentine Codex* (*CF* I:unnumbered) with respect to those of the earlier Primeros memoriales that served as direct models (*Historia de las cosas* 6:23–36):

The bodily proportions of the *Florentine Codex* figures adhere more closely to European figural conventions, with heads smaller in proportion to total body height and legs longer than their *Primeros memoriales* counterparts. Also notable is the adoption of a three-quarter view and the technique of foreshortening to provide a more spatial rendering of the figures. In contrast to indigenous graphic practices, the emphatic modular line that typically defined pre-Hispanic forms is here thinner, lighter, and more curvilinear, suggesting actual bodily contours. . . . [T]he body is depicted as an organic, substantial whole, not merely a prop on which to display costume elements. The effort to convey the proportions, mass, and rounded forms of the human body thus departs from indigenous pictorial techniques that had produced the flat, schematic figural depictions still evident in the *Primeros memoriales*. (263–64)

It is easy to see why the increased humanization—by Western standards—of the deity images would appeal to Sahagún. Even though the deity images of the *Primeros memoriales* could easily be depictions of deity-impersonators, to European eyes the individualized images in the *Florentine Codex* emphasize more the idea of ordinary human beings "dressed up" like gods. In Book I of the *Florentine Codex*, for example, the Nahua informants—presumably eager to please the friars—emphasize that some of the old gods like Huitzilopochtli were "only men" (e.g., *FC* I:1).[17] Sahagún and his companions could easily have perceived—if only unconsciously—the indigenous imitation of European artistic techniques as a way of unmasking the deity-impersonators.

The deity images in the *Primeros memoriales* are probably direct copies of other (possibly pre-Hispanic) indigenous drawings (Nicholson, "Iconography," 231). The deity images in the *Florentine Codex*, however, are more than mere copies of the earlier images in the *Primeros memoriales*. Quiñones Keber, for example, has demonstrated that a drawing of the goddess Chalchiuhtlicue in the *Florentine Codex* implements changes (like the addition of jade beads in the skirt) that reveal the artist's knowledge of pre-Hispanic traditions

(Quiñones Keber, 268). On the one hand, it is possible to say that the Europeanized deity images of the *Florentine Codex* are twice removed from the now lost, "more authentic" pre-Hispanic images. On the other hand, examples like Quiñones Keber's demonstrate that the artists of the *Florentine Codex* were *enriching* the Europeanized, human-looking depictions of deities in some places with details that lent them greater authority or authenticity. In medieval iconography, saints seldom look truly human because they are modeled after the invisible reality of a typos hieros. This idea is still ingrained enough in Western consciousness to provoke the assumption that the very human mundaneness or realism of the deity images in the *Florentine Codex* reveals their lack of true divinity—but could it be otherwise?

Tezcatlipoca is one of the important Central Mexican deities depicted in both the *Primeros memoriales* and the *Florentine Codex* (*Historia de las cosas* 6:23; *CF* I:unnumbered). He was a patron god of rulers, priests, and warriors. He was considered an omnipotent and omnipresent god of discord but also whimsically bestowed fame and prosperity (*CF* I:1r–2v). In Book II of the *Florentine Codex* there is a detailed, illustrated description of how deity-impersonators were chosen and prepared to embody the god Tezcatlipoca (*CF* II: 30r–37v). The most surprising aspect of this description is the amount of care taken to choose the most suitable candidate for impersonating Tezcatlipoca. Here is only part of a much longer description:

In the time of Toxcatl there was Tezcatlipoca's great festival. At that time he was given human form; at that time he was set up. . . .

Indeed he who was thus chosen was of fair countenance, of good understanding, quick, of clean body, slender, reed-like, long and thin, like a stout cane, like a stone column all over, not of overfed body, not corpulent, not very small, nor exceedingly tall.

Indeed it became his defect if someone were exceedingly tall. The women said to him "Tall fellow; tree-shaker; star-gatherer." He who was chosen as impersonator was without defects.

He was like something smoothed, like a tomato, like a pebble, as if sculptured in wood; he was not curly-haired, curly-headed; his hair was indeed straight, his hair was long. He was not rough of forehead; he had no pimples on his forehead; he did not have a forehead like a tomato; he did not have a baglike forehead. He was not long-headed; the back of his head was not pointed; his head was not like a carrying net; his head was not bumpy; he was not broad-headed; he was not rectangular-headed; he was not bald; he was not of rounded forehead; he was not of swollen eyelids; he was not of enlarged eyelids; he was not swollen-cheeked; he was not of injured eyes; he was not of injured cheeks; he was not bulging of eye; he was not cloven-chinned; he was not gross-faced; he was not of downcast face; he was not flat-nosed; he did not have a nose with wide nostrils; he was not Roman-nosed; he was not concave-nosed; he was not twisted-nosed; not bent-nosed, not crooked-nosed; but his nose was averagely placed; he was straight-nosed. He was not thick-lipped, he was not gross-lipped, he was not big-lipped. (*FC* II:66–67)

Deity-impersonators were not impersonators in the modern, almost pejorative sense of the word. Through their impersonation, human beings became one with the omnipresent gods and affirmed their collective place in a mythic cosmic order. Unlike Christianity, the Central Mexican cosmology was more a system of balances between dualisms than a struggle to the end between forces of good and evil. The primary purpose of the elaborate rituals was to safeguard or restore balance in the universe. The detailed criteria used to choose the Tezcatlipoca impersonator reveals the emphasis placed on performing the rituals in a preordained manner in order to appease the gods. It also reveals a sense that certain individuals were mimetically better predisposed to embodying the god than were others. Unlike the West's persistent struggle or inability to reconcile the human with the divine (especially noticeable in iconographic representations of holy figures and the endless debates over the nature of Christ's humanness), the text cited above does not lead one to believe that the Nahuas were uncomfortable with the idea of human beings with designated individual characteristics becoming—if only temporarily—gods.

The detailed verbal description of what kind of individual is best suited to impersonate Tezcatlipoca finds its visual parallel in the increased individuality of the Europeanized deity images of the *Florentine Codex*. The description of the Tezcatlipoca impersonator should lead one to suspect that the individuality of the human beings in the *Florentine Codex*'s deity images does not downplay their divinity, as it would in a Western schema, but actually sustains or reaffirms the intricate and pervasive web of divine, mimetic correspondences in the Central Mexican cosmos.

The Nahua artists of the *Florentine Codex* were probably converts, but it seems improbable that the fervor and dexterity with which they mimetically appropriated European artistic techniques was governed solely by a desire to expose deity-impersonators as idiosyncratic, ordinary mortals dressed in fancy costumes. It is more likely that the appropriation of European artistry was seen—unconsciously or otherwise—as a way of heightening a sense of the "magical" mimetic correspondences that permeated the world of both the colonial and precolonial Nahuas—mimetic correspondences Westerners are now in a position to detect sometimes, but which, nevertheless, remain just beyond the grasp of modern viewers.

3. The Crisis of Exemplarity

In *The Slippery Earth: Nahua-Christian Moral Dialogue in Sixteenth-Century Mexico*, Louise Burkhart acknowledges the value of studies that attempt to reconstruct authentic pre-Hispanic Nahua culture, but she also notes that these studies tend to elide the importance of native language texts—especially doctrinal texts—that clearly bear the stamp of European influence (5). After the conquest, Nahua culture entered into a kind of opaque moral dialogue with European culture through the presence of Christian missionaries such as Sahagún. As I have shown, interlocutors from both sides of this dialogue interpreted their interaction in terms of their own cultural preconceptions, but these preconceptions were subtly transformed as the missionaries quixotically struggled to convey their message accurately in Nahuatl. Burkhart ably demonstrates that the Nahuas'

ethical beliefs were not the only ones that were mimetically transformed in the years after the conquest. When the friars were confronted with the impossible task of remolding an entire culture in
their own image, they "responded by, to some extent, remaking
themselves" (184). Both indigenous and European beliefs survived
the conquest of Mexico, but—to use Burkhart's phrasing—Christianity was "conquered" as well through both the ways in which it
was modified to suit Nahua culture and the changes effected on the
friars' worldview.

In what follows, I will examine one specific problem that ensued
from Sahagún's moral dialogue with Nahua culture: namely, the crisis
of exemplarity that critics normally associate with the sociopolitcal
situation of early modern Europe. My brief analysis of Sahagún's
Historia universal and *Psalmodia christiana* will show that the entirety of
his missionary work is threatened by an underlying crisis of exemplarity that is similar to the early modern European one in some
respects, but which is primarily galvanized by the particular nature
of his interaction with the Nahua world. In this sense, I hope to
reverse the stereotype that, in all facets of its worldview, Europe
produced its own modernity and then, and only then, exported it to
the New World. Moreover, I hope to show that even when the
indigenous authenticity of Nahuatl texts such as the *Historia universal*
or the *Psalmodia christiana* turns out to be elusive, these texts nevertheless prove quite revealing of what happens when Western and
non-Western worlds collide.

The missionary ideals of the Franciscans during the Middle Ages
are characterized by a surprising degree of continuity. E. Randolph
Daniel has shown that medieval Franciscans cultivated a unique
missionary ideal that emphasized conversion through example. Even
though Franciscan missionary theory was informed by the various
rationalistic and apocalyptic approaches to conversion that were
common during the Middle Ages, the Franciscan ideal stood out in
the sheer degree of emphasis it placed on the cultivation of a personal spiritual perfection. Franciscans believed that the primary

mode of conversion would occur through the perfection of a "joy-fully suffering" self modeled on Christ and Saint Francis, which would, in a sense, disseminate itself through the purity of its unspoken exemplarity. All in all, the Franciscans' tendency toward the simple, unadorned preaching of penitence during the Middle Ages was meant to reinforce their ideal of preaching through their works and not their words (Daniel, 38).

Given the Franciscan emphasis on example as the path to both spiritual perfection and conversion, it is not surprising that Franciscan preachers were primarily responsible for developing the use of *exempla* in sermons during the great preaching revival of the thirteenth century and for organizing them in the form of handbooks during the fourteenth (Bremond, Le Goff, and Schmitt). One of the primary purposes of the medieval *exemplum*, or example, was to unite the particularity of the everyday world of the parishioners with the universal message of Christian eschatology. Karlheinz Stierle has described the medieval example as the minimum narrative unit linking history as a universal, cohesive system and history as the realm of the everyday, the concrete, the pragmatic (180–85). In short, the example was one way in which medieval women and men confirmed their pars pro toto relationship with the universe—their understanding of themselves as a microcosm of God's macrocosm.

Medieval exempla were understood to be self-enclosed, authentic components of knowledge that could be moved from one discursive context to another without losing their essence or viability (Bremond, Le Goff, and Schmitt, 36–37). Stierle points out that there are two fundamental and interrelated assumptions in the use of medieval examples. First, the readily transferable and autonomous nature of medieval examples defies the modern notion that texts are fixations of verbal actions that only gain meaning through their interaction with various contextual situations. Second, because of the claim that the particularity of exempla reveals a universal moral code, the use of them assumes that there is a single point of view shared by all those involved in the production, conveyance, and reception of the text in question (187).

In a lengthy article entitled "Menschliches Handeln und göttliche Kosmologie: Geschichte als Exempel," Gumbrecht argues that
what is now perceived as the contradictory and remarkably unexemplary nature of many medieval examples stems from the lack in
medieval thought of the idea that individual perspective plays a role
in the production of knowledge—including the idea of what constitutes normal behavior. The recent works of Karlheinz Stierle,
John D. Lyons, and Timothy Hampton all argue that the crisis of
exemplarity in the early modern period is a result of the emerging
recognition that the mind, without divine revelation, is the primary
locus—and later an agent or constitutive element—in the production of knowledge. By way of example, an easily identifiable—but
nonetheless complex—form of this recognition can be found in the
emergence of linear perspectival techniques in early modern art
(Panofsky, *Perspective*; Damisch). In religious painting, the imple-
mentation of such perspectival techniques partially transferred the
locus of meaning away from the sacred archetype and toward the
skill and intentions of the individual artist (Belting).

Stierle, Lyons, and Hampton all show that many of the so-called
foundational texts of the early modern period in Europe share in
common the newly found preoccupation with what—if anything—
makes an example exemplary. Montaigne in his *Essais*, for instance,
consistently renders problematic the notion that examples link the
particularity of the everyday world to some universal lesson of history. He attempts to substitute the didactic failure of examples with
the uniformity of the very *process* of cogitation he self-consciously
stages in his essays (Hampton, 134–97; Lyons, 118–53; Stierle,
190–98).

In most respects, the European crisis of exemplarity only existed
in an inchoate form when the first Franciscans made their way to
New Spain in 1524. The Twelve Apostles embarked on their journey
to the New World steadfast in their conviction that all the
civilizations and histories of the world were part and parcel of a
single, unified history, whose meaning only the advent of Christianity could provide. As discussed in chapter 3, the twelve friars did

not see their mission as an open-ended, unpredictable adventure so much as the preordained final step before the End of the World (Phelan; Baudot, *Utopía*).

In the context of the last chapter I looked briefly at a text that now merits further scrutiny. In this text, the friars, who were about to set out for the New World, were given instructions by the general minister, Fray Francisco de los Ángeles. The general minister was careful to address the friars on the day of Saint Francis in a convent that took its name in the imitation of one in Assisi, Italy (Mendieta, 200). The general minister projected the friars' mission as a reenactment of the pilgrimages of the disciples of both Saint Francis and Christ. The general minister's words are permeated with the theme of example. The friars are both following the example of past holy men and embodying the notion of exemplarity for others: "And for this, if you could be together in a city, it would be better; because the harmony and good example that they see in your life and conversation would be as much a part in the conversion as your words and preaching" (quoted in Mendieta, 202). On the eve of the friars' departure, the general minister accentuated the idea that their mission would help bring about the long-awaited End of the World and repeated his emphasis on the importance of example (204–5). Example, in short, was the key to securing the eschatological cohesiveness of the friars' mission.

The juxtaposition in the general minister's instructions of conversion through example and the apocalyptic significance of the friars' journey is not a coincidence. During the Middle Ages, the Bible did not represent reality, it *was* reality. As Brian Stock has pointed out, beginning in the eleventh century, all interpretation of Christian history and reality was textually grounded—even if one could not read (34). With this in mind, it is clear why the friars who were heading for New Spain were expected to follow example, set an example, and operate as a kind of embodied exemplum in the preinscribed trajectory of history they were following. All of these forms of example were part of a single textual model. It is therefore not so surprising that Sahagún recurred to a textual model—*the*

Model, as Lewis saw it in *The Discarded Image* (11–12)—when he underwent his missionary crisis and pronounced the entire church in New Spain a fraud. Sahagún's fear or suspicion that a single idea could mean radically different things in different cultures is linked to one of the most important realizations of early modernity. In particular, it is one of the most important factors in what the critics I have discussed refer to as the early modern crisis of exemplarity. Lyons, for instance, argues that the purpose of examples in general is to establish or reaffirm a "common ground" or shared reality between the various participants of any discursive action. He goes on to say that the early modern period is characterized by its struggle—if not inability—to reach this common ground (x). Sahagún responded to this problem by recurring to the unifying methods of high scholasticism and, most notably, the generalized technique of manifestatio. I would now like to show that much, if not all, of Sahagún's work must also be understood as his attempt to ward off the increasing erosion of the unifying value of examples and exemplarity in the mission of New Spain.

Book XI of the *Historia universal* is ostensibly the most mundane and, hence, least important of Sahagún's *magnum opus*. This book—the longest of the twelve books of the *Historia*—is a combination bestiary, herbal, and lapidary that also includes other "natural things." Sahagún, however, did not regard Book XI as the least important part of his *Historia*:

In order to give examples and make comparisons, the knowledge of natural things certainly is not the least noble jewel of the coffer, of the preaching of the Gospel—as we have seen the Savior use them. And the more these examples and comparisons are familiar to the hearers, and the more they are used and said amongst them through words and language, the more they will be efficacious and beneficial. This is why this treasure was made with labor and travail—this volume in which are written in the Mexican language: the exterior and interior properties and manners that could be obtained of the best known and most used animals, birds, fish, trees, herbs, flowers and fruits of all the land; wherein there is a copious

selection of words and much language that is very proper and very common and very pleasing material. (*CF* XI:"Prologo")

    At the beginning of his *Historia*, Sahagún states that the purpose of
his work is to serve as a tool for preachers and confessors who hope
to "cure" the Nahuas of their spiritual "illnesses." The above quotation from the prologue to Book XI makes even clearer to the modern
reader that Sahagún's work was meant to serve as a compendium of
exempla that reveal both the internal and the external properties of
the various cultural domains of the Nahua world. Overall, the work
was meant to function as a collection of examples like those com-
piled by the Franciscans in fourteenth-century Europe. But much like
the fourteenth-century collections, it is not clear what exactly is
exemplary about many of the exempla collected. At certain junctures,
Sahagún is even conscious of this problem. In Book X, for instance,
he states, "The prudent reader should not be offended that only
words, and not sentences [morals], are listed above and other parts
further along, because this treatise is meant principally to apply the
Castilian language to the Indian language so that one knows how to
use the words of this material of *viciis et virtutibus* [vices and virtues]"
(*CF* X:2v). When Sahagún felt unsure about the exemplarity—or
negative exemplarity—of a particular passage, he could affirm its
linguistic usefulness. Nevertheless, this linguistic usefulness is still
tied to the problem of exemplarity. Sahagún notes above that the
material is concerned with Nahua "vices" and "virtues"—the
Nahuas' own realm of exemplarity. For Sahagún, language serves as
the starting point for mapping out the Nahua domain of exemplarity
in order subsequently to mend it where necessary.

    In the continuation of the earlier quotation from Book XI,
Sahagún reveals that his collection is driven by a desire to recon-
textualize the foreign connotations of Nahuatl within a Christian
framework:

This work will also prove very useful in revealing to them the value of
creatures so they do not attribute them with divinity, because they call

Teutl—which means god—any creature they perceive to be eminent in good or evil. Hence, they call the sun "teutl" for its beauty, also the sea for its size and ferociousness, and also they call many other animals by this name because of their frightening disposition and wildness. It is inferred from this that the noun teutl is taken as either good or bad. And this is even more recognizable when it is in composite form—such as in this noun, *teûpiltzintli*, very pretty child. Or: *teuhpiltontli*, a very mischievous or bad boy. Many other words are composed in this fashion—from whose meaning it can be conjectured that this word, teutl, means something extreme in either good or evil. (CF XI:"Prologo")

Sahagún's analysis of the compound forms of *teo-tl* ("god") forces Nahua ethics into an alien good-versus-evil schema (see Burkhart, 37). The good-versus-evil schema is most apparent in Book X, where it serves as Sahagún's central structuring principle for Nahua social roles (see López Austin, "Research," 141–42; Robertson, 624–25).

In the prologue to Book X, Sahagún states that his goal is to sort out the Nahua virtues from the vices so that preachers can "persuade" with one and "dissuade" with the other (*CF* X:"Prologo"). This explicit agenda of example collecting is most interesting where it breaks down. In chapter 27 of Book X, Sahagún lists the parts of the body in Nahuatl without providing his normal loose translation. In *The Human Body and Ideology: Concepts of the Ancient Nahuas*, Alfredo López Austin demonstrates the integral and extremely complex relationship between the Nahua body and their system of ethics. Sahagún does more than simply avoid this complexity: he substitutes his translation with his famous "Relacion del autor digna de ser notada" ("An Account by the Author Worthy of Note"). In this piece, Sahagún attributes the failure of the Nahuas' Christian education to their inherent, "vigorous sensuality" ("*briosa sensualidad*"; *CF* X:75r). By doing this, Sahagún replaces in one fell swoop Nahua moral beliefs about the body with Christianity's leitmotiv of the oppositional struggle between the spirit and the evils of the body. Historians have been so delighted to have the information on the Colegio de Santa Cruz that Sahagún provides in his "Relacion," they have systematically failed to see its skewed connection to the catalogue of body parts and functions. The entire piece is a tacit admission of partial defeat for Sahagún in the face of his incomprehension of Nahua morality. Sahagún's stated goal of rendering the world of the Nahuas in terms of examples and exemplarity—whether negative or positive—simply broke down when it came to the Nahua body. In this moment, the Nahuas displayed an extreme form of alterity or Otherness that held no place in the medieval Christian cosmology's sense of itself as a unified, all-encompassing, coherent whole.

Sahagún began work on his *Psalmodia christiana* at about the same time he began work on his *Historia universal*. Like the *Historia*, the *Psalmodia* is driven by the problem of example or exemplarity. The *Psalmodia* is a collection of exemplary canticles written in Nahuatl around the middle of the sixteenth century in an attempt to thwart or simply substitute the perceived (unexemplary) idolatry of songs like the *Cantares mexicanos*.[18]

Hagiographic literature of the Middle Ages was always composed with a didactic intent. Nevertheless, most medieval vernacular "saints' lives" contain a great deal of material whose exemplary value is not immediately clear. For instance, when medieval French authors turned to the Latin hagiographic tradition in order to compose their vernacular versions, they favored "dramatic events and exotic adventures at the expense of religious moralization" (Cazelles, 7). Medieval hagiography could afford these diversions because the overall exemplarity of the saints was never in question.

Sahagún's *Psalmodia* is extremely remarkable in its tendency to spell out at every step of the way the exemplary value of the attributes of the saints. Unlike medieval saints' lives, Sahagún's *Psalmodia* never foregoes religious moralization at any point for the sake of a good story. The canticle/sermon for Saint Mark the Evangelist provides an interesting case of how Sahagún frequently used the everyday world of the Nahuas to set a saint apart as an example. Sahagún first introduces the subject of his canticle: "Let us pay honor to the matchless merchant, God's beloved Saint Mark the Evangelist."[19] He then directs the discourse to the Nahuas themselves:

> You merchant, you vanguard merchant, you who reach far distant places, you who penetrate far places to gain your livelihood, who wind about the coastlands, who cross the seas:
>
> There you seek all kinds of precious birds, all kinds of feathers— trogon [black and green], troupial [black and gold], rosy spoonbill, yellow parrot chick feathers, blue cotinga.
>
> There you acquire what grows there, perhaps cacao, or species of vanilla, "big-ear" spice, or various kinds of fruit.
>
> You afflict yourself no little; you discover gorges, mountains, as you seek what you require; you go exhausted, shedding your sweat, pressing on though overtired, dropping to the ground exhausted. In your sweat you force yourself to travel. . . .
>
> If you were to undergo your torment to help God's vassals and have pity on the poor, you would be saved. (124–25)

Sahagún reprimands the Nahua merchants for their greed and then presents Saint Mark as a counterexample: "He went to Rome. Not quetzal [plumes], not all kinds of precious stones did he go to seek, but just the Holy Gospel" (126–27).

Sahagún next sets up Saint Mark as part of a chain of exemplars imitating exemplars: "But he did not emulate just anyone as he gained his wealth; he became the pupil of God's beloved Saint Peter himself" (126–27). Sahagún subsequently tells the fuller story of Saint Mark, contrasting his spiritual riches to the material riches of the Nahua merchants throughout. Sahagún ends with the description of Saint Mark's torments and God's final intervention. The spiritually motivated torments of Saint Mark that come at the end both round out and counter the merchants' mundane sufferings from the beginning of the canticle.

The entire *Psalmodia* is riddled with various Nahuatl translations of the word "example" or "exemplify": "*mixcuitia*" (82), "*machiotl*"

(84), "*octacatl*" (84), and so forth. In other instances, the saints "guided them in righteous living" (331), changed "men's ways of living through their preaching, through their way of living" (221), "became an example for the women wishing to be chaste" (239); and Sahagún offers Saint Martin's dying words: "When I die I only need a bed of ashes, and this is an example that I leave to you. It is needful that you do it, too" (332–33).

Since the Nahuas did not share Christianity's morally laden distinction between the material and the spiritual world, the *Psalmodia* is replete with passages that carefully draw out the difference: "Very great, very admirable was God's beloved Antony, for he repelled, he overcame his body and the devil and the world" (178–79). This distinction was extended to include, among other things, remnants of Nahua animism: "Understand [and] realize, you various people, that Christianity, unlike precious green stones, bracelets, emerald-green jade, even rubies smoking like quetzal plumes, is a heavenly thing, a marvelous miracle that the Lord God, that Jesus Himself, came here on earth to give us" (16–17).

Throughout the *Psalmodia*, Sahagún emphasizes the Christian tradition of figural interpretation in which every important event of the Christian era is prefigured in the Old Testament. Erich Auerbach defines medieval *figura* as "something real and historical which announces something else that is also real and historical. The relation between the two events is revealed by an accord or similarity" (29). Here is just one example from Sahagún's *Psalmodia*: "Moses represented our Lord Jesus Christ, Whom God the Father, His beloved Father, told to make, to set up the holy Church. He set the model, the example, as it was to be. And He set in place, commanded those who were to work there" (84–85).

The most important feature of *figura* is its ability to establish an essential rapprochement or identification between diverse phenomena over a distance of time and culture. *Figura*, in short, enables the Christian Middle Ages to read the entire course of history as a self-enclosed, unified whole whose entire meaning is only provided by the advent of Christ. Sahagún's emphasis on *figura* in the *Psalmodia* is designed to counteract any alternative, non-Christian understanding of history. The fact that Sahagún explicitly presents the *figura* of the above quote as exemplary is particularly resonant for my arguments. In the end, Sahagún's generalized, heightened emphasis on the exemplarity of the saints indicates that he felt that their role in the Christian episteme was no longer readily transparent. The most threatening thing about Sahagún's worry is the fact that an example whose exemplarity is unclear is, in reality, not much of an example. Simply put, Sahagún was worried that exemplarity in general could no longer be taken for granted.

For better or worse, Sahagún's crisis of exemplarity led to the creation of a new, hybrid form of indigenous or pseudoindigenous literature. It turns out to be extremely difficult to determine what— if anything—remains of authentic Nahua culture in Sahagún's work. This is even true for the *Historia universal*, since in numerous instances it is not clear when European or Nahua schemata are being used to both elicit and shape knowledge about the Nahua world. Nevertheless, Sahagún's work is extremely revealing of what can happen when radically different worlds are forced into an uneasy coexistence.

Much like a dormant virus that turns into a full-blown infirmity only when certain environmental conditions are met, the potentially unstable European rhetoric of example burgeoned into a highly contagious disease when it was brought into the context of New Spain. Unlike the arrival of the common cold in the New World, however, the crisis of exemplarity affected the moral health of Nahuas and Europeans alike. Much more rapidly and dramatically than in Europe, friars such as Sahagún were forced to contend with the fragmentation of their unified Christian worldview. After the arrival of the Spaniards, the idea of example, for both the Nahuas and the friars, could never again be a simple, transparent affair. Sahagún's need to orchestrate and monitor both the presentation and contextual application of examples only served to erode the medieval notion that exempla are autonomous units of knowledge and morality.

Those friars who chose not to walk away from the failures of the mission in New Spain were forced to acknowledge some of the cultural gaps that separated Nahuas from Spaniards as a first step toward bridging them. The didactics of exemplarity that Sahagún attempted to instigate and rigidify did not come without a price. It meant that he inevitably had to engage himself directly with Nahua culture. The search for a common moral ground meant that Sahagún could only enter into the implied alternate world of Nahua ethics by adapting his own standards to the linguistic reality and possibilities of Nahuatl. The problem of establishing an unequivocal realm of exemplarity forced the friars, including Sahagún, into a precarious and uncanny mimetic interchange whose nature and import is only now becoming apparent. Even Saint Francis, who was now in the *Psalmodia* an animistic *"teuiutica aueuetl"* (sacred cypress tree), would never be quite the same (158–59).

5

SAHAGÚN, THE DEVIL, AND THE DISINTEGRATION OF A MEDIEVAL CONCEPTUALIZATION OF KNOWLEDGE

It is certainly a thing of great astonishment that our Lord God kept hidden for so many centuries a forest of so many idolatrous peoples, whose abundant fruits only the devil has gathered and holds as treasures in the fires of Hell. Nor can I believe that the church of God will not prosper where the synagogue of Satan has had such prosperity. In conformity with this, Saint Paul writes: "Grace will abound where wickedness (once) abounded." (*CF* I:"Prologo")

In the first prologue to the *Florentine Codex*, Sahagún marveled that God had kept the indigenous peoples of the New World hidden from Europeans for so many centuries. What surprised him even more, perhaps, was the notion that the devil had been given free rein in the Americas until the arrival of the Spaniards. The quotation above draws out several features of Sahagún's thinking that I would like to explore in some detail in this chapter. First, Sahagún interprets the pre-Hispanic world of the Nahuas in terms of the machinations of the devil. Second, he establishes a historical, and even cosmological, symmetry between the reign of Satan and the reign of Christianity. Third, Sahagún confesses that there is something startling about the idea that God could leave the indigenous population of the New World at the mercy of Satan's wiles for so long.

Like many of his contemporaries, Sahagún used the devil to explain the existence of what seemed like unimaginably evil indigenous practices, such as institutionalized human sacrifice. As John

Elliott has noted, this enabled the friars to shift the blame for idolatry away from ideas of inherent deficiencies and toward the deceptive powers of the devil. In Elliott's words, "If the responsibility for bestial acts could be attributed to the devil, the Indian could be presented as a man who was deluded rather than deficient" ("Discovery," 60). The use of the devil as a versatile explanatory tool came at a price, however. The more the devil was used to explain untoward phenomena in the New World, the more powerful and the more ubiquitous became Satan's reach—at least in the eyes of the friars.

Historians have long been aware of the surge of purported witchcraft and diabolism in early modern Europe, and historians as early as Jules Michelet have been fascinated by the relationship between these practices and the advent of modern forms of knowledge and intellectual discovery. The devil's historical trajectory in sixteenth-century New Spain is inevitably related to diabolism in the Old World, but it is not identical in every respect. It is misleading for two important reasons to think of diabolism in New Spain as a mere cultural export from Europe. First, friars only began to emphasize the purported role of the devil in pre-Hispanic culture after they began to lose their illusions about an immediate, miraculous conversion of the indigenous population. Europe's demons were used as an interpretive response to a dilemma that grew out of, and was shaped by, the unique missionary situation of New Spain. Second, once diabolism took hold in New Spain, it took on a life of its own as it was combined with indigenous traditions and conceptions of morality. *The Devil in the New World: The Impact of Diabolism in New Spain*, by Fernando Cervantes, is the most detailed analysis of this phenomenon so far. Cervantes shows that the indigenous population actually—indeed, paradoxically—aided in their own demonization as a culture by developing their own "demonic ethos" out of the friars' obsessions with the pervasiveness of evil. Since the Nahuas were concerned with keeping the cosmos in a constant state of equilibrium, they were inclined to honor Satan as much as God (47).

Sahagún's work stands at an interesting intersection between diabolism and larger conceptualizations of knowledge. His obsession with the devil grew out of his conviction that evil, idolatrous practices lurked under Nahua appropriations of Christian culture. This obsession led him to delve into the Nahuas' historical past to find the roots of this idolatry. Sahagún, however, was not convinced that everything about Nahua culture was demonic. He was, in fact, as interested in the good qualities of the pre-Hispanic Nahuas as he was in what he saw as the bad qualities. Sahagún's investigations into Nahua culture were governed by a two-fold purpose: identifying idolatrous practices and identifying positive attributes that justified the friars' efforts to bring the Nahuas into the fold of Christianity. Sahagún's novel inquiries into Nahua culture constitute an attempt—sometimes preliminary—to sift the good from the bad. This process resulted in a work that seems remarkably modern to the present-day observer. In many places—especially in the latter books—Sahagún's *Historia universal* seems like a work driven by a profound sense of unfettered curiosity—a sense of intellectual discovery that is normally identified as one of the primary features of the modern period. The apparent irrelevance of much of the information he gathered to the immediate needs of proselytization creates the illusion that Sahagún pursued knowledge for its own sake. On closer examination, however, his experience of intellectual discovery would have been very different from the understanding of the nature and purpose of knowledge circulating now, or even during the Enlightenment.

My chief interest in this chapter is the way in which Sahagún's interest in the evil of the Nahua practices was symbiotically related to the erosion of a medieval conceptualization of knowledge as a preexisting, static whole that "man"[1] could learn, guard, and elucidate—but never produce. Sahagún stands on the threshold between a medieval conviction that *curiositas* was a vice and the (modern) need to look to the world itself for answers to life's essential questions. The pivotal contemporary notion that curiosity is a positive attribute that is essential for knowledge and progress had its obscure

beginnings in a situation in which human beings pursued knowledge in a manner that was functionally equivalent to—but not
identical with—the idea that God is impotent or absent from the
world. My argument—which owes an intellectual debt to the work
of Hans Blumenberg—reverses the common understanding of the
role curiosity played in the advent of a modern conceptualization
of knowledge. Normally, scholars interpret the phenomenon of
curiosity breaking free from blind dogma and superstition as the
advent of a modern form of knowledge. Nevertheless, this falsely
presupposes that medieval thinkers secretly valorized unfettered
curiosity and would have unleashed their imaginations if only medieval learning had not been so stifling. Actually, in the beginning,
intellectual curiosity was a by-product of a situation in which the
Middle Ages' traditional way of answering certain fundamental
questions no longer seemed adequate to the task.

In short, I believe that Sahagún is symptomatic of the transition
to a modern form of knowledge, but this transition—as seen in his
work—cannot be properly interpreted teleologically in terms of a
contemporary assessment of what the pursuit of knowledge is, or
should be, all about. On the contrary, Sahagún's work must be
interpreted in the context of the other side of this threshold of
knowledge—the disintegrating knowledge of the Middle Ages—in
order to avoid the pitfall of seeing his work as a modern conceptualization of knowledge now held in high esteem. In order to make
this argument, in the first section of this chapter I explore the role
the devil played in Sahagún's thinking. In the second section I tie
Sahagún's way of thinking to his shifting relationship to different
forms of knowledge.

1. Demons

Elliott's essay "The Discovery of America and the Discovery of
Man" takes its title from a quotation by Jules Michelet that argues
that "[t]wo things belong to this age [the sixteenth century] more
than to all its predecessors: the discovery of the world, the discovery
of man" (42). Elliott notes, however, that the body of European

knowledge was surprisingly unperturbed by the vast array of information available from the New World that stood in direct contradiction to the Christian and classical traditions.[2] Those people who
were caught up in the fray of cultural interaction with the New
World, however, were forced by "circumstance and opportunity" to
apply their minds to the foreign, unprecedented peoples and objects
they encountered. Most inquiries by Spaniards into the nature of
indigenous culture—including inquiries by missionaries such as
Sahagún—were driven by pragmatic considerations. But, Elliott
argues, the initial typifications used to understand the indigenous
population were bound to be altered through prolonged contact.
Spaniards in the sixteenth-century New World began altering their
previously monolithic view of the role of the indigenous population in the cosmos and came up with a number of variations. By the
end of the sixteenth century, Europeans were increasingly obsessed
with "the idea of a graded, and then of an evolutionary, scale of
being" (48). The very humanity of the indigenous population came
into question as Spaniards stacked their political deck by increasingly defining living "like a man" as living "like a Spaniard" (53).[3]
The unfavorable comparison between the Nahuas and the Spaniards
became the justification for using (or abusing) the autochthonous
peoples as a cheap form of wage labor.

Elliott argues that the only way that Europeans could break out
of the pattern of permanently relegating the indigenous population
to a life of suffering was by introducing a historical dimension to
their understanding of the New World's first inhabitants. Nevertheless, much of the indigenous world became explicable to the few
who chose this path only when theological interpretations of the pre-
Hispanic era were introduced. In Elliott's words, the devil became a
diabolus ex machina, capable of making sense of any puzzling feature of
the indigenous world and locating it at the same time in a cosmic
struggle between the forces of good and evil (59). For Europeans
like Sahagún, the devil served as a vehicle for salvaging the dignity
and humanity of the indigenous population. The indigenous population was viewed as emerging from an era of diabolic deception

under the guidance of the missionaries rather than as remaining trapped in the chains of the inherent deficiencies most Spaniards attributed to the Nahuas by the end of the sixteenth century.

Essentially, and perhaps ironically, the devil became a diabolus ex machina—or hermeneutic wild card—for precisely those Europeans who felt a certain degree of sympathy for the plight of the indigenous population. As children of Adam who had been led astray by the devil, the indigenous population became the responsibility of the more morally fortunate religious community sent by God's grace to the New World for the very purpose of bringing them back into His fold. The devil, however, was used as a hermeneutic wild card by different writers with varying degrees of emphasis, and with some degree of functional difference. In 1607, for example, Gregorio García, a Dominican friar, argued in his *Origen de los indios del Nuevo Mundo* that the devil incited the original inhabitants of the New World to invent their diabolically difficult languages as a way to hide and distort the true word of God. García hence interpreted all the linguistic enterprises of the missionaries in the New World in terms of the Christian struggle between good and evil forces (52–53).[4] In this view, wherever indigenous languages failed to coincide with European expectations of semantic content, the devil could be invoked to explain the discrepancy—a discrepancy, as I explained in chapter 3, that some missionaries had a hard time accepting for deeply held theological reasons.

The best approach to Sahagún's own peculiar use of the devil as a hermeneutic wild card is by way of comparison. Diego Durán, another Dominican friar, was a contemporary of Sahagún who was born in Seville but spent most of his life in New Spain. His *Historia de las Indias de Nueva España e Islas de la Tierra Firme* is commonly considered the most important ethnographic source on the colonial and precolonial Nahuas after Sahagún. Durán's history is replete with references to the devil. His principle contention, like Sahagún's, is that idolatrous practices lurk just below the surface of the Nahuas' purportedly Christian acts of devotion. Durán claims that the church in New Spain must begin as a tabula rasa because the Nahuas "join the Christian faith with something of the cult of the devil" (I:3). For Durán, the pre-Hispanic gods were demons (I:59), the indigenous priests were "ministers of Satan" (I:24), and their rites were "diabolic ceremonies" that parodied Christian rituals such as Holy Communion (I:35). Durán even extends the epithet "demonic" to indigenous ointments (I:52), musical sounds (I:54), and the use of flowers in ceremonies (I:151). Nevertheless, despite the frequent references in Durán's work to demonic practices, the devil does not bear the primary hermeneutic weight in the author's attempt to understand the alienness of Nahua culture. The pre-Hispanic period was a time when Satan reaped the fruits of the New World, but Durán turns to another—not unrelated—historical interpretation to explain the idiosyncrasies of Nahua culture and locate the Nahuas more squarely in Christianity's historical and theological trajectory. In Durán's eyes, the alienness of Nahua culture is primarily explainable in terms of their "Hebrew" past and fleeting contact with the sojourning apostle Saint Thomas, who was rebuffed in his efforts to convert such an obstinate people (I:11).

Durán delights in establishing parallels between Hebrew and Nahua customs, and he goes so far as to say that the Nahuas do not differ from the Hebrews in any respect:

In order to examine the certain and true account of the origin and beginning of these Indian nations which is so hidden from us and doubtful—in order to be able to establish the mere truth—some kind of divine revelation would be necessary, or a spirit of God who would teach it and make it understood. However, lacking these, it will be necessary to approach suspicions and conjectures, in the ample occasions that this people gives us, with their extremely low mode and manner of treatment, and of their such low conversation, so much belonging to that of the Jews, that we could ultimately affirm that they are originally Jews and Hebrew people. And I believe that he would not make a major error he who affirmed this, if it is taken into consideration their mode of living, their ceremonies, their rites and superstitions, their auguries and hypocrisies so related and belonging to those of the Jews, and which do not differ in any respect. For proof of this, Sacred Scripture will be a witness, where clearly and openly we will withdraw the truth of this opinion, and we will give some sufficient reasons to explain this. (II:13)

Durán goes on to claim that the most convincing indication that the Nahuas are of Hebrew descent is the obstinacy with which they cling to their idolatries and superstitions—in his opinion, the same Jewish practices that are documented in Holy Scripture (II:18). If the precolonial Nahuas were servants of Satan, they served him as Jews: it is as members of the ten lost tribes of Israel that the apparent idiosyncrasies of the Nahuas become meaningful in a profound and articulate way for Durán.

Like Durán and many other writers of the period, Sahagún may have entertained the idea that the Nahuas were of Jewish origin. Nevertheless, Sahagún does not share his contemporaries' penchant for wild speculation on this topic.[5] Rather, the interpretive weight of Sahagún's arguments is shifted in a different direction. Sahagún places more explanatory emphasis on the role of the devil in pre-Hispanic culture than Durán does. He also calls into play a different hermeneutic tradition in order to give his demonization of the Nahuas the depth and nuance necessary to explain the highly complex nature of precolonial religious beliefs and practices. Whereas the devil functions in Durán as a loose epithet with some vaguely defined referentiality, the devil in Sahagún's *Historia universal* is the object of a more scrutinizing analysis. One of the primary functions of the *Historia universal* is—especially in the early books—to serve as a demonology for Nahua idolatry.

Sahagún's conviction that the devil played a powerful role in pre-Hispanic Mexico—that the devil, alone and unchallenged before the coming of the friars, won the souls of the Nahuas—creates certain theological problems for him. The more power is attributed to the devil, the more he threatens the notion of an omnipotent God. As Jeffrey Burton Russell has emphasized in *Lucifer: The Devil in the Middle Ages*, "Intensely mystical, unitive modes of religious thought tend to find little place for an active spirit of evil in a cosmos where all things proceed from God and return to him" (32). The notion of a powerful, uninhibited devil threatens the very core of monotheism. Christian theologians from early on and throughout the Middle Ages countered the problem of dualistic religious thought by repeatedly affirming that evil is, essentially, "nothing." Augustine, John of Damascus, Aquinas, and other pillars of orthodox Christianity all held that evil was nothing more than the absence of good—the ultimate form of non-being—since God, from Dionysius on, is defined simply as He who *is* (Russell, 30).[6]

But, if evil is "nothing," then how is it that it exerts such power—why is it a threat at all? The church's complex answers to this question sometimes took theologians far away from the nuts and bolts of life's everyday problems, but one solution in particular mediated the tension between the palpable feeling of evil and the definition of evil as the anti-ontological privation of good. Medieval thinkers such as Isidore of Seville assigned a hierarchy of ranks and grades to evil spirits or demons. Evil and evil spirits were envisioned in terms of a quasi-social hierarchy that placed them at increasingly far distances from God and with greater degrees of impotence and nonexistence. Hence, as Russell notes, Dante's absurdly depicted Lucifer adheres more to theology than to popular sentiment in his state of pathetic, essential ignorance and lack of being as he lays trapped at the furthest remove from God (227–30). The medieval emphasis on a hierarchy of both celestial and infernal entities (a kind of personification of virtues and vices) enabled people to determine that, no matter how much power was attributed to forces of evil, no matter how present the devil and his band of demons seemed to be in the world, God was always in control at the pinnacle of the cosmic order.

Sahagún's emphasis on describing and identifying the Nahua gods in Book I of the *Florentine Codex* grew out of this kind of tension. If Sahagún was going to attribute so much power in the New World to the devil and yet avoid the heretical pitfalls of dualism— the belief that evil exists on par with good—it was going to be necessary to expose and delineate a comprehensive hierarchy of evil

Nahua demons that made sense in terms of medieval theology. For a model to map out and pinpoint the vagaries of the devil and his legion of demons in New Spain, Sahagún turned to one of the most important canonical texts of the Christian tradition: Saint Augustine's *City of God*.

Sahagún scholars have paid scant attention to the prologue of Book III of the *Florentine Codex*, in which Saint Augustine is singled out as an auctor who lends theological legitimacy to the kind of demonology Sahagún envisioned.[7] The prologue is worth quoting in its entirety, because it sets forth clearly the relationship between Saint Augustine's *City of God* and the first five books of the *Florentine Codex*:

The divine Augustine did not consider it a superfluous or vain thing, the treatment of the fabulous theology of the gentiles in the sixth book of the *City of God*. Because, as he says, if the vain fables and fictions that the gentiles held with respect to their faked gods are known, then they could easily be made to understand that they were not gods, nor could they provide rational creatures with anything beneficial. For this reason, in this third book, the fables and fictions that these natives held concerning their gods are written down, because, understanding the vanities that they held for faith concerning their lying gods, they will come more easily, through the doctrine of the Gospel, to know the true God, and that those who they held as gods were not gods but lying and deceiving demons, and if someone thinks that these things are so forgotten and lost, and that the faith in one God is so implanted and rooted among these natives that there will be no need at any time to speak of these things—this I piously believe, but I know for sure that the devil never sleeps nor has he forgotten the honor these natives paid him, and he is waiting for the opportunity to be able to come back to the kingdom he had held. And at that time, it would be an easy thing for him to awaken all the things that are said to be forgotten about idolatry. And for such an occasion it is good that we keep our weapons at the ready in order to go out and meet him in the attack. And for this, not only will what is written in this third book be useful but what is written in the first, second, fourth, and fifth as well. Nor will there be an opportunity then for his disciples to deceive the faithful and the preachers with gilding, with lies and trickery, with the vanities and improprieties that they held with respect to the faith of their gods and their cult, because the clean and pure truths that declare who their gods were and what services they demanded, as they are contained in the aforementioned books, will appear. End of prologue. (*CF* III:"Prologo")

This passage is especially important for understanding Sahagún's mentality because it is virtually the only place where Sahagún makes an explicit reference to an author he used as a model for his own work.

Augustine's *City of God* provided Sahagún with a useful conceptual framework for interpreting Nahua religion. For example, as an auctor—a canonical author within the Christian tradition who lends legitimacy to an idea or practice—Augustine was almost without par. Given its content, the *City of God* could easily serve as a justification for delving into the religious past of a non-Christian culture like that of the Nahuas. Augustine set forth in elaborate detail the beliefs surrounding the deities of antiquity in order to expose their falsehood and subject them to ridicule. Sahagún states quite clearly that this is his intention as well. Contrary to the wishful thinking of many critics, Sahagún did not write in detail about Nahua deities because he admired their religion.[8] He did admire the fervor with which the Nahuas adored their gods, but most of his admiration for their culture lay elsewhere.

Sahagún shared with Augustine—and most people of the Middle Ages[9]—the idea that the pagan gods were not just false, they were actual demons intent on deceiving human beings. Hence, in the prologue cited above, Sahagún states his fear that the devil and his "satelites" (demons) only lie waiting for the opportunity to return to their "*señorio*" (dominion/estate). Since Sahagún perceives the devil as an evil ruler with a spiritually perverse polity of demons under his command, the best way to prepare for their return is to establish their hierarchical order and unmask their deceptions beforehand:

This god, called Huitzilopochtli was another Hercules. (*CF* I:1r)

This god, called Painal, was like a military right-hand-man of the afore-mentioned because he dictated as the highest captain when there would be war against certain provinces. (1r–1v)

The third chapter treats the god called Tezcatlipoca, who generally was held to be a god by these natives of New Spain: he is another Jupiter. (1v)

The seventh chapter treats the goddess who was called Chicome Coatl: she is another Ceres. (3r)

The eleventh chapter treats the goddess of water, who was called Chalchiuhtlicue: she is another Juno. (5r)

The twelfth chapter treats the goddess of carnal things, who was called Tlazalteotl: she is another Venus. (10r)

Sahagún's comparison between the Nahua gods and the gods of antiquity (inevitably) does not constitute a perfect one-on-one correspondence, but it does represent something much more profound than a polite gesture to European readers who might need help interpreting the alien nature of his material.[10] By identifying the Nahua gods with the gods of antiquity, Sahagún lends more credibility to the notion that the indigenous gods are actual demons capable both of demanding perverse honors and of possessing individuals. For example, the god Tezcatzoncatl is identified with Bacchus in the corner of the illustration depicting him (*CF* I: unnumbered), and Sahagún argues that the Nahuas did not consider drinking or drunken acts a sin because it meant they were possessed by this god, "or, better said, the devil" (*CF* I:23v). Sahagún interprets this defense as a form of moral irresponsibility, but he sometimes sympathizes with the Nahuas' inability to resist the machinations of a powerful devil:

I do not believe that there is a heart so hard that on hearing of a cruelty so inhumane, more than bestial, and demonic like the one described above it would not soften and be moved to tears, horror, and fright. And certainly it is a lamentable and horrible thing to see our human nature brought down so low and base: that parents, on the suggestion of the devil, kill and eat their children without thinking they were committing any offense, but rather thinking they were doing a great service to their gods. The blame of this cruel blindness that was executed through these unfortunate children should not so much be placed on the cruelty of the parents, who shed many tears and with much pain in their heart did this, so much as on the extremely cruel hatred of our age-old enemy Satan, who with extremely evil cleverness persuaded them to do such an infernal thing. (*CF* II:17v)

Sahagún exposes the falsehood of some of the Nahua gods—Quetzalcoatl, for example—by arguing that they were really nothing more than mortals whom the Nahuas worshiped as gods under the guidance of the devil (*CF* I:2r–v; 35v–36r). This also finds a parallel in the *City of God*. In his critique of Marcus Terentius Varro, for example, Augustine argues that the human origin of several pagan gods undermines their veracity and that the absurd practice of worshiping mortals was brought on by demons (243). Augustine believes in general that the "demons' greatest desire is to deceive" (176), and that they are willing to go to any length—no matter how grotesque—in order to drag others down with them.[11] In order to expose the machinations of the demons and demonstrate the falsehood of the Roman gods, Augustine does not rely solely on the message of Christianity. His method is systematically to turn the classical sources against themselves in order to expose the absurd, contradictory nature of idolatry—a nature that is a grotesque inversion of true religion.[12] This, too, is Sahagún's general technique, except that in his case, his sources must first be culled from oral sources and then written down.

The relevance of Sahagún's use of Augustine as a model becomes clearest in his appendix to Book I of the *Florentine Codex*. In order to refute the idolatry of the Nahuas, Sahagún relies on the authority of the Bible. He chooses in particular chapters 12 through 15 of the Book of Wisdom. Nevertheless, although these chapters make a strong case against idolatry, the Book of Wisdom does so by emphasizing the distinction between God and the created world, not the machinations of evil spirits. The central argument against idolatry is that idolaters worship lifeless, human-made objects. In one passage, idolaters are described as "being deceived, like silly children," but the text does not make any explicit reference to a deceiver (Wis 12:24). Rather, the blame is placed squarely on the shoulders of the idolaters themselves: "*naturally* stupid are all men who have not known God and who, from the good things that are seen, have not been able to discover Him-who-is" (Wis 13:1, my emphasis). The Book of Wisdom is an apt choice for refuting idolatry, because it treats the topic in a clear, pithy manner, but it fails on the whole to explain any role the devil might play in idolatrous cultures. In general, the Book of Wisdom adheres quite well to the orthodox view that evil, literally, is nothing. Sahagún remedies this limitation, however, by inserting references to the devil in his commentary and paraphrastic version of the text.

The appendix to Book I is designed for Nahua ears and friars' mouths. The prologue to it, written in Nahuatl with a Spanish translation that follows, argues that the purpose of the appendix is to save the Nahuas from the devil's grasp so that they can rule with God in heaven (*CF* I:24v). The text then consists of passages from the Book of Wisdom in Latin and a loose Nahuatl translation. One passage from the Book of Wisdom seems to be of particular interest to Sahagún: "Hence judgement shall fall on the idols themselves of the heathen, since, although part of God's creation, they have become an abomination, snares for the souls of men, a pitfall for the feet of the reckless" (Wis 14:11).[13] Even though the greater context of the Book of Wisdom would imply that the idols are mere *things* that God now holds in abomination,[14] Sahagún interprets the idols to be actual demons in his translation of the passage into Nahuatl: "These, *the demons*, were the cause of idolatry. For never will God have mercy upon them" (*FC* I:58, my emphasis). In a sense, Sahagún's insertion of a clarification in this short passage serves as the conceptual bridge to the refutation of idolatry that follows the quotations from the Book of Wisdom in Sahagún's appendix.

At the beginning of this next section in the appendix, Sahagún declares that the texts from the Book of Wisdom are sufficient for demonstrating the "great evil" of idolatry and idolaters, but he believes a different version is necessary for less intelligent people: "But in order to come down to the level of people of low understanding, it is suitable to refute this cursed vice with its great specificity" (*CF* I:29v–30r). Sahagún believes that he is merely applying the ideas of the Book of Wisdom to the particular context of New Spain, but his version for "less intelligent" people places him squarely in the tradition of Augustine and others who saw pagan gods as actual, powerful demons who could be labeled and unmasked. Sahagún begins his confutation by repeating "*amo teutl*" ("is not a god") after the name of each deity. He then states in a passage that is more likely from *The City of God* than the Bible: "For all are demons, evil spirits, as it is in the word of God: *Omnes dii gentium demonia*; that is to say, All whom the idolaters worship, all are devils, demons, evil spirits" (*FC* I:64).

This sets the tone for the entire section, and Sahagún proceeds to refute the divinity of the Nahua gods one by one. He identifies Tezcatlipoca with the devil himself:

Likewise we know that in times past, everywhere here in New Spain, there was worship of Tezcatlipoca. And they [also] named him Titlacauan, and Yaotl, Necoc yaotl, Moyocoya, Neçaualpilli. This Tezcatlipoca, the ancients went on to say, was a true god; his abode was everywhere—in the land of the dead, on earth, in heaven. When he walked upon the earth he quickened war; he quickened vice, filth; he brought anguish, affliction to men; he brought discord among men, wherefore he was called "the enemy of both sides." He mocked men, he ridiculed men. He was called wind, shadow. This wicked Tezcatlipoca, we know, is Lucifer, the great devil who there in the midst of Heaven, even in the beginning, began war, vice, filth. From there he was cast out, from there he fell. But he walketh here upon the earth deceiving men, tricking men. For so is the word of God: Factum est proelium magnum in coelo. Apoc., 12. That is, a great war was fought in the midst of Heaven, which Lucifer began. This Tezcatlipoca Titlacauan is a great devil. The ancients worshipped him, and they celebrated his feast day when [it was the month of] Toxcatl, and they slew his representation, whom they named Titlacauan. So much were the ancients in confusion. (*FC* I:67–68)

Sahagún continues on in this vein with other gods until the end, when he asks all Nahuas who know of the idolatry he has described to denounce sinners to the holy church. He argues that those who know of idolatry and refuse to denounce it are devils ("*diablome*") themselves (FC I:75).

The appendix of Book I ends with a prayer written in Nahuatl for those neophytes who hope to leave behind the demonic realm of sin that Sahagún has just described. In the prayer, Nahuas are asked to lament the lies and error that had reigned in New Spain for over eight hundred years and to contemplate "the hatred of the demon of the air, of Satan, for men" (*FC* I:76). Sahagún even inserts a question for God in the prayer: "Why hast Thou not known them [the people of New Spain]?" (*FC* I:76). It is unclear to Sahagún why God could let the people of New Spain stay in spiritual darkness for so long, but Sahagún does have clear, graphic ideas about what the nature of this darkness was.

Sahagún needed his dissection of Nahua deities to be comparable to Augustine's in order to affirm his sense that evil was a concrete enemy who "walked" among the "heathen" of New Spain and yet retain the idea that the devil (Satan/Lucifer)[15] and his army of demons were hierarchically subservient to God and his court of celestial entities. The enormous amount of power that Sahagún ascribes to the devil is related to a more general phenomenon of early modernity, but his use of Augustine as a model to construct a demonology is somewhat unique. In early modern Europe—especially during the second half of the sixteenth century and first half of the seventeenth—the theological notion that the devil was essentially impotent or was a mere figurehead for the privation of good began to break down. Learned Europeans were given the church's support to write and employ numerous demonologies for the express purpose of checking the devil's growing influence. As Jean Delumeau puts it in *La peur en Occident*, "Unmasking Satan was one of the great enterprises of the beginning of the modern times" (319). Such works as Heinrich Kramer and James Sprenger's *Malleus Maleficarum* (1484) and Martín del Río's *Disquisitionum Magicarum* (1599) served as models for a growing progeny of manuals and treatises that sought to prove that the devil really was a puppet of God or God's ape (*simia dei*) despite the perceived increase in phenomena that seemed to indicate the contrary view. Much of the content of this new genre centered on the problem of what evil spirits were actually capable of doing versus what they could trick people into thinking they could do.[16]

All in all, the exhaustive details of these manuals constitute an attempt to catalogue, sort, and explain the increasingly strange phenomena of an increasingly complex social world. To early modern Europeans, the world seemed increasingly evil and threatening.[17] The devil, and the witches possessed by him, took up the interpretive slack needed to explain why God could seem so much like an absentee landlord in the affairs of mortals.

Throughout the Middle Ages, social institutions in general (including knowledge) were perceived as fundamentally unchanging. This reification of the social order led to a situation in which the world of institutions appeared to merge with the world of nature. As Peter Berger and Thomas Luckmann have noted in *The Social Construction of Reality*, certain social and historical factors like overall institutional crises, social marginality, and contact between previously segregated societies favor the dereification of the social world (90–92). In general, the growing prevalence of the devil in early modernity can be interpreted as an attempt to make sense of a dynamic, complex natural and social world that no longer corresponded to the reified vision of society presented by the dominant tradition of the Middle Ages. Sahagún's use of the devil as a hermeneutic wild card is symptomatic of this general phenomenon of the transition to modernity, but he also stands apart from his European contemporaries for the important and interesting reason that his obsession grew out of the unique context of proselytism in New Spain. The devil constituted a post hoc way for the friars to reconcile the alienness of Nahua culture with the Christian tradition, but Sahagún's exaggerated emphasis on the role of the devil in New Spain led him to construct an unparalleled hermeneutic scaffolding to support the idea. Sahagún's demons are far more nuanced and have far more substance than the demons of contemporaries such as Durán, but Sahagún also wrote a kind of demonology that differs in many respects from the demonologies being written in Europe at the time. Unlike most European authors of demonologies, Sahagún felt profound admiration for many of the Nahuas' accomplishments as a civilization, which complicated his assessment of the Nahua world. This aspect of Sahagún's thinking was an important factor in his shaping of the *Historia universal* as a demonology as well as in his evolving notion of the nature of knowledge.

2. Knowledge

The title *City of God* has led some scholars to the false conclusion that Augustine was antistate or that he wanted to contrast the City of God with the City of Man in a strict good-versus-evil binarism.[18] This misconception can lend authority to the kind of contempt-of-the-world (*contemptus mundi*) spiritualism that has resonated in Europe at least from the twelfth century, when Bernard of Cluny wrote his satirical *De contemptu mundi* (ca. 1140). However, this interpretation is based on a profound misreading of Augustine's purpose. Augustine does indeed single out "the city of this world" for condemnation, but this is because mortals, through the sin of pride, have misconstrued their achievements to be the product of their own doing or the doings of false gods rather than *gifts* from God. The argument in the *City of God*, in fact, is shaped by

Augustine's need to reconcile what he admitted were Rome's achievements with its unacceptable polytheism. In order to do this, for example, he argues at one point that virtuous Romans earned the increase of their empire (a temporal reward) as a gift from God even though they did not worship Him (196–224).

Augustine's professed admiration for certain aspects of Roman culture was perhaps inevitable since this was the culture that first shaped him. Accepting Christianity in its entirety initially presented a difficult hurdle for Augustine for this very reason. For example, since he was steeped in the Roman rhetorical tradition, he initially found the low style of the Latin translation of Holy Scripture to be unpalatable. Augustine overcame this initial aversion by arguing, in *On Christian Doctrine* and elsewhere, that the low style of Holy Scripture was actually an intentional use of language that paralleled Jesus Christ's state as the human embodiment of God. The low style of Scripture represented the true, sublime "humility" that was required for any rapprochement to God.[19]

Augustinian thought, then, was defined by a need to sort the bad from the good in pre-Christian Roman culture in order to reconcile his conversion with his Roman formation. Any attribute of Roman culture, or any attribute of his own, that he did not wish to discard needed to be providentially subsumed to the God of the Christians. This, in brief, is the aspect of Augustinian thought that proved most appealing—and even necessary—to Sahagún. Nahua culture presented Sahagún with many of the same dilemmas that pre-Christian European culture did. Namely, why did God deny to some parts of human history the redemption provided by the birth of Jesus Christ? Or, phrased differently, why did God permit the devil and his bands of demons to roam the earth unchallenged by the Savior for so long? And, most important for Sahagún, how could any aspect of pre-Christian Nahua culture be worthy of safeguarding if the Nahuas' world was governed by the Prince of Evil?

Augustine provides an answer to this dilemma in a way that contemporary European demonologies did not. Whereas European demonologies of the early modern period are primarily concerned with ferreting out demonic practices and knowledge in order to destroy them, Augustine sets forth a way to unmask the machinations of demons and yet indirectly attribute any positive features of a pagan culture to the benevolence of God. For Sahagún, this was more than an idle question because he needed to prove to himself and others that the Nahuas as a culture had produced something that made them worthy of the full benefits of conversion rather than the systematic destruction or enslavement that many Europeans advocated.

It is no accident that the principal features of Nahua culture that Sahagún admires are their government, their rhetoric, and their philosophy. These attributes parallel the elements of antiquity that Augustine hoped to preserve in a selective or renovated fashion. Sahagún writes that the almost total destruction of the Nahuas by the Spaniards has led to the false impression that they are "barbarians" or a people of very base mettle, while, in reality, "in political things, they are a step ahead of many other nations" (*CF* I:"Prologo"). Sahagún goes on to compare their history directly to antiquity:

This famous and great city of Tula—very rich, with a wise people, and very forceful—had the adverse fortune of Troy. The Chololtecas, who are those who escaped from there, have had the outcome of the Romans, and like the Romans built the capitol as their fortress. . . . Many years afterward the Mexicans built the City of Mexico, which is another Venice, and in knowledge and government, they are other Venetians. (*CF* I:"Prologo")

He makes these same comparisons in the prologue to Book VIII of the *Florentine Codex*—the book that treats the Nahua lords and kings.

Something similar happens in the prologue to Book VI, where Sahagún argues that the Nahuas had an extremely advanced level of rhetoric and moral philosophy comparable to "the Greeks, Latins, Spaniards, French, and Italians: there are books full of this material."

In a manner similar to Augustine, Sahagún argues that these "virtues" explain how the Nahuas established an empire (*CF* VI:"Prologo"). But like "our forefathers," the Greeks and Latins, the Nahuas fell, and were led, into sin despite their virtues:

It is clear through their own writings that the gentiles, our ancestors—the Greeks as much as the Latins—were foolish in their knowledge of the created world. Their writings tell us of the ridiculous fables they invented about the sun, the moon, (and some) the stars, the water, earth, fire, and air, and of other creations, what is worse, they attributed them with divinity, and they adored them, made offerings to them, sacrificed to them, and heeded them as if they were gods.

This was a result, in part, of the blindness into which we fell through original sin, and in part through the malice and the age-old hatred of our adversary Satan, who always manages to drive us to vile, ridiculous, and very blameworthy things. (*CF* VII:"Prologo")

The most interesting thing about this passage is the use of the inclusive first-person plural. Sahagún maintains that the Nahuas are essentially no different than "our" own antecedents, the Greeks and Latins. The Nahuas stand together with the ancient Greeks and Romans—with both their virtues and their vices—on the other side of a fence that was posted in time with the arrival of Christ and Christianity. For Sahagún, Christianity redeems and completes the limited virtues of the Nahuas the same way it recuperates the achievements of antiquity in a book like the *City of God*—virtues and achievements that were possible in spite of Satan's reign of evil.

Sahagún's use of Augustine as a model provides room for a positive kind of knowledge that early modern Europe's demonologies did not permit. Sahagún shares with his contemporary demonologists the desire to unearth evil practices, but this goal is balanced by the need to demonstrate the Nahuas' worthiness. In the very passage where Sahagún points to Augustine as an auctor, he divides his *Historia universal* into two characteristically different segments. Books I through V are directly designed to set forth the absurdity of Nahua paganism in the manner of Augustine (*CF* III:"Prologo"). The following books, which deal with more worldly matters, leave more room for praise of Nahua culture.

This division follows the Augustinian idea of the limits of what is achievable in a culture without the direct intervention of Christianity. For Sahagún, the devil ruled antiquity in the same way he ruled pre-Hispanic New Spain, but, in spite of their "blindness," both cultures were able to achieve a certain degree of moral success as civilizations. Nevertheless, this strange symmetry creates certain cognitive problems for an author such as Sahagún who is steeped in the learning and manners of the medieval worldview. Augustine enables Sahagún to recuperate many facets of Nahua culture as something compatible with medieval knowledge even though the inherited canon does not directly refer to the Nahuas. However, this encapsulation of the Nahuas as a people similar in some profound sense to the Greeks and Romans inevitably stretched the very limits of the medieval conceptualization of knowledge. The crucial difference between Augustine's reconciliation with certain features of the Roman world and Sahagún's acceptance of certain Nahua achievements is the fact that the very existence of Rome as a civilization was not in doubt when Augustine wrote the *City of God*. Roman and Greek culture was manifest as both an oral and written tradition—a body of knowledge—that needed to be negotiated in order to accept the then alien tenets of Christianity. Sahagún, however, was faced with the challenge of proving that a civilization in New Spain that was comparable in some respects with Rome even existed in the past. Sahagún, in essence, needed to provide proof that a corpus of knowledge worthy of European scrutiny and approbation existed among the Nahuas before the Spaniards turned their world upside down. This led to Sahagún's famous use of indigenous informants—a *concession* that was prompted by the fact that the Nahuas had no written tradition in the eyes of the Spaniards.

Walter Mignolo has noted that the European tradition encoded knowledge in the written word whereas the Nahuas encoded knowledge in the world itself—in the constellations, for example ("Signs," 253). Another way of saying this is that knowledge for the Nahuas was more "life-worldly" (grounded in immediate expression) than medieval European forms of knowledge, which were primarily concerned with the afterlife and the *inner* coherency of texts handed down from the past. This distinction is interesting because it is similar to a distinction Blumenberg makes between medieval and modern knowledge systems in *The Legitimacy of the Modern Age*. Blumenberg argues that the strength of the medieval system that is epitomized by scholasticism lay in its relative indifference to life-worldly success or failure (i.e., applications of knowledge to the world). Medieval knowledge is characterized by the self-contained nature of its logic and a complex process of arbitration that long defers the ramifications of any contradiction. This aspect of medieval knowledge is even apparent in relatively mundane genres. Alfonso X's *Lapidario*, for instance, is notable for its indifference to whether or not the stones described actually exist in the world, despite the fact that they are attributed with curative powers.

The strength of the modern system, in contrast, "lay in its being oriented toward continued, almost daily confirmations and 'life-worldly' successes of its 'method'" (Blumenberg, 472–73). Sahagún's use of indigenous informants seems modern at first because it pushes his work into the cognitive realm of the life-worldly, but it is important to note that the life-worldly character of Sahagún's *Historia universal* was immediately checked by features that are primarily indicative of a medieval form of knowledge. Once Sahagún had gathered his information—once he had established his Nahuatl canon, in a sense—he seemed more interested in subjecting it to the demands of *internal logic* set forth by a medieval knowledge system. This internal logic was provided in part by the imposition of European structuring devices (like the ones I outlined in chapters 2 and 3). It was also provided by the ironing out of wrinkles that inevitably revealed the naturally diverse, contradictory nature of Nahua culture—a diversity that was facilitated by the fact that Nahua

culture was not grounded in a relatively more stable (but not necessarily better) alphabetized book culture.[20]

One of the (unconscious) appeals of Sahagún's *Historia universal* for
ethnohistorians is its combination of rich detail and homogeneity.
Sahagún seems like the last word on Nahua culture in part because
his material so seldom contradicts itself. Nevertheless, it would be a
mistake to assume that this homogeneity was the natural result of
the internal coherence of Nahua culture. Durán's continual emphasis
on regional differences in his own history, for example, belies the
notion that such constructs as the Nahua pantheon of deities
found in Sahagún were equally applicable to all areas of the Nahua
world. Moreover, the fact that Sahagún spent much more time
organizing and editing his materials than gathering them should
create a certain amount of healthy suspicion among present-day
scholars. Sahagún spent two years in Tepepulco gathering his original
information and then a year and a half in Tlaltelolco with Nahuas
who "amended, explained, and supplemented" the original information (*CF* I:"Prologo"). But then, off and on, Sahagún tinkered
with the history over the course of the rest of his uncommonly
long life. In short, after Sahagún's brief concession to using the life-
worldly experiences of Nahua informants to gather his material, he
retreated into what is a decidedly unmodern systematization of this
new-found knowledge. The original information was no longer
tested against the world, but rather tested against itself in an
attempt to smooth over internal discrepancies. From the perspective
of modern academic disciplines, it is difficult to understand why or
how Sahagún could choose to do this; and it is small wonder that
Sahagún scholars have tended to emphasize his use of informants
and to downplay his own substantial input. The only way to understand this aspect of Sahagún, however, is to try to stop interpreting
his methodology in terms of the telos of present-day ideas about
the nature of knowledge.

Sahagún did not emerge from a cultural situation in which knowledge for its own sake was considered an acceptable alternative—or

even a supplement—to knowledge that led one closer to God. In fact—as Blumenberg has shown—from Augustine to the end of the Middle Ages, curiosity (*curiositas*) was considered a vice because it turned one's attention outward to the world rather than inward to one's spiritual well-being (Blumenberg, 309–23). Augustine states it this way at one point in his *Confessions*, when he criticizes the Manichees for attributing to themselves humanly produced knowledge:

O Lord God of truth, if a man is to please you, surely it is not enough that he should know facts like these? Even if he knows them all, he is not happy unless he knows you; but the man who knows you is happy, even if he knows none of these things. And the man who knows you, and knows these things as well, is none the happier for his knowledge of them: he is happy only because he knows you, and then only if he has knowledge of you and honours you and gives you thanks as God and does not become fantastic in his notions. (94–95)

Curiosity also signals that there is a disjunction between a person and the cosmological order—a subjective eccentricity to the world that has profound ethical implications for a medieval schema in which everyone and everything has a proper, divinely ordained place in the universe: "Only the metaphysical suspicion that nature could function without regard to man in its lawfully regulated processes makes urgent and necessary a knowledge of nature that can examine each state of affairs merely for its *potential* relevance to man" (Blumenberg, 318, his emphasis). Blumenberg shows that Augustine—and subsequent thinkers of the Middle Ages—opposed memory (*memoria*) to curiosity because "only by memory can what gets lost in dispersion be grasped; memory gives man the authentic relation— which makes him independent of the world—to his origin, to his metaphysical 'history,' and thus to his transcendent contingency" (315). During the Middle Ages, curiosity was perceived as nothing more than a distraction from true knowledge—a knowledge that can only be revealed by God and safeguarded with the memory provided by the written word.

Sahagún's use of informants is a concession that is not easily embraced because—as he notes himself in the prologue to Book II—it is only the result of the Nahuas' lack of a written canon (memoria, in the medieval sense of the word) that is safeguarded by "authorities." Sahagún's aversion to the kind of knowledge now characterized positively as modern is even more explicit in the prologue to Book V. Here, more than anywhere else, Sahagún sets forth his disapproval of a knowledge produced by unfettered curiosity:

Because of their appetite to know more, our first parents deserved to be deprived of the original knowledge that had been given to them and to fall into the very dark night of ignorance in which they left all of us. Still not having lost that appetite, we do not cease to persist, to want to investigate, rightly or wrongly, that which we ignore—that which concerns natural things and that which concerns supernatural things. And even though to know many of these things we have many ways, and very certain ones, we are not happy with this. Rather, through illicit and forbidden ways we manage to know the things which our God is not served by us knowing, such as things of the future and secret things. And this is learnt sometimes via the devil. (*CF* V:"Prologo")

The kind of intellectual "appetite" or curiosity that Sahagún condemns inspired a kind of profound moral fear at the end of the Middle Ages that is difficult to appreciate now. Blumenberg gives the example of Petrarch, who climbed a mountain for the sheer thrill of discovering something unknown—"purely out of the desire to see the unusual altitude of this place"—and thought better of it (quoted in Blumenberg, 341). Petrarch opens an edition of Augustine's *Confessions* to a passage in Book X and is overcome with remorse for having admired earthly things. He turns his attention inward, and "Nature now shrinks into insignificance: 'Et vix unius cubiti altitudo visa est prae altitudine contemplationis humanae' [And it appears scarcely a cubit in height in comparison to the loftiness of human contemplation]" (342).

Petrarch's struggle with the temptations of curiositas finds its parallel in the New World. Durán describes in a similar manner the resistance nature sets forth when human beings turn to the world for (idle) knowledge. Durán recounts the story of a Spaniard who tried to climb a volcanic mountain in New Spain "in order to consummate and give satisfaction to his passion—which I myself have" (*Historia* I:164). The volcano, however, erupted just as he was reaching the summit. Durán notes that several others have failed as well and decides that he will not pursue this "passion." The sinfulness of this passion is made even more clear when Durán notes that only witches and necromancers could possibly reach the summit (I:164). The friars were suspicious of the demonic nature of the mountains in New Spain because the Nahuas venerated them as gods. When Sahagún climbs to the top of a mountain—as he says he does in Book XI—its altitude is described as "monstrous" and as a place of "much idolatry" (*CF* XI:232v).

Blumenberg notes that curiosity did not become a positive attribute of knowledge in the modern age until the scholastic notion that reality was transcendent became fully eroded (353). The idea that human beings had a fundamental *right* to knowledge did not begin to emerge until the seventeenth century, with such thinkers as Francis Bacon. Even so, Bacon rearranged the biblical paradise as a utopian goal of human history in order to justify human curiosity (386). Bacon only valorized human curiosity as a vehicle for returning from exile to a union with a God who had become hidden from view. Curiosity was not depersonalized as the driving power of humanity's progress and knowledge until the Enlightenment. By the end of the eighteenth century, the world was no longer perceived as something made for human beings, and curiosity was interpreted as a vital, distinctly human attribute that was necessary for wresting knowledge from an indifferent world (396–405). Blumenberg asserts that by the nineteenth century God ceased to be the primary object of the "beyond" of knowledge to which curiosity drives humanity (439).

It is this very recent sense of the self-explanatory value of curiosity—its indifference to any kind of transcendental legitimization—

that scholars have tried to attribute retroactively to Sahagún. Sahagún's work, however, is shaped by the very fact that he was uncomfortable with this kind of godless curiosity. The fact that God had hidden himself from the Nahuas for so long, and hidden the Nahuas from Europeans as well, prompted Sahagún to fill in this empty space in the existing stock of medieval knowledge in a manner that was as unobjectionable to his medieval sensibilities as possible. The popular notion that the European format of the *Historia universal* was Sahagún's way of mediating the alienness of Nahua culture for a European audience is a deceptive half-truth. Sahagún was mediating Nahua culture as much for himself as for anyone else. A corpus of Nahua knowledge could only be acceptable to the extent it made sense in terms of the prevailing, medieval view of the world. Sahagún did not look into the worldly matters of the Nahuas out of idle curiosity; he looked into the world of the Nahuas for the sole purpose of establishing what their relationship to God's Christian order was. Anything that looks like the functional equivalent of the modern sense of curiosity in the *Historia universal* is potentially fulfilling one of two purposes, from Sahagún's standpoint: Either it is necessary to look into the world of the Nahuas—not knowing what one will find—in order to determine what damage Satan has done, or it is necessary to discover what aspects of Nahua culture exist that guarantee them a place in God's preexisting order.

The intentions I attribute here to Sahagún, however, inevitably differ to some degree from what can actually be seen in the *Historia universal*. Since the utter futility of trying to press the world of the Nahuas into a European scheme of things seems obvious today, it is easy to spot the elements of Sahagún's work that defy easy classification. This, however, does not mean that Sahagún wanted or encouraged information that made no sense in terms of European structures and ideas. Rather, it is indicative of a cultural tension that Sahagún was finally unable to overcome. Descriptions like that of the good turkey seller versus the bad turkey seller in Book X exhibit just how desperately Sahagún struggled to impose some order on a body of information that, from a European vantage, seemed to be flying out of control.

In his book *Satanism and Witchcraft*, Jules Michelet directly credits demonic practices with the birth of modern knowledge: "The Devil is now popular, and active everywhere; he appears to have won the day. But does he really profit by his victory? Does he gain in actual, substantial influence? Yes! from the view of that scientific revolt that is to give us the bright, light-bringing renaissance" (142). With much irony, he contrasts demonic knowledge favorably with the "barren dogmas of Aquinas" and an obstinate church that was unable to keep up with the immediate needs of a suffering populace (72). In Michelet's view, true knowledge could only come about by revolting against the church and turning to Satan's domain: nature and science. Michelet tells the story of this revolt, however, with the nineteenth century as his clear telos. He rejects the idea that medieval knowledge could be judged by any criterion other than a modern one defined by progress. For him, medieval knowledge is "paralysed": "Between Abelard and Occam the progress made is—nil!" (xviii).

Progress, however, was not the goal of medieval knowledge. Preservation and elucidation were. Sahagún stands on a threshold of knowledge because his experience with the Nahuas tested the limits of a knowledge that was primarily defined through *memoria*. It is misleading, however, to interpret Sahagún as a foundational figure of modern knowledge. The notion of a foundational figure assumes a complete or near-complete rupture with the past, but this kind of rupture was the last thing Sahagún intended. If Michelet's devils mark the beginning of modern knowledge, Sahagún's devils—in tandem with his novel use of antiquity—mark the desperate attempt to shore up a medieval conceptualization of knowledge that could no longer bear the weight of complex, contradictory, life-worldly information like that found among the Nahuas in sixteenth-century New Spain.

NOTES

Introduction

1. This is now spelled Tlatelolco.

2. For the most thorough description of this corpus, see Jesús Bustamante García's "La obra etnográfica " and *Fray Bernardino*.

3. This necrological tradition often took the form of menologies—a genre in which brief biographical descriptions of holy people, normally saints, are assigned to the days of a calendar. Sahagún, for example, is included in Fray Agustín de Vetancurt's seventeenth-century menology, *Teatro mexicano*. See the entry for 23 October.

4. Here, if more explicitness is needed, is the definition on which I rely: "Reality" can be defined as "phenomena that we recognize as having a being independent of our volition (we cannot 'wish them away')" (Berger and Luckmann, 1). Nevertheless, human beings perceive and interact with reality according to the structural contours and limitations of our embodied cognitive faculties. Moreover, these faculties have a phylogenetic and ontogenetic history that is complicated—but not doomed—by the fact that no one can ever see the world entirely from someone else's perspective. In short, what constitutes knowledge of the "real" will partly depend on the individual, the culture, the time, and the circumstances in question.

5. For example, no one knows whether or not Fray Junípero Serra will be canonized in the end, but the current drive in this direction is in part responsible for the enrichment and improved focus of the holdings of an archival center in Southern California.

6. See, for example, Jacques Le Goff's essay "For an Extended Middle Ages."

7. This element of Sahagún's work draws into question the appropriateness of the historically embedded term "modernity," but, for lack of a better word, it will be employed throughout.

8. The early stage of the increasingly active role over time that the "modern" individual plays in the determination of knowledge is often articulated in

Renaissance studies in terms of the "dignity of man" topos. After the eighteenth century—and most notably with Nietzsche—the role of subjectivity in the production of knowledge was more fully or radically articulated as the notion that the human mind is *inescapably* an active, constitutive element in the production of knowledge. The emphasis on this inescapability undermined the very possibility of knowledge based on Truth, and hence the "dignity" of the human mind has been subjected to a more variegated array of interpretations.

9. Elsewhere, Geertz directly applies this notion of cultural relativism to thinking in all of its multifarious forms and argues for the viability of an "ethnography" of the thought processes. See "The Way We Think Now."

10. "Alterity" connotes a lack of *identification* with a given community, culture, gender, or anything else that is perceived as "other" than oneself.

11. See Wlad Godzich, "The Semiotics of Semiotics."

12. Clifford uses the term "ethnographic" in a cross-disciplinary sense.

Chapter 1. Sahagún's Entrances into History

1. For Saint Francis, "the carnal, the flesh, the body meant what savored of the earthly, of self-seeking" (Habig, 36n).

2. See Daniel.

3. There is one possible exception. Sahagún is depicted in the *Cardona Codex*, but this potentially useful document has yet to be authenticated and remains in private hands. Most depictions of Sahagún are based on a posthumous painting housed in Mexico City's Museo Nacional de Historia.

4. The standard biography on Sahagún is by Nicolau d'Olwer. The most up-to-date summary of Sahagún's life is Bustamante García, *Fray Bernardino*. This work by Bustamante and A. Hernández de León-Portilla, "Las primeras biografías de Bernardino de Sahagún," are the two best sources for the evolution of Sahagún's biographies. Vicente Castro and Rodríguez Molinero offer the most extreme example of the phenomenon to which I am referring. See the bibliography for the titles of the numerous other biographies or biographical statements on Sahagún.

5. *Converso* refers to a Christian of Jewish ancestry.

6. Closer examination, however, reveals the problematic nature of this claim. Nevertheless, Sahagún sought to create this impression. This point will be examined in more detail in the second part of the book.

7. See, for example, the paper read by Miguel León-Portilla at the 1966 dedication in Salamanca ("Significado").

8. Many medieval chronologies or some Mesoamerican genealogies, for example, could be considered nonnarrative, or barely narrative, histories.

9. "The everyday life-world is the region of reality in which man can engage himself and which he can change while he operates in it by means of his animate organism" (Schütz and Luckmann, 1:3).

10. Living systems always "perceive" and interact with their environment in terms of their own structures. In the case of human beings, we refer to these structures as typifications. Humberto R. Maturana and Francisco J. Varela have introduced the important concept of "structural coupling" to explain how the structure of the environment only *triggers* changes in a living system rather than directing or determining them. See their *Autopoiesis* and *Tree of Knowledge*.

11. Even in such otherwise sound analyses of the confiscation of the *Florentine Codex* as Enrique Florescano's *Memory, Myth, and Time in Mexico* (95–99), there is a tendency to take for granted the universal status of a *romantic* individual-versus-society paradigm. Florescano assumes that the historian's perspective is inevitably antithetical to the "narrow limits of group interests" (99), but this particular construct of the fundamentally eccentric role of the historian vis-à-vis society is a result of intellectual and cultural tensions of the post-Enlightenment period.

12. Jesús Bustamante García has satisfactorily determined that it was in fact the *Florentine Codex* that was confiscated and not a now missing manuscript. See Bustamante García, *Fray Bernardino*, 334–46.

13. I am grateful to José Luis de Rojas for this insight.

14. The positivization of law refers to the historical emergence of law as a *normative* structure that is distinct from society as a factual life. In a sense, it is the opposite of the concept of natural law, in which law and society are perceived as one and the same.

15. For example, in *Ecological Communication*, Luhmann argues that responses to major environmental disasters will always be inadequate and overdue because each of society's "systems" (politics, economics, law, etc.) only can and only will deal with disasters in terms of their own semiautonomous structures, and there is no longer any metasystem from which these responses can be coordinated. Ironically, one of the consequences of this phenomenon is the heightened need among citizens to feel that one individual is still in control of the various separate social systems. It is no accident that Philip II felt the need to generate—for himself and others—an image of centralized control, when, for example, a great deal of autonomy was simultaneously being conceded to Spanish municipalities. See Nader, *Liberty in Absolutist Spain*, on this latter point.

16. Luhmann notes that sixteenth-century bureaucracy is characterized by an attempt to *rigidify* and transfer a hierarchically centered distribution of authority to organizational systems, but this process is precisely a response to the growing

NOTES TO PAGES 32–38

arbitrariness of political power produced by the increasing complexity of society (*Teoría*, 61).

17. See, for example, Ricard, 40–45; and chapter 2, section 3, of this book for more on this. Miguel León-Portilla—incorrectly, in my view—attributes the confiscation of the *Florentine Codex* directly to "the old jealousies of those other friars who had accused him of facilitating the preservation of idolatry" (*Bernardino de Sahagún*, 120).

18. Bureaucracy, of course, existed in Spain on a *limited* scale before Sahagún's time. Nevertheless, it is no coincidence that the science of statistics was invented in Spain during the reign of Philip II.

19. I point this out, in part, to demonstrate that the highly contrary theories of Schütz and Luckmann and of Luhmann are compatible at least in this sense.

20. The *physical* side of the presence and immediacy of human understanding is often overlooked, although this was not always the case. Drew Leder (*The Absent Body*) points out that, at least since René Descartes, the West has tended to neglect the ontological relationship between the mind and the body, and the fact that the human body's primarily "ecstatic" nature lends itself to a sense of identity built around interaction with others and the outside world.

21. *Criollismo* refers to the development and politicization of a Creole identity.

22. For the fullest treatment of Mendieta's views, see Phelan.

23. See A. Hernández de León-Portilla, "Las primeras," 239–44.

24. Asención Hernández de León-Portilla also makes this point in connection with biographies of Sahagún ("Las primeras," 244–45).

25. Cline's comment was made more than twenty years ago, and although the picture has changed some, his comment still holds true for much of the current historical debate. The period Cline refers to is often currently referred to as the "Mexican Renaissance"—a label that implies both a reverence and a certain distance vis-à-vis a historiographical past.

26. Michael Coe in *Breaking the Maya Code* offers the following appreciation of Eduard Georg Seler: "Incredibly well prepared for his research (he knew most of the major languages of Mesoamerica and gave classes in Maya and Nahuatl), blessed with an encyclopedic mind, and an exceptionally good visual memory, Seler was the founder of Mesoamerican iconographic research: he was the first to demonstrate from preconquest art and books that there was a fundamental unity to Mexican and Maya thought and religion. His output was stupendous: his collected essays alone fill five very thick volumes, and all of them are still worth reading" (120). Seler's enormous corpus is currently being edited and translated for publication in English.

27. Those interested in Seler's life and work should consult H. B. Nicholson's "Eduard Georg Seler, 1849–1922."

28. See A. Hernández de León-Portilla, "Las primeras," 246–47.

29. Beltrami's publications of his travels through North America were very popular in their day and surely inspired him to continue on through Mexico. In a note in *Le Mexique* Beltrami has been kind enough to provide us with transcriptions of numerous newspaper clippings that attest to the importance and resonance of his discoveries and travels. See his "Préface" (1:xv–xxxii). All further page references to *Le Mexique* will be given in parentheses after the text. The only recent study on Beltrami of which I am aware is Augusto P. Miceli's *The Man with the Red Umbrella*. Although Miceli's attempt to reconstruct Beltrami's journey through North America began by chance when he tried to figure out how an Italian name was chosen for Beltrami County, Minnesota, his interest soon turned into an attempt to vindicate the life, travels, and scientific contributions of Beltrami against the few scattered descriptions of Beltrami as a quixotic eccentric (Miceli, 7–8).

30. Gerbi, whose work is truly encyclopedic in scope, was apparently unaware of the existence of *Le Mexique*.

31. See Michel Foucault's *Les mots et les choses*.

32. Sahagún's tomb no longer exists, but, during Beltrami's lifetime, it was probably nothing more than an engraved stone inside the convent. It is improbable that anyone—including Nahuas—paid much attention to it at the time.

33. Beltrami seems to use the word "science" throughout his work as if it were magic.

34. I think Beltrami exaggerates once again here in a passage where dust and librarians are conflated into a negligible whole: "In the place where I myself discovered it, in a library where only dust and librarians of the Casti Abbey presided" (2:175).

35. I am grateful to Wayne Ruwet for these bibliographical details.

36. I attempted to be quite thorough in my reading of Beltrami in this sense. With the exception of Fray Bartolomé de Las Casas, one Franciscan (1:145), and one secular Spaniard (1:170–71), whom Beltrami is simply *amazed* to discover are "honest" (1:145), peninsular-born Spaniards and Spanish priests are rarely treated with kind words.

37. Beltrami's depictions in *Le Mexique* of Mexican "Indians" and mestizos are no less two-dimensional and can be compared to Beltrami's depictions of "Indians" in his *Alle sorgenti del Mississippi* and *Notizie e lettere*. See Gerbi (60n, 216n, 260n, 272n, 342n, 358, 378n, 553). See Beltrami's "Préface" to *Le Mexique* for his own analysis of his objectivity.

38. Here is the passage in question: "The principle is no doubt, as regards its occasion, derived from experience, viz. from that methodized experience called observation; but on account of the universality and necessity which it ascribes to such purposiveness, it cannot rest solely on empirical grounds, but must have as its basis an *a priori* principle, although it be merely regulative and these purposes lie only in the idea of the judging [subject] and not in an effective cause. We may therefore describe the aforesaid principle as a *maxim* for judging of the internal purposiveness of organized beings" (223, brackets in original).

39. These texts include, for example, a dictionary housed at the Newberry Library in Chicago and a pictorial catechism that is unlikely the product of someone so adept at Nahuatl as Sahagún was. The latter is reproduced in Resines Llorente, *Catecismos*.

Chapter 2. Paternity Suits and Cases of Mistaken Identity

1. During the 1991–92 school year at a public school in Palo Alto, California, thirteen-year-old Marcos G. Real was asked to write an essay on the topic "Columbus: Hero, Villain, or Fool?" Against the advice of his parents, Marcos argued that Columbus was a hero. As his parents had foreseen, Marcos's argument met with great disapproval from his teacher.

2. See "The Talk of the Town," *New Yorker*, 25 Jan. 1993, 31.

3. Sahagún is even a pivotal character in a recent opera written by Myron Fink and Donald Moreland, The Conquistador. The opera, which had its world premiere in San Diego, California, in 1997, opens with Sahagún contemplating the plight of those who defend the oppressed:

Don Luis [the conquistador of the title], whose life must soon end. Not from old age but at the very height of his powers. And for what cause? Aiding and protecting Jews.

Better I should die in his stead . . . for a lifetime of teaching and defending the Indian. That too, it seems, has become a crime against the State!

O Spain, what are we doing?
Where are we heading?
Where is the kingdom of God?

(*A large Catholic SUNBURST or ROYAL COAT OF ARMS has descended. MERCHANTS, CLERGY, and NOBLEMEN appear.*)

(Fink and Moreland, *The Conquistador*, 8)

4. In reality, many Renaissance thinkers alternated between humanist and scholastic modes of discourse depending on the audience being addressed. See Kristeller, *Medieval*, 25.

5. Thomas Kuhn's notion of a scientific paradigm was instrumental in the sixties and seventies in undermining the idea that scientists contribute to a cumulative development of science by objectively discovering, refining, and augmenting laws and characteristics that are autonomously set forth by nature itself. One of Kuhn's most suggestive arguments lies in his comparison of scientific paradigms to Wittgensteinian language games (Kuhn, 44–46).

6. See Keber, "Sahagún and Hermeneutics."

7. Throughout the chapter I utilize the expression "father of modern anthropology" because it is this odd, patriarchic expression that is used repeatedly in Sahagún criticism.

8. Manuel Marzal's *Historia de la antroplogía indigenista: México y Perú*, for example, stages itself as a polemic against European or North American claims of having founded the discipline of anthropology. I will have more to say about this book further along in the discussion.

9. There certainly are some interesting parallels between inquisitors and anthropologists, but I question the value of any prolonged comparison. In "From the Door of His Tent: The Fieldworker and the Inquisitor," Renato Rosaldo first mapped out some of the similarities between anthropologists and inquisitors, but in a more balanced and more appropriately unenthusiastic way than does Ginzburg. Ginzburg's article is, in part, a response to Rosaldo (Ginzburg, 22on. 1), since Rosaldo (rightly, in my opinion) questions the way some historians use the aura of the discipline of anthropology to legitimate their use of certain kinds of ethnographic material from the past.

10. Although I would never deny that knowledge is a form of power, Rabasa's late-Foucauldian claim skirts the whole problem of *degrees* of power. Power, in its most fundamental form, manifests itself as a direct threat to someone's biological, corporeal existence. All other forms of power derive from this threat, but they never surpass it. There is a difference—if only of degree—between a soldier who kills someone and an anthropologist who distorts someone's culture through the dialogic process of extracting information. In my view, providing modern anthropology with "perverse genealogies" as a response to the hollow-sounding claims of an idealized founding father for the discipline is a step in the wrong direction.

11. Miguel León-Portilla affectionately refers to J. Jorge Klor de Alva as his disciple, for example, in Sahagún, *Coloquios*, 12.

12. Klor de Alva's argument is patterned after Hayden White's notion of historical "emplotment" in his work on nineteenth-century historiography, *Metahistory*.

13. See de Man (215) on the contagiousness of an ironic interpretation of a text.

14. I analyze the importance of the three-column structure in more detail in chapter 3.

15. See Pardo for analysis of confession in the context of New Spain. I analyze the imposition of (textual) structuring devices as a response to certain kinds of social complexity in a different context in chapter 3.

16. In what follows, my own reading of Foucault's importance is based, in part, on White's essay "Foucault Decoded."

17. Human interpretation in the Middle Ages was unacceptable unless it could somehow refer back to divine revelation. Hence, the medieval obsession with "authorities."

18. White says that Foucault is correct in asserting that the "human sciences, as they unfold between the sixteenth and twentieth century, can be characterized in terms of their failure to recognize the extent to which they are each captive of language itself, their failure to see language as a problem" (251). Each successive episteme banks its success on a certain understanding of the relationship between language and the world, yet the more any one of these understandings is applied, the more it reveals its limitations and failure to capture the truths of the world, and the more it reveals the gaps in which the subsequent episteme will take up residence.

White argues that different rhetorical tropes determine how each of Foucault's epistemes will enact their particular determination of the relationship between "words" and "things," and that when any one of these tropes is stretched too far in its application, it will inevitably give way to the use of another trope. For example, the emphasis on similitude that was used in putting together the lists and tables that characterize early modern knowledge produced the side effect of also highlighting the *differences* between things. The more these lists attempted to be thorough, the more differences came to light. White argues that since "the very search for similitudes is inconceivable in the absence of any sense of differtness (sic), the category of differentness is implicitly endowed with just as much authority as the category of similarity in the science constructed as the solution to the problem of the relations obtaining among things" (252–53). Sooner or later, the differences were bound to outweigh the similarities, break down the system of similitude, and leave science open to a new mode of operation in which the only apparent relationship between things would be determined by their "mode of contiguities, i.e., spatial relationships" (White, 253). Whereas a science based on the mechanics of similitude is characterized by the trope "metaphor," White argues that the trope "metonymy" comes to typify the subsequent episteme—the episteme of the eighteenth century—since it "connotes a mode of linguistic usage by which the world of appearances is broken down into two orders of being, as in cause-effect or agent-act relationships." The epistemological projections inherent in the eighteenth-century search for a "universal grammar," the "true basis of wealth," and "the essences of organic species in the contemplation of their external attributes" are nothing if not metonymical (253).

19. Sociologists often point to the same individuals as do anthropologists in the search for founding fathers.

20. I say "superficial" because any good research scientist is driven—at least in part—by a sense of esthetics particular to his or her own field of inquiry.

21. See Bustamante García, "Retórica."

22. See Kristeller, Medieval Aspects, 13, on the popularity of the dialogue form for humanists. The full title of the Coloquios is: "COLLOQVIOS Y DOCTRI // na christian conque los do // ze frayles de san francis // co enbiados por el papa Adriano sesto y por el Em // perador Carlo qujnto: // côvertierô alos indi // os de la Nueva Espa // na ēlēgua Mexica // na y Española." Miguel León-Portilla's critical edition contains a facsimile of the surviving portion (Sahagún, Coloquios 37–68).

23. See also Bustamante García, Fray Bernardino.

24. The early modern emphasis on human agency is intertwined with the rise of the modern state and the shifting political roles of individuals. This is quite explicit in Valla: "I, on the contrary, think it is fairer to let the princes despoil you [the Pope] of all the empire you hold. For, as I shall show, that Donation whence the supreme pontiffs will have their right derived was unknown equally to Sylvester and to Constantine" (Valla, 27). The document in question was a medieval forgery in which great privileges and possessions were conferred on the Pope and the Roman church by the Emperor Constantine the Great. The document was considered authentic until the fifteenth century, when Valla proved with certainty that it was a forgery.

25. The "faithfulness" of a translation to the original was seldom an issue in medieval texts. The content of medieval translation was often governed by its place or "creative reception" in specific social contexts.

26. Bustamante is correct when he points out that the work of Saint Augustine—who is far from being a Renaissance humanist—represents the most apt articulation of Sahagún's own system of ethics. Saint Augustine is one of the few authorities Sahagún cites in his works (Bustamante García, "Retórica," 347–65).

27. As Geertz has astutely noted in "Anti Anti-Relativism," cultural relativism in general does not inevitably lead to nihilism as proponents of absolutist positions would often have it. Nevertheless, emerging from an absolute, unified

Christian cosmology, Sahagún and his contemporaries would have interpreted cultural relativism—or anything, for that matter, that threatened Christianity's coherency—as a cause for concern.

28. For Zaballa Beascoechea's analysis of the historicity of the *Coloquios* see Zaballa Beascoechea, 45–62.

29. See, for example, Lepenies.

30. See, for example, Klor de Alva's translation of Sahagún's *Coloquios*, "Aztec-Spanish Dialogues," 104–105, 112. All future quotations from the *Coloquios* are from this edition unless otherwise indicated.

31. The complexities surrounding this recognition are analyzed in more detail in the next chapter.

32. I disagree with Christian Duverger's contention that Sahagún's text is "*insidieusement anti-espagnol*" because the conquistadores are depicted as a calamity sent by God to punish the indigenous population (Duverger, 49–50). Sahagún, in fact, was a great admirer of Hernán Cortés and his feats.

33. These residues of oral discourse are prevalent in early colonial Nahua texts. See, for a comparable case, the *Codex Chimalpopoca*.

34. For the connotations of *yolli* (heart), see López Austin, *The Human Body*, 2:213–31.

35. Much of the original manuscript is missing, including the text of this chapter.

36. See, for example, León-Portilla, "Significado," 20.

37. I will return to a discussion of this figure in the second section of chapter 4.

38. I first encountered the term "pagan summa" in Le Clézio (49), but it is possible that someone applied the term earlier to Sahagún's work. Medieval summas were works meant to be summations of all knowledge, which in turn was exclusively derived from God through revelation.

39. Bear in mind that the medieval notions of *auctor* (author, authority) and creativity (creation)—and, hence, originality—are not those of modern times. On the notion of the "author function," see Foucault, "What Is an Author?" For a description of several of the problems the term "creativity" produces, see Gumbrecht, "Fichier."

40. The first printing presses in New Spain in no way competed with the European presses, for their primary function was the dissemination of evangelical tools such as catechisms, dictionaries, grammars, and so forth (Leonard, 198). Most of these printed works have not survived since they suffered the wear and tear of daily use and were not regarded as "treasures" the way a book such as the

Florentine Codex—for better or worse—would be. The advent of printing in Europe contributed to certain important epistemological changes or shifts in "mentalities"—the most important of these being the fragmentation of the holism represented by the medieval dream of a unified church. This fragmentation was partially the irreversible consequence of rapidly circulating and highly visible Reformation literature (Eisenstein; Giesecke). Also, at various rates in particular social situations, the advent of printing eclipsed "the body" as a locus for the production of "textual" meaning, substituting it with the now-familiar notion of a (disembodied) "author's intent" (Gumbrecht, "Body"). Nevertheless, the changes wrought by print culture in Europe were slower to take root among the friars who arrived in New Spain in the first quarter of the sixteenth century. Essentially, the friars did not experience print as a rupture with scriptorial traditions but as an added bonus for the dissemination of certain kinds of literature. Any influence print might have had on altering Sahagún's worldview was far outweighed by more serious influences and problems, which will be discussed in the first section of the next chapter.

Chapter 3. When Worlds Collide

1. For an extremely thorough overview of the relationship between European and colonial New Spain confessional and penitentiary practices, see chapter 3 of Osvaldo Pardo's "Nueva teología es menester."

2. In fact, the further European scholars were from the New World, the easier it was for them to make sense of its "discovery." See Gumbrecht "Wenig Neues." Also, on closer examination, Montaigne's essay reveals more about Europe than the New World.

3. There is nothing simple about the way nineteenth-century European imperialism justified itself. Even though ethnographic information was often gathered for imperialistic purposes, ironically, its diversity constituted the biggest threat to any nation's claim to have the "natural" right to rule over other peoples. Nineteenth-century European empires put into play extremely complex modes of discourse—including literary ones—in order to balance the tension between the desire to exploit cultural differences and the ensuing threat to the legitimacy of univocal political structures. For a recent analysis in literary studies of just how complex these modes of discourse could be, see Said.

4. See, for example, S. L. Cline, 7.

5. In the ensuing discussion of the Franciscan millennial movement in New Spain, I follow in many respects Baudot (*Utopía*, 83–128) and Phelan. Nevertheless, as will become apparent, my interpretation of Sahagún's

relationship to this movement differs from both of these scholars' mutually opposing views.

6. On the whole, I have followed Bustamante García's thorough analysis of the confusion surrounding Sahagún's title. For his analysis of the Tolosa manuscript, see *Fray Bernardino*, 328–34.

7. Cobarruvias defines *"fábrica"* in terms of *"any sumptuous edifice/ building"* (578).

8. This is one of Bustamante García's most salient leitmotivs in *Fray Bernardino* and "La obra."

9. There appear to be some "universal" constraints to all languages, but these constraints do not in and of themselves imply any transcendent origin for meaning, because they may be determined by physical or corporeal conditions that all human beings share. For a useful introduction to linguistics directed specifically to students of literature, see Traugott and Pratt; for this point in particular, see Traugott and Pratt, 7–8. The extent to which the conventional aspects of language (including the arbitrariness of the linguistic sign, as described by Ferdinand de Saussure [also see Culler on Saussure]) affects what gets signified, and how, is still a topic of much debate. Some—if not most— thought clearly takes place without language, but it is unclear at just which point different languages begin to shape the very reality (the signified) that humans perceive. The idea that the makeup of a particular language will affect how reality is perceived has recently been subjected to much scorn and ridicule by Steven Pinker in *The Language Instinct*, but I am suspicious of the extreme nature of his own position.

10. Some scholars feel that the persistence of the doctrine of significatio hobbled progress in medieval sign theory (Kretzmann, Kenny, and Pinborg, 173). But much, if not most, of medieval linguistics would probably never have developed if medieval scholars had not tried to bridge the gap between the contextual uses of language and the transcendental universals they assumed must exist.

11. I have relied throughout this section on the clearly organized section of *The Cambridge History of Later Medieval Philosophy* entitled "Logic in the High Middle Ages: Semantic Theory" (Kretzmann, Kenny, and Pinborg, 159–269). Since Sahagún is often deemed a humanist (see the second part of my second chapter), a statement from a later section of *The Cambridge History of Later Medieval Philosophy* is relevant to our topic: humanists were never hostile to the notion of a universal language or the belief that all languages share certain basic grammatical categories (815). In general, the so-called antipathy between humanism and scholas-

ticism is an exaggeration. A single author might indulge in either "scholastic" or "humanist" modes of discourse according to the public being addressed (Kristeller, *Medieval*, 25).

12. Sahagún's tripartite structure is discernible throughout much of the other texts gathered together in *Historia de las cosas de Nueva España*, edited by Paso y Troncoso.

13. Sahagún used—somewhat unsuccessfully—a European good-versus-evil schema to structure the information he elicited from his Nahua informants. I return to a discussion of this approach in chapter 4.

14. Anderson and Dibble offer the following rendering of the Nahuatl text into English:

THE GREAT-GRANDFATHER
[He is] decrepit, in his second childhood.
The good great-grandfather [is] of exemplary life, of fame, of renown. His good works remain written in books. He is esteemed, he is praised. He leaves a good reputation, a good example.
The bad great-grandfather [is] forgotten, worthy of being detested, cursed, ridiculed; worthy after death of complaints, worthy of murmurs in his absence. There are ridicule, spitting, anger because of him. (*FC* X:5)

15. Theirs was distorted because of the trickery of the devil. See chapter 5.

16. See also Le Goff, *Les intellectuels au Moyen Âge*, 100.

17. This is an example of how Panofsky's approach to art history often foreshadows the work of Foucault in *Les mots et les choses*, although Panofsky garners more respect in so-called "antitheoretical" circles of scholarship than Foucault does. This is principally for stylistic reasons. Panofsky couches his sweeping statements in a plethora of documented examples—his endnote and illustration pages longer are often longer than his main text. Foucault is notorious for his lack of explicit documentation.

18. Music, in fact, was one of the areas of medieval knowledge that underwent a transformation similar to scholasticism and Gothic architecture in the thirteenth century. At that time, music began to be "articulated through an exact and systematic division of time" (Panofsky, *Gothic*, 38–39).

19. See, for example, Ballesteros Gaibrois et al.; Glass; and Bustamante García, *Fray Bernardino* and "La obra" (part 1).

20. See López Austin, "The Research Method."

21. Although it is perhaps unpleasant to think about, the relationship of Sahagún's aides to other Nahuas is of the utmost relevance. These aides—listed by name by Sahagún—were educated from a very young age by the Franciscans in

the Colegio de Santa Cruz (CF II:1r–2v). In a different passage of the history, Sahagún recounts how the Nahua children educated by the Franciscans terrorized the other Nahuas when they were set loose in their villages in order to find and destroy idols or break up indigenous celebrations: "The fear was so great that the common folk had of these boys who were reared by us, that after a few days it was not necessary to go with them, nor send many, when there was a celebration or drunken debauchery at night" (CF X:77r–78v). It is unreasonable to assume that the presence of these frightening boys, during the gathering of information for the history, would elicit the most forthright responses. This passage is perhaps the most overlooked or conveniently ignored statement about Sahagún's helpers in the works of critics bent on proving Sahagún's objectivity and the scientific rigor of his methods (see the first part of chapter 2).

22. I have borrowed the wording in quotation marks from Panofsky (50, 58).

23. Much of the vast storehouse of information on Nahua economics, for example, could only be remotely relevant to actual evangelism. It is probable that much of this information was included simply because it was being gathered for other purposes. At this time, the Spanish crown was very interested in anything that pertained to the economics of New Spain, and it is probable that some of the same people who worked with Sahagún worked on contributions to the *Relaciones geográficas*.

24. Lewis is referring specifically to Dante's *Divine Comedy* as well as Aquinas's *Summa Theologica*.

25. In this process memory played a quintessential role during the Middle Ages.

26. As I noted in the last section, this is made extremely explicit by Aquinas in part 1, question 1, article 8 of the *Summa Theologica* (5).

27. The growing reliance on, or recognition of, the role of human sign conceptions in the production of knowledge from the Renaissance to the present has led to what can only be described as an idiosyncratic history of what constitutes truth or scientism. Foucault brought this problem to the foreground in his "archaeology" of the human sciences, *Les mots et les choses*. For a concise, but informative, account of some of the prominent sign conceptions in everyday European culture from the Renaissance on, see Gumbrecht "Sign-Conceptions."

28. For an introduction to medieval disputation, see Kretzmann, Kenny and Pinborg, 21–33.

29. This might be compared to the way all French students today are systematically taught to apply a single structuring technique to the philosophical part of their "bac" (baccalauréat) and the way in which, in turn, this structure governs a great deal of their post–high school and nonphilosophical thinking.

30. This is Charles Dibble's contention. See his "Sahagún's Appendices," 117.

31. The fourteenth century in Europe is commonly characterized as being a time of crisis—if not *the* crisis of the Middle Ages. This is the century of the Black Plague, the growth of cities and ensuing social reshuffling, numerous confusing and seemingly endless wars, and so forth. For a collection of studies that try to adapt the general notion of a fourteenth-century crisis to the specificity of different social, economic, and national spheres, see Seibt and Eberhard, *Europa 1400: La crisis de la baja Edad Media.*

Chapter 4. Problems of Mimesis and Exemplarity in Sahagún's Work

1. An *auto sacramental* is an allegorical religious play closely associated with the liturgical calendar and the celebration of Holy Communion.

2. On the Iberian peninsula, these generalizations about alterity in the Middle Ages hold true, too, but there is room for a more nuanced assessment. The unique situation of *convivencia*—Muslims, Jews, and Christians living in close proximity to one another—coupled with Spain's singular problems of noble genealogy led to intervals during which Spanish culture can be said to have "dabbled" in alterity. For example, the early *muhwashshaha* poetry from al-Andalus, the thirteenth-century Alphonsine corpus, and the fifteenth-century Castilian court literature bear traces of a moderate ability to see one's own cultural situation from a distance. More often than not, these interspersed "exceptions" to the rule of medieval alterity are visible in contextual, cultural "play-situations" that are retroactively referred to as "literature." On the whole, however, Otherness was normally not consciously thematized on the peninsula as an experience with any depth. For the most nuanced analysis of alterity in medieval Spain, see Gumbrecht, *Eine Geschichte*, 29–167.

3. As Costa Lima points out, Aristotle's definition was actually misinterpreted by Renaissance thinkers.

4. Sahagún scholars routinely and incorrectly divide the corpus into evangelical versus ethnographic works.

5. I have retained the original spelling of the titles of these works.

6. Although it is clear that some sixteenth-century missionaries were influenced by Erasmus (Bataillon, 807–31), there is a more interesting question for my purposes: what role were certain forms of religiosity supposed to play when they were projected onto the Nahuas?

7. All quotations from the *Addiciones, Apéndiz,* and *Exercicios* refer to the collection edited and translated into Spanish by Arthur J. O. Anderson, and all English translations of the Nahuatl are derived from Anderson's.

8. Roughly, "He who is doubtful in faith is an infidel."

9. In the *Apéndiz*, for example, Sahagún instructs the Nahuas on how to walk properly, holding their heads high (104).

10. See, for example, Memmi, *The Colonizer and the Colonized*, 119–41; or Césaire, *Discourse on Colonialism*, 21–25.

11. For orientation here, see the essays collected in Klor de Alva, Nicholson, and Quiñones Keber, 199–293. I will refer to some of these insightful essays further along in this section.

12. See, for instance, Díaz del Castillo's description of Moteuczomah in his *Historia verdadera de la conquista de la Nueva España* (1:322).

13. See, for example, the illustrations in Durán, *History* (between 308 and 309).

14. See, for example, the illustration of Moteuczomah from the Tovar manuscript at the John Carter Brown Library at Brown University (Providence, Rhode Island) that is reproduced in Hassig, *Aztec*, 220.

15. Whether or not it is correct, the assumption that handwriting tells us something about a person's character is still quite widespread. Many top universities, for example, still ask applicants for undergraduate admissions to submit a personal statement written in their own hand.

16. Maturana and Varela's *Tree of Knowledge* is the most accessible of their works.

17. Others are "devils." See chapter 5 for further discussion.

18. The *Cantares mexicanos* is a collection of indigenous songs in Nahuatl from the sixteenth century. These songs were possibly collected by Sahagún himself and bear the stamp of both preconquest traditions and European influence. The fact that their semantic content is extremely esoteric led many friars to be extremely suspicious of their nature and has forced modern translators to interpret the songs on an extremely speculative level.

19. All translations of the *Psalmodia* are Arthur J. O. Anderson's.

Chapter 5. Sahagún, the Devil, and the Disintegration of a Medieval Conceptualization of Knowledge

1. It is interesting to note that the nineteenth-century historian Jules Michelet—whose work I will touch on further along—credits women with the birth of a modern, truer form of knowledge. One of the leitmotivs of *Satanism and Witchcraft* is the notion that the "sorceress" gained true knowledge at the end of the Middle Ages by rejecting church dogma and experimenting with the possibilities of nature and the world.

2. Elliott makes this point in much greater detail in *The Old World and the New, 1492–1650*.

3. In the previous chapter, I analyzed this phenomenon in terms of a shift from a medieval form of mimesis to a modern one. Anthony Pagden's *Fall of Natural Man* and *European Encounters with the New World* are splendid sources for the evolution of European views of the indigenous population of the New World. See also Gerbi's equally comprehensive *Dispute of the New World*.

4. I am grateful to Doug Smith for informing me of the existence of this passage in García's work.

5. The Jewish origin of the original inhabitants of the New World turned out to be an extremely durable hypothesis. The driving force behind Lord Kingsborough's publication between 1831 and 1848 of his *Antiquities of Mexico* was an obsessive desire to prove that pre-Hispanic Mexico had been colonized by the Jews. See Keen, 348–49.

6. Aquinas defines goodness as actuality. See Russell, 193.

7. The notable exception is Bustamante García. Bustamante García, however, is primarily interested in establishing a link between Sahagún's thinking and Augustine's conception of rhetoric and socially determined linguistic meaning in *De Doctrina Christiana*. See his "Retórica," 355–64.

8. Tzvetan Todorov's influential idea in *La conquête de l'Amérique* that Sahagún's alternate use of the terms "god" and "devil" for Nahua deities is a sign of his neutrality vis-à-vis the Nahuas' religious beliefs (237) is groundless. Augustine himself uses the terms indiscriminately without conceding that the pagan gods of antiquity are due any respect. Compare Augustine's own comment on the writing of the *City of God* with a passage Todorov unduly emphasizes from Sahagún's first prologue: Augustine: "I write against those who maintain that the worship of the gods—I would rather say, of the evil spirits (*daemones*)—leads to happiness in this life" (quoted in *City*, xxxvi); and Sahagún: "I wrote twelve books on divine, or better said, idolatrous and human and natural things of this New Spain" (*CF* I:"Prologo"). See Keber's "Sahagún and Hermeneutics" (57–58) for an excellent critique of Todorov's argument.

9. See, for example, Canto I of the "Inferno" of Dante's *Divine Comedy* (I:6).

10. This, essentially, is Klor de Alva's view in "Sahagún and the Birth of Modern Ethnography" (51). Klor de Alva mistakenly assumes that the Spanish text was included exclusively for the benefit of a European audience and that Sahagún did not really believe his own interpretation of a "fit" between Nahua deities and the deities of antiquity.

11. According to Augustine, demonic deception was behind most Roman theater (168).

12. See, for example, *City of God*, 135.

13. Sahagún presents a shorter version of this passage in Latin (*CF* I:26v).

14. If, in fact, evil can be credited with having any supernatural agency at all in the Book of Wisdom, it is only in a very weak sense.

15. Like many people of the period, Sahagún conflates these figures.

16. See, for example, the bizarre, elaborate theories developed about whether or not demons could procreate with mortals in Kramer and Sprenger (21–28), del Río (312–27), and finally, from the second half of the seventeenth century, Sinistrari's monograph *Demonality* (*De Daemonialitate, et Incubis et Succubis*). The scandalous views expressed in this latter work probably explain why it was not published until 1875.

17. For a detailed analysis of this general point, see Delumeau's book-length study *La peur en Occident*.

18. See John O'Meara's introduction to Henry Bettenson's translation of Augustine's *City of God* for a brief discussion of this misunderstanding and its proponents (xxi–xxvi).

19. Augustine's notion of *sermo humilis* (the humble sermon) became one of the general, constitutive features of medieval rhetoric. The most important analysis of this rhetorical recuperation of Christian works is Auerbach's *Literary Language and Its Public in Late Antiquity and in the Middle Ages*, 25–81.

20. For an introduction to the kind of profound social changes brought about by literacy and, subsequently, print culture, see Ong, *Orality and Literacy*.

BIBLIOGRAPHY

Alfonso X. *Lapidario*. Ed. María Brey Mariño. 2nd ed. Madrid: Castalia, 1983.

————. *Primera crónica general de España*. Ed. Ramón Menéndez Pidal. 2 vols. Madrid: Gredos, 1978.

————. *Las siete partidas*. Ed. Gregorio López. Facs. ed. 3 vols. Madrid: Boletín Oficial del Estado, 1985.

Anderson, Benedict. *Imagined Communities: Reflections on the Origin and Spread of Nationalism*. London: Verso, 1983.

Aquinas, Saint Thomas. *Summa Theologica*. Trans. Fathers of the English Dominican Province. 5 vols. Westminster, Md.: Christian Classics, 1948.

Ares, Berta, Jesús Bustamante, Francisco Castilla, and Fermín del Pino. *Humanismo y visión del otro en la España moderna*. Madrid: Consejo Superior de Investigaciones Científicas, 1992.

Auerbach, Erich. *Literary Language and Its Public in Late Latin Antiquity and in the Middle Ages*. Trans. Ralph Manheim. Princeton: Princeton University Press, 1965.

————. *Mimesis: The Representation of Reality in Western Literature*. Trans. Willard R. Trask. Princeton: Princeton University Press, 1953.

————. *Scenes from the Drama of European Literature: Six Essays*. New York: Meridian Books, 1959.

Augustine of Hippo, Saint. *Concerning the City of God against the Pagans*. Trans. Henry Bettenson. London: Penguin, 1984.

————. *Confessions*. Trans. R. S. Pine-Coffin. London: Penguin, 1961.

————. *On Christian Doctrine*. Trans. D. W. Robertson, Jr. New York: Macmillan, 1986.

Baird, Ellen T. *The Drawings of Sahagún's "Primeros Memoriales": Structure and Style*. Norman: University of Oklahoma Press, 1993.

Ballesteros Gaibrois, Manuel. *Vida y obra de fray Bernardino de Sahagún*. Madrid: Cátedra, 1991.

Ballesteros Gaibrois, Manuel, and Germán Vázquez Chamorro. *Fray Bernardino de Sahagún: Misionero y sabio antropólogo (hechos y significación de la vida de un leonés de pro)*. León: Mijares, 1990.

Ballesteros Gaibrois, Manuel, et al. *Códices matritenses de la Historia general de las cosas de la Nueva España de Fr. Bernardino de Sahagún: Trabajo realizado por el Seminario de Estudios Americanistas bajo la dirección de Manuel Ballesteros Gaibrois*. Vol. 1. Madrid: Ediciones José Porrúa Turanzas, 1964.

Bartholomaeus Anglicus. *On the Property of Things: John Trevisa's Translation of Bartholomaeus Anglicus "De Propietatibus Rerum."* Gen. ed. M. C. Seymore. 3 vols. Oxford: Clarendon, 1975.

Bataillon, Marcel. *Erasmo y España: Estudios sobre la historia espiritual del siglo XVI*. Trans. Antonio Alatorre. Mexico: Fondo de Cultura Económica, 1950.

Baudot, Georges. "Fray Toribio Motolinía denunciado ante la Inquisición por Fray Bernardino de Sahagún en 1572." *C. M. H. L. B. Caravelle* 55 (1990): 13–17.

———. *Utopía e historia en México: Los primeros cronistas de la civilización mexicana (1520–1569)*. Trans. Vicente González Loscertales. Madrid: Espasa-Calpe, 1983.

Belting, Hans. *Likeness and Presence: A History of the Image before the Era of Art*. Trans. Edmund Jephcott. Chicago: University of Chicago Press, 1994.

Beltrami, Jules-Césaire (Giacomo Costantino). *Le Mexique*. 2 vols. Paris: Delaunay, 1830.

———. *A Pilgrimage in America, Leading to the Discovery of the Sources of the Mississippi and Bloody River; with a Description of the Whole Course of the Former, and of the Ohio*. Chicago: Quadrangle Books, 1962.

Benjamin, Walter. "On the Mimetic Faculty." In *Reflections*, ed. Peter Demetz, trans. Edmund Jephcott, 333–36. New York: Schocken Books, 1978.

Berger, Peter L., and Thomas Luckmann. *The Social Construction of Reality: A Treatise on the Sociology of Knowledge*. New York: Doubleday, 1966.

Bernard of Cluny. *De contemptu mundi*. East Lansing, Mich.: Colleagues Press, 1991.

Blumenberg, Hans. *The Legitimacy of the Modern Age*. Trans. Robert M. Wallace. Cambridge: MIT Press, 1983.

Brading, D. A. *The First America: The Spanish Monarchy, Creole Patriots, and the Liberal State 1492–1867*. Cambridge: Cambridge University Press, 1991.

Bremond, Claude, Jacques Le Goff, and Jean-Claude Schmitt. *L'«exemplum»*. Typologie des sources du moyen âge occidental, ed. L. Genicot, vol. 40. Turnhout, Belgium: Brepols, 1982.

Burkhart, Louise M. *The Slippery Earth: Nahua-Christian Moral Dialogue in Sixteenth-Century Mexico*. Tucson: University of Arizona Press, 1989.

Bustamante García, Jesús. *Fray Bernardino de Sahagún: Una revisión crítica de los manuscritos y de su proceso de composición.* México: Universidad Nacional Autónoma de México, 1990.

———. "La obra etnografica y lingüística de fray Bernardino de Sahagún." Ph.D. diss., Universidad Complutense de Madrid, 1989.

———. "Retórica, traducción y responsibilidad histórica: Claves humanísticas en la obra de Bernardino de Sahagún." In *Humanismo y visión del otro en la España moderna*, ed. Berta Ares, Jesús Bustamante, Francisco Castilla, and Fermín del Pino, 243–375. Madrid: Consejo Superior de Investigaciones Científicas, 1992.

Cantares Mexicanos: Songs of the Aztecs. Trans. John Bierhorst. Palo Alto: Stanford University Press, 1985.

Capel, Horacio. *La física sagrada: Creencias religiosas y teorías científicas en los orígenes de la geomorfología española.* Barcelona: Serbal, 1985.

Cazelles, Brigitte. *The Lady as Saint: A Collection of French Hagiographic Romances of the Thriteenth Century.* Philadelphia: University of Pennsylvania Press, 1991.

Certeau, Michel de. *The Writing of History.* Trans. Tom Conley. New York: Columbia University Press, 1988.

Cervantes, Fernando. *The Devil in the New World: The Impact of Diabolism in New Spain.* New Haven: Yale University Press, 1994.

Césaire, Aimé. *Discourse on Colonialism.* Trans. Joan Pinkham. New York: Monthly Review Press, 1972.

CF. See Sahagún, Fray Bernardino de. *Códice florentino.*

Chavero, Alfredo. "Apuntes sobre la bibliografía mexicana." *Boletín de la Sociedad de Geografía y Estadística de la República Mexicana* 6 (3ª época, 1882), 5–42. Mexico: Francisco Díaz de León.

———. *Sahagún.* México: Imprenta de José Mareia Sandoval, 1877.

Clifford, James. *The Predicament of Culture: Twentieth-Century Ethnography, Literature, and Art.* Cambridge: Harvard University Press, 1988.

Cline, Howard F. "Selected Nineteenth-Century Mexican Writers on Ethnohistory." In *Handbook of Middle American Indians*, Robert Wauchope, gen. ed., Howard F. Cline, vol. ed., vol. 13, 370–427. Austin: University of Texas Press, 1973.

Cline, S. L. *Colonial Culhuacan, 1580–1600: A Social History of an Aztec Town.* New Mexico: University of New Mexico Press, 1986.

Cobarruvias, Sebastián de. *Tesoro de la lengua castellana o española: Primer diccionario de la lengua.* 1611. Madrid: Ediciones Turner, 1984.

Codex Chimalpopoca: The Text in Nahuatl with a Glossary and Grammatical Notes. Ed. John Bierhorst, and *History and Mythology of the Aztecs: The Codex Chimalpopoca.* Trans. John Bierhorst. Tucson: University of Arizona Press, 1992.

Coe, Michael D. *Breaking the Maya Code.* New York: Thames and Hudson, 1992.

Costa Lima, Luiz. *Control of the Imaginary: Reason and Imagination in Modern Times.* Trans. Ronald W. Sousa. Minneapolis: University of Minnesota Press, 1988.

―――. *The Dark Side of Reason: Fictionality and Power.* Trans. Paulo Henriques Britto. Stanford: Stanford University Press, 1992.

Culler, Jonathan. *Ferdinand de Saussure.* Rev. ed. Ithaca: Cornell University Press, 1986.

Curtius, Ernst Robert. *European Literature and the Latin Middle Ages.* Trans. Willard R. Trask. Princeton: Princeton University Press, 1953.

Damisch, Hubert. *The Origin of Perspective.* Trans. John Goodman. Cambridge: MIT Press, 1994.

Daniel, E. Randolph. *The Franciscan Concept of Mission in the High Middle Ages.* Lexington: University of Kentucky Press, 1975.

Dante Alighieri. *The Divine Comedy.* Trans. Charles S. Singleton. 3 vols. Princeton: Princeton University Press, 1970–75.

Deleuze, Gilles. "Plato and the Simulacrum." In *The Logic of Sense,* ed. Constantin V. Boundas, trans. Mark Lester with Charles Stivale, 253–66. New York: Columbia University Press, 1990.

Del Pino, Fermín. "Humanismo renacentista y orígenes de la etnología: A propósito del p. Acosta, paradigma del humanismo antropológico jesuita." In *Humanismo y visión del otro en la España moderna,* ed. Berta Ares, Jesús Bustamante, Francisco Castilla, and Fermín del Pino, 377–429. Madrid: Consejo Superior de Investigaciones Científicas, 1992.

Delumeau, Jean. *La peur en Occident (XIVᵉ–XVIIIᵉ siècles).* Paris: Fayard, 1978.

De Man, Paul. *Blindness and Insight: Essays in the Rhetoric of Contemporary Criticism.* 2nd rev. ed. Minneapolis: University of Minnesota Press, 1983.

Díaz del Castillo, Bernal. *Historia verdadera de la conquista de la Nueva España.* Ed. Miguel León-Portilla. 2 vols. Madrid: Historia 16, 1984.

Dibble, Charles E. "Sahagún's Appendices: 'There Is No Reason to Be Suspicious of the Ancient Practices.'" In *The Work of Bernardino de Sahagún: Pioneer Ethnographer of Sixteenth-Century Aztec Mexico,* ed. J. Jorge Klor de Alva, H. B. Nicholson, and Eloise Quiñones Keber, 107–18. Austin: University of Texas Press, 1988.

Di Camillo, Ottavio. *El humanismo castellano del siglo XV.* Valencia: Fernando Torres, 1976.

Durán, Fray Diego. *Historia de las Indias de Nueva España e Islas de la Tierra Firme.* 1581. Ed. Ángel María Garibay K. 2nd ed. 2 vols. Mexico: Porrúa, 1984.

———. *The History of the Indies of New Spain.* Trans. Doris Heyden. Norman: University of Oklahoma Press, 1994.

Duverger, Christian. *La conversion des Indiens de Nouvelle Espagne avec le texte des "Colloques des douze" de Bernardino de Sahagún (1564).* Paris: Seuil, 1987.

Eisenstein, Elizabeth L. *The Printing Press as an Agent of Change: Communications and Cultural Transformation in Early-Modern Europe.* Cambridge: Cambridge University Press, 1979.

Elliott, John H. "The Discovery of America and the Discovery of Man." In *Spain and Its Worlds 1500–1700,* 42–64. New Haven: Yale University Press, 1989.

———. *The Old World and the New 1492–1650.* Cambridge: Cambridge University Press, 1970.

Esteve Barba, Francisco. *Historiografía indiana.* 2nd rev. ed. Madrid: Gredos, 1992.

FC. See Sahagún, Fray Bernardino de. *Florentine Codex.*

Fernández del Castillo, Francisco, ed. *Libros y libreros en el siglo XVI.* Mexico: Fondo de Cultura Económica, 1982.

Fink, Myron (composer), and Donald Moreland (librettist). *The Conquistador* (libretto). Premiered on 1 March 1997, San Diego Opera, San Diego, California.

Florescano, Enrique. *Memory, Myth, and Time in Mexico: From the Aztecs to Independence.* Trans. Albert G. Bork. Austin: University of Texas Press, 1994.

Foucault, Michel. *Les mots et les choses: Une archéologie des sciences humaines.* Paris: Gallimard, 1966.

———. "What Is an Author?" In *The Foucault Reader,* ed. Paul Rabinow, 101–20. New York: Pantheon, 1984.

García, Gregorio. *Origen de los indios del Nuevo Mundo.* Mexico: Fondo de Cultura Económica, 1981.

García Icazbalceta, Joaquín. *Bibliografía mexicana del siglo XVI.* Ed. Agustín Millares Carlo. Mexico: Fondo de Cultura Económica, 1981.

García Mora, Carlos, ed. *La antropología en México: Panorama histórico.* 15 vols. México: Instituto Nacional de Antropología e Historia, 1987.

Garibay K., Ángel María. *Historia de la literatura náhuatl.* 2 vols. Mexico: Porrúa, 1987.

Geertz, Clifford. "Anti Anti-Relativism." *American Anthropologist* 86 (1984): 263–78.

———. *Local Knowledge: Further Essays in Interpretive Anthropology.* New York: Basic Books, 1983.

————. "The Way We Think Now: Toward an Ethnography of Modern Thought." In *Local Knowledge: Further Essays in Interpretive Anthropology*, 147–63. New York: Basic Books, 1983.

Gellrich, Jesse M. *The Idea of the Book in the Middle Ages: Language Theory, Mythology, and Fiction*. Ithaca: Cornell University Press, 1985.

Gerbi, Antonello. *The Dispute of the New World: The History of a Polemic, 1750–1900*. Trans. Jeremy Moyle. Rev. ed. Pittsburgh: University of Pittsburgh Press, 1973.

Geremek, Bronislaw. "Le marginal." In *L'homme médiéval*, ed. Jacques Le Goff, 381–413. Paris: Seuil, 1989.

Giesecke, Michael. *Der Buchdruck in der frühen Neuzeit: Eine historische Fallstudie über die Durchsetzung neuer Informations- und Kommunikations technologien*. Frankfurt am Main: Suhrkamp, 1991.

Ginzburg, Carlo. "The Inquisitor as Anthroplogist." In *Clues, Myths, and the Historical Method*, trans. John and Anne Tedesci, 156–64. Baltimore: Johns Hopkins University Press, 1989.

Glass, John B. *Sahagún: Reorganization of the Manuscrito de Tlatelolco, 1566–1569*. Part I. Contributions to the Ethnohistory of Mexico, vol. 7. Lincoln Center, Mass: Conemex Associates, 1978.

Godzich, Wlad. "The Semiotics of Semiotics." In *The Culture of Literacy*, 193–216. Cambridge: Harvard University Press, 1994.

Grafton, Anthony, with April Shelford and Nancy Siraisi. *New Worlds, Ancient Texts: The Power of Tradition and the Shock of Discovery*. Cambridge: Harvard University Press, 1992.

Gumbrecht, Hans Ulrich. "The Body versus the Printing Press: Media in the Early Modern Period, Mentalities in the Reign of Castile, and Another History of Literary Forms." *Poetics* 14, 3/4 (1985): 209–27.

————. "Eccentricities: On Prologues in Some Fourteenth-Century Castilian Texts." *The South Atlantic Quarterly* 91, 4 (1992): 891–907.

————. "Fichier créativité." *Théologiques* 2, 1 (1994): 61–80.

————. *Eine Geschichte der spanischen Literatur*. 2 vols. Frankfurt am Main: Suhrkamp, 1990.

————. "Literary Translation and Its Social Conditioning in the Middle Ages: Four Spanish Romance Texts of the Thirteenth Century." *Yale French Studies* 51 (1974): 205–22.

————. "Menschliches Handeln und göttliche Kosmologie: Geschichte als Exempel." In *La littérature historiographique des origines à 1500. Grundriss der romanischen Literaturen des Mittelalters*. Vol. 11/3, ed. Hans Ulrich Gumbrecht,

Ursula Link-Heer, and Peter Michael Spangenberg, 869–951. Heidelberg: Carl Winter and Universitätsverlag, 1986.

―――. "Narrating the Past Just as if It Were Your Own Time." In *Making Sense in Life and Literature*, trans. Glen Burns, 54–75. Minneapolis: University of Minnesota Press, 1992.

―――. "Sign-Conceptions in European Everyday Culture between the Renaissance and the Early Nineteenth Century." In *Semiotik: Ein Handbuch zu den zeichentheoretischen Grundlagen von Natur und Kultur*, ed. R. Posner, K. Robering, and T. A. Sebeok. Berlin, 1992.

―――. "Wenig Neues in der Neuen Welt: Über Typen der Erfahrungsbildung in spanischen Kolonialchroniken des XVI. Jahrhunderts." In *Die Pluralität der Welten: Aspekte der Renaissance in der Romania*, ed. Wolf-Dieter Stempel und Karlheinz Stierle, 227–49. Munich: Wilhelm Fink Verlag, 1987.

Habig, Marion A., ed. *St. Francis of Assisi. Writings and Early Biographies: English Omnibus of the Sources for the Life of St. Francis*. 4th rev. ed. Quincy, Ill: Franciscan Press, 1991.

Hampton, Timothy. *Writing from History: The Rhetoric of Exemplarity in Renaissance Literature*. Ithaca: Cornell University Press, 1990.

Hassig, Debra. "Transplanted Medicine: Colonial Mexican Herbals of the Sixteenth Century." *Res* 17/18 (1989): 30–53.

Hassig, Ross. *Aztec Warfare: Imperial Expansion and Political Control*. Norman: University of Oklahoma Press, 1988.

Hernández de León-Portilla, Ascensión. "Las primeras biografías de Bernardino de Sahagún." *Estudios de cultura náhuatl* 22 (1992): 235–52.

―――, ed. *Bernardino de Sahagún: Diez estudios acerca de su obra*. México: Fondo de Cultura Económica, 1990.

Hodgen, Margaret T. *Early Anthropology in the Sixteenth and Seventeenth Centuries*. Philadelphia: University of Pennsylvania Press, 1964.

Isidoro de Sevilla, San. *Etimologías*. Ed. and trans. José Oroz Reta and Manuel-A. Marcos Casquero. 2 vols. Bilingual ed. Madrid: Biblioteca de Autores Cristianos, 1982.

The Jerusalem Bible. Alexander Jones, gen. ed. Garden City, N.Y.: Doubleday, 1966.

Jiménez Moreno, Wigberto. "Fr. Bernardino de Sahagún y su obra." Fr. Bernardino de Sahagún, *Historia general de las cosas de Nueva España*, vol. 1. Mexico: Pedro Robredo, 1938. xiii–liv.

Kant, Immanuel. *Critique of Judgement*. Trans. J. H. Bernard. New York: Hafner Press, 1951.

Keber, John. "Sahagún and Hermeneutics: A Christian Ethnographer's Understanding of Aztec Culture." In *The Work of Bernardino de Sahagún: Pioneer Ethnographer of Sixteenth-Century Aztec Mexico*, ed. J. Jorge Klor de Alva, H. B. Nicholson, and Eloise Quiñones Keber, 53–63. Austin: University of Texas Press, 1988.

Keen, Benjamin. *The Aztec Image in Western Thought*. New Brunswick: Rutgers University Press, 1971.

Kingsborough, Edward King, Viscount. *Antiquities of Mexico*. London: Robert Havell and Conaghi, 1831–48.

Klor de Alva, J. Jorge. "La historicidad de los 'Coloquios' de Sahagún." In *Bernardino de Sahagún: Diez estudios acerca de su obra*, ed. Ascensión Hernández de León-Portilla, 180–218. Mexico: Fondo de Cultura Económica, 1990.

———. "Sahagún and the Birth of Modern Ethnography: Representing, Confessing, and Inscribing the Native Other." In *The Work of Bernardino de Sahagún: Pioneer Ethnographer of Sixteenth-Century Aztec Mexico*, ed. J. Jorge Klor de Alva, H. B. Nicholson, and Eloise Quiñones Keber, 31–52. Austin: University of Texas Press, 1988.

———. "Sahagún's Misguided Introduction to Ethnography and the Failure of the Coloquios Project." In *The Work of Bernardino de Sahagún: Pioneer Ethnographer of Sixteenth-Century Aztec Mexico*, ed. J. Jorge Klor de Alva, H. B. Nicholson, and Eloise Quiñones Keber, 83–92. Austin: University of Texas Press, 1988.

Klor de Alva, J. Jorge, H. B. Nicholson, and Eloise Quiñones Keber, eds. *The Work of Bernardino de Sahagún: Pioneer Ethnographer of Sixteenth-Century Aztec Mexico*. Austin: University of Texas Press, 1988.

Koselleck, Reinhart. *Futures Past: On the Semantics of Historical Time*. Trans. Keith Tribe. Cambridge: MIT Press, 1985.

Kramer, Heinrich, and James Sprenger. *The Malleus Maleficarum*. 1484. Trans. Montague Summers. New York: Dover, 1971.

Kretzmann, Norman, Anthony Kenny, and Jan Pinborg, eds. *The Cambridge History of Later Medieval Philosophy: From the Rediscovery of Aristotle to the Disintegration of Scholasticism 1100–1600*. Cambridge: Cambridge University Press, 1982.

Kristeller, Paul Oskar. *Medieval Aspects of Renaissance Learning*. Ed. and trans. Edward P. Mahoney. New York: Columbia University Press, 1992.

———. *Renaissance Thought and Its Sources*. Ed. Michael Mooney. New York: Columbia University Press, 1979.

Kuhn, Thomas S. *The Structure of Scientific Revolutions*. 2nd rev. ed. Chicago: University of Chicago Press, 1970.

Le Clézio, J.-M. G. *The Mexican Dream, or, The Interrupted Thought of Amerindian Civilizations.* Trans. Teresa Lavender Fagan. Chicago: University of Chicago Press, 1993.

Leder, Drew. *The Absent Body.* Chicago: University of Chicago Press, 1990.

Le Goff, Jacques. "For an Extended Middle Ages." In *The Medieval Imagination,* trans. Arthur Goldhammer, 18–23. Chicago: University of Chicago Press, 1988.

———. *History and Memory.* Trans. Steven Rendall and Elizabeth Claman. New York: Colombia University Press, 1992.

———. *Les intellectuels au Moyen Âge.* 1957. Paris: Éditions de Seuil, 1985.

———. *Medieval Civilization 400–1500.* Trans. Julia Barrow. Oxford: Basil Blackwell, 1988.

Leonard, Irving A. *Books of the Brave: Being an Account of Books and of Men in the Spanish Conquest and Settlement of the Sixteenth-Century New World.* 1949. Berkeley: University of California Press, 1992.

León-Portilla, Miguel. *Bernardino de Sahagún.* Madrid: Historia 16/Quorum, 1987.

———. "Significado de la obra de fray Bernardino de Sahagún." *Estudios de Historia Novohispana* 1 (1966): 13–27.

Lepenies, Wolf. *Between Literature and Science: The Rise of Sociology.* Trans. R. J. Hollingdale. Cambridge: Cambridge University Press, 1988.

Lewis, C. S. *The Discarded Image: An Introduction to Medieval and Renaissance Literature.* Cambridge: Cambridge University Press, 1964.

Lockhart, James. *The Nahuas after the Conquest: A Social and Cultural History of the Indians of Central Mexico, Sixteenth through Eighteenth Centuries.* Stanford: Stanford University Press, 1992.

———. "Some Nahua Concepts in Postconquest Guise." *History of European Ideas* 6, 4 (1985): 465–82.

López Austin, Alfredo. *The Human Body and Ideology: Concepts of the Ancient Nahuas.* Trans. Thelma Ortiz de Montellano and Bernard Ortiz de Montellano. 2 vols. Salt Lake City: University of Utah Press, 1988.

———. "The Research Method of Fray Bernardino de Sahagún: The Questionnaires." In *Sixteenth-Century Mexico: The Work of Sahagún,* ed. Munro S. Edmonson, 111–49. Albuquerque: University of New Mexico Press, 1974.

Luhmann, Niklas. *A Sociological Theory of Law.* Trans. Elizabeth King-Utz and Martin Albrow. London: Routledge and Kegan Paul, 1985.

———. *Ecological Communication.* Trans. John Bednarz, Jr. Chicago: University of Chicago Press, 1989.

————. *Teoría política en el Estado de Bienstar*. Trans. Fernando Vallespín. Madrid: Alianza Editorial, 1993.

Lyons, John D. *Exemplum: The Rhetoric of Example in Early Modern France and Italy*. Princeton: Princeton University Press, 1989.

Marzal, Manuel M. *Historia de la antropología indigenista: México y Perú*. Barcelona: Editorial Anthropos, 1993.

Maturana, Humberto R., and Francisco J. Varela. *Autopoiesis and Cognition: The Realization of the Living*. Dordrecht, Holland: D. Reidel Publishing Company, 1980.

————. *The Tree of Knowlege: The Biological Roots of Human Understanding*. Trans. Robert Paolucci. Rev. ed. Boston and London: Shambhala, 1992.

Memmi, Albert. *The Colonizer and the Colonized*. Trans. Howard Greenfeld. Boston: Beacon Press, 1967.

Mendieta, Fray Gerónimo de. *Historia eclesiástica indiana*. Ed. Joaquín García Icazbalceta. 2nd facs. ed. Mexico: Porrúa, 1980.

Miceli, Augusto P. *The Man with the Red Umbrella: Giacomo Costantino Beltrami in America*. Baton Rouge: Claitor's Publishing Division, 1974.

Michelet, Jules. *Satanism and Witchcraft*. 1862. Trans. A. R. Allinson. New York: Citadel Press, 1992.

Mignolo, Walter. "Cartas, crónicas y relaciones del descubrimiento y la conquista." In *Historia de la literatura hispanoamericana 1: Época colonial*, ed. Luis Íñigo Madrigal, 57–116. Madrid: Cátedra, 1982.

————. "Signs and Their Transmission: The Question of the Book in the New World." In *Writing without Words: Alternative Literacies in Mesoamerica and the Andes*, ed. Elizabeth Hill Boone and Walter D. Mignolo, 220–70. Durham: Duke University Press, 1994.

Miller, Mary, and Karl Taube. *The Gods and Symbols of Ancient Mexico and the Maya: An Illustrated Dictionary of Mesoamerican Religion*. London: Thames and Hudson, 1993.

Montaigne, Michel de. *Essais*. 3 vols. Paris: Garnier-Flammarion, 1969.

Moorman, John. *A History of the Franciscan Order from Its Origins to the Year 1517*. Oxford: Clarendon Press, 1968.

Motolinía, Fray Toribio de Benavente o. "Carta de Fray Toribio de Motolinía al Emperador Carlos V." In *Memoriales e Historia de los Indios de la Nueva Espana*, 335–45. Madrid: Biblioteca de Autores Espanoles, 1970.

————. *Historia de los indios de la Nueva España*. 1541. Ed. Georges Baudot. Madrid: Clásicos Castalia, 1985.

————. *Memoriales e Historia de los indios de la Nueva España*. Madrid: Biblioteca de Autores Españoles, 1970.

Nader, Helen. *Liberty in Absolutist Spain: The Hapsburg Sale of Towns, 1516–1700.* Baltimore: Johns Hopkins University Press, 1990.

Nicholson, H. B. "Eduard Georg Seler, 1849–1922." In *Handbook of Middle American Indians,* Robert Wauchope, gen. ed., Howard F. Cline, vol. ed., vol. 13, 348–69. Austin: University of Texas Press, 1973.

———. "The Iconography of the Deity Representations in Fray Bernardino de Sahagún's *Primeros Memoriales*: Huitzilopochtli and Chalchiuhtlicue." In *The Work of Bernardino de Sahagún: Pioneer Ethnographer of Sixteenth-Century Aztec Mexico,* ed. J. Jorge Klor de Alva, H. B. Nicholson, and Eloise Quiñones Keber, 229–53. Austin: University of Texas Press, 1988.

Nicolau d'Olwer, Luis. *Fray Bernardino de Sahagún (1499–1590).* Trans. Mauricio J. Mixco. Salt Lake City: University of Utah Press, 1987.

Nicolau d'Olwer, Luis, and Howard F. Cline. "Sahagún and His Works." In *Handbook of American Indians,* Robert Wauchope, gen. ed., Howard F. Cline, vol. ed., vol. 13, 186–206. Austin: University of Texas Press, 1973.

Northrop, F. S. C., and Helen H. Livingston, eds. *Cross-Cultural Understanding: Epistemology in Anthropology.* New York: Harper and Row, 1964.

Ong, Walter J. *Orality and Literacy: The Technologizing of the Word.* London: Routledge, 1982.

Pagden, Anthony. *European Encounters with the New World: From Renaissance to Romanticism.* New Haven: Yale University Press, 1993.

———. *The Fall of Natural Man: The American Indian and the Origins of Comparative Ethnology.* Cambridge: Cambridge University Press, 1982.

Panofsky, Erwin. *Gothic Architecture and Scholasticism: An Inquiry into the Analogy of the Arts, Philosophy, and Religion in the Middle Ages.* New York: Meridian, 1951.

———. *Perspective as Symbolic Form.* Trans. Christopher S. Wood. New York: Zone Books, 1991.

Pardo, Osvaldo Fabian. "Nueva teología es menester: Cultura cristiana y evangelización en México. Siglo XVI." Ph.D. diss., University of Michigan, Ann Arbor, 1993.

Parker, Geoffrey. *Felipe II.* Trans. Ricardo de la Huerta Ozores. Madrid: Alianza Editorial, 1978.

Phelan, John Leddy. *The Millennial Kingdom of the Franciscans in the New World.* 2nd rev. ed. Berkeley: University of California Press, 1970.

Pico della Mirandola, Giovanni. *On the Dignity of Man: On Being and the One; Heptaplus.* Trans. Charles Glenn Wallis, Paul J. W. Miller, and Douglas Carmichael. New York: Bobbs-Merrill, 1965.

Pinker, Steven. *The Language Instinct: How the Mind Creates Language*. New York: Harper Perennial, 1995.

Polo, Marco. *The Travels of Marco Polo (the Venetian)*. Ed. Manuel Komroff, trans. Marsden. New York: Liveright, 1926.

Pratt, Mary Louise. *Imperial Eyes: Travel Writing and Transculturation*. London: Routledge, 1992.

Quiñones Keber, Eloise. "Deity Images and Texts in the *Primeros Memoriales* and *Florentine Codex*." In *The Work of Bernardino de Sahagún: Pioneer Ethnographer of Sixteenth-Century Aztec Mexico*, ed. J. Jorge Klor de Alva, H. B. Nicholson, and Eloise Quiñones Keber, 255–72. Austin: University of Texas Press, 1988.

Rabasa, José. "Dialogue as Conquest: Mapping Spaces for Counter-Discourse." *Cultural Critique* 6 (1987): 131–59. Revised and reprinted in *Inventing America: Spanish Historiography and the Formation of Eurocentrism*, 83–124. Norman: University of Oklahoma Press, 1993.

Reinhard, Wolfgang. "Sprachbeherrschung und Weltherrschaft. Sprache und Sprachwissenschaft in der europäischen Expansion." In *Humanismus und Neue Welt*, ed. Wolfgang Reinhard (Mitteilung XV der Kommission für Humanismusforschung. Acta humaniora). Weinheim: VCH Verlagsgesellschaft, 1987.

Resines Llorente, Luis. *Catecismos americanos del siglo XVI*. 2 vols. Madrid: Junta de Castilla y León, 1992.

Ricard, Robert. *The Spiritual Conquest of Mexico*. Trans. Leslie Byrd Simpson. Berkeley: University of California Press, 1966.

Rico, Francisco. *El sueño del humanismo: De Petrarca a Erasmo*. Madrid: Alianza Universidad, 1993.

Río, Martín del. *La magia demoníaca (Libro II de las "Disquisiciones Mágicas")*. 1599. Trans. Jesús Moya. Madrid: Hiperión, 1991.

Robertson, Donald. *Mexican Manuscript Painting of the Early Colonial Period: The Metropolitan Schools*. New Haven: Yale University Press, 1959.

———. "The Sixteenth Century Mexican Encyclopedia of Fray Bernardino de Sahagún." *Cahiers d'Histoire Mondiale/Journal of World History/Cuadernos de Historia Mundial* 9 (1966): 617–27.

Rosaldo, Renato. *Culture and Truth: The Remaking of Social Analysis*. Boston: Beacon Press, 1989.

———. "From the Door of His Tent: The Fieldworker and the Inquisitor." In *Writing Culture: The Poetics and Politics of Ethnography*, ed. James Clifford and George E. Marcus, 77–97. Berkeley: University of California Press, 1986.

Rowe, John Howland. "The Renaissance Foundations of Anthropology." *American Anthropologist* 67 (1965): 1–20.

Ruiz, Juan. *Libro de buen amor*. Ed. Joan Corominas. Madrid: Gredos, 1967.

Ruiz, Ramón Eduardo. *Triumphs and Tragedy: A History of the Mexican People*. New York: Norton, 1992.

Russell, Jeffrey Burton. *Lucifer: The Devil in the Middle Ages*. Ithaca: Cornell University Press, 1984.

Sahagún, Fray Bernardino de. *Adiciones, Apéndice a la postilla y Ejercicio cotidiano*. Ed. and trans. Arthur J. O. Anderson. Mexico: Universidad Nacional Autónoma de México, 1993.

———. "The Aztec-Spanish Dialogues of 1524 [*Coloquios*]." Trans. J. Jorge Klor de Alva. *Alcheringa: Ethnopoetics* 4.2 (1980): 52–193.

———. *Breve compendio de los ritos idolátricos que los indios de esta Nueva España usaban en tiempo de su infidelidad*. Ed. María Guadalupe Bosch de Souza and Guillermo Rousset Banda. Mexico: Lince, 1990.

———. *Códice florentino. [Historia universal de las cosas de la Nueva España.]* Facs. ed. Mexico and Florence: Casa Editorial Giunti Barbèra and Archivo General de la Nación, 1979. Abbreviated as CF.

———. *Coloquios y doctrina cristiana con que los doce frailes de San Francisco, enviados por el papa Adriano VI y por el emperador Carlos V, convirtieron a los indios de la Nueva España. En lengua mexicana y española. Los diálogos de 1524, dispuestos por fray Bernardino de Sahagún y sus colaboradores Antonio Valeriano de Azcapotzalco, Alonso Vegerano de Cuauhtitlán, Martín Jacobita y Andrés Leonardo de Tlatelolco, y otros cuatro ancianos muy entendidos en todas sus antigüedades*. Ed. Miguel León-Portilla. Facs. ed. Mexico: Universidad Autónoma de México, 1986.

———. *Florentine Codex: General History of the Things of New Spain*. Ed. and trans. Arthur J. O. Anderson and Charles E. Dibble. Monographs of the School of American Research, Number 14. 13 vols. Santa Fe and Salt Lake City: School of American Research and University of Utah Press, 1950–82. Abbreviated as *FC*.

———. *Historia de las cosas de Nueva España*. Ed. Francisco del Paso y Troncoso. Vols. 6–8. Madrid: Hauser y Menet, 1905–07.

———. *Historia general de las cosas de Nueva España*. Ed. Alfredo López Austin and Josefina García Quintana. 2 vols. Madrid: Alianza Editorial, 1988.

———. *Psalmodia Christiana (Christian Psalmody)*. 1583. Trans. Arthur J. O. Anderson. Salt Lake City: University of Utah Press, 1993.

Sahlins, Marshall. *Islands of History*. Chicago: University of Chicago Press, 1985.

Said, Edward W. *Culture and Imperialism*. New York: Alfred A. Knopf, 1993.

Saussure, Ferdinand de. *Cours de linguistique générale.* Ed. Tullio de Mauro. Paris: Payot, 1982.

Schütz, Alfred, and Thomas Luckmann. *The Structures of the Life-World.* Trans. Richard M. Zaner, H. Tristram Engelhardt, Jr., and David J. Parent. 2 vols. Evanston: Northwestern University Press, 1973, 1989.

Seibt, Ferdinand, and Winfried Eberhard, eds. *Europa 1400: La crisis de la baja Edad Media.* Alfredo Mateos Paramio. Barcelona: Crítica, 1993.

Seler, Eduard Georg. *Collected Works in Mesoamerican Linguistics and Archeology.* Gen ed. Frank E. Comparato. 6 vols. Culver City, Calif.: Labyrinthos, 1990.

Siméon, Rémi. *Diccionario de la lengua náhuatl o mexicana.* 1885. Trans. Josefina Oliva de Coll. Mexico: Siglo XXI Editores, 1977.

Sinistrari, Lodovico Maria. *Demoniality (De Daemonialitate, et Incubis et Succubis).* Trans. Montague Summers. New York: Dover, 1989.

Solano, Francisco de, and Pilar Ponce, eds. *Cuestionarios para la formación de las Relaciones geográficas de Indias siglos XVI/XIX.* Madrid: Consejo Superior de Investigaciones Científicas, 1988.

Stierle, Karlheinz. "L'histoire comme exemple, l'exemple comme histoire: Contribution à la pragmatique et à la poétique des textes narratifs." Trans. Jean-Louis Lebrave. *Poétique* 10 (1972): 176–98.

Stock, Brian. *Listening for the Text: On the Uses of the Past.* Baltimore: Johns Hopkins University Press, 1990.

Stocking, George W., Jr. *Victorian Anthropology.* New York: Free Press, 1987.

"The Talk of the Town." *The New Yorker,* 25 Jan. 1993, 31.

Taussig, Michael. *Mimesis and Alterity: A Particular History of the Senses.* New York: Routledge, 1993.

Taylor, William B. *Drinking, Homicide, and Rebellion in Colonial Mexican Villages.* Stanford: Stanford University Press, 1979.

Todorov, Tzvetan. *La conquête de l'Amérique: La question de l'autre.* Paris: Éditions du Seuil, 1982.

Torquemada, Fray Juan de. *Monarquía indiana.* 1615. Ed. Miguel León-Portilla. 5th ed. 3 vols. Mexico: Porrúa, 1975.

Traugott, Elizabeth Closs, and Mary Louise Pratt. *Linguistics for Students of Literature.* San Diego: Harcourt Brace Jovanovich, 1980.

Valdés, Juan de. *Diálogo de la lengua.* Ed. Cristina Barbolani. 3rd ed. Madrid: Cátedra, 1987.

Valla, Lorenzo. *The Treatise of Lorenzo Valla on the Donation of Constantine.* Trans. Christopher B. Coleman. Toronto: University of Toronto Press, 1993.

Vetancurt, Fray Agustín de. *Teatro mexicano: Descripción breve de los sucesos ejemplares históricos y religiosos del Nuevo Mundo de las Indias. Crónica de la provincia del Santo Evangelio de México. Menologio franciscano de los varones más señalados, que con sus vidas ejemplares, perfección religiosa, ciencia, predicación evangélica en su vida, ilustraron la provincia del Santo Evangelio de México.* 2nd facs. ed. México: Porrúa, 1982.

Vicente Castro, Florencio, and J. Luis Rodríguez Molinero. *Bernardino de Sahagún: Primer antropólogo en Nueva España (Siglo XVI).* Salamanca: Universidad de Salamanca, 1986.

Weckmann, Luis. *La herencia medieval de México.* 2 vols. Mexico: El Colegio de México, 1984.

White, Hayden. "Foucault Decoded: Notes from Underground." In *Tropics of Discourse: Essays in Cultural Criticism,* 230–60. Baltimore: Johns Hopkins University Press, 1978.

———. *Metahistory: The Historical Imagination in Nineteenth-Century Europe.* Baltimore: Johns Hopkins University Press, 1973.

Xirau, Ramón. *Idea y querella de la Nueva España.* Madrid: Alianza Editorial, 1973.

Zaballa Beascoechea, Ana de. *Transculturación y misión en Nueva España: Estudio histórico-doctrinal del libro de los "Coloquios" de Bernardino de Sahagún.* Pamplona: Ediciones Universidad de Navarra, 1990.

Zink, Michel. *La prédication en langue romane avant 1300.* Paris: Éditions Honoré Champion, 1976.

INDEX

Corn section, in *Florentine Codex*, 136–37

Cortés, Hernán, 58, 82

Costa Lima, Luiz, 144, 145, 164

Council of Indies, 29, 30, 33;
Motecuhzoma's petition to, 28

Creation, biblical account of, 47–48

Creoles (*criollos*): Beltrami's view of, 45, 46,
51; foundations of identity of, 36;
Nahua past idealized by, 157; travel
narratives and, 43

Criollismo, 218n.21. *See also* Creoles

Critiques (Kant), 47, 48

Cultural conjuncture, 72

Cultural identity, scholarly work and, 12

Cultural relativism, 54, 81, 109; and
missionary endeavors, 86

Culture, 69

Culture and Truth (Rosaldo), 68

Curiosity, 187–88, 209–12

Curtius, Ernst Robert, 133

Daniel, E. Randolph, 173–74

Dante, depiction of Lucifer by, 193

De contemptu mundi (Bernard of Cluny), 202

Deities, Nahua, 193, 195–200, 231n.8

Deity images, in Sahagún's work, 169, 170,
172

"Deity Images and Texts in the *Primeros
Memoriales* and *Florentine Codex* (Quiñones
Keber), 168

Deity-impersonators, Nahua, 169, 170–72

Deleuze, Gilles, 164–65, 166, 168

Delumeau, Jean, 201

Demonology. *See* Devil

De Propietatibus Rerum (Anglicus), 93–94, 126

"Des cannibales" (Montaigne), 109

"Determination of the Philosophy of a
Culture, The" (conference, 1962), 57

Devil, 185–204, 206; demonic practices and
birth of modern knowledge, 213

*Devil in the New World: The Impact of Diabolism
in New Spain, The* (Cervantes), 186

Devil's advocate, 8

Diabolism. *See* Devil

Diálogo de la lengua (Valdés), 85

"Dialogue as Conquest: Mapping Spaces
for Counter-Discourse" (Rabasa), 58

Dialogue form, Sahagún's use of, 82, 83,
84, 86–90

Differentiation, mimesis and, 144

Dignity of man, Renaissance notion of
the, 78

Dionysius, 193

Discarded Image, The (Lewis), 130, 177

"Discovery of America and the Discovery
of Man, The" (Elliott), 188

Disputation, medieval (*Disputatio*), 135–36,
138

Dispute of the New World, The (Gerbi), 39

Disquisitionum Magicarum (Río), 201

Divine Comedy (Dante), 85

Donation of Constantine, 78

Double mistaken identity, Lockhart's
notion of, 106, 110

Double prologues, 139–40, 141

Drawings of Sahagún's "Primeros Memoriales," The
(Baird), 94

Drinking, of postconquest Nahuas, 155–58,
196

Dualism, 193

Durán, Diego, 27, 59, 190–91, 202, 208, 211

"Eccentricities: On Prologues in Some
Fourteenth-Century Castilian Texts"
(Gumbrecht), 139

Education, 108. *See also* Colegio de Santa
Cruz de Tlaltelolco

Elliott, John, 186, 188–89

Empiricism, 55, 133–34; and Kant's theory,
49; and transcendentalism, 48

Enlightenment, the: episteme of, 67; Kant
as final stage of, 51–52; and New World
nationalism, 46

Enríquez, Martín, 26

Episteme, 66–68, 222n.18

Epistemology. *See* Knowledge

Erasmian spirituality, 151

Escalona, Alonso de, 97, 103

Escaray, Antonio de, 156

Ethics, humanism and, 76–79